Fighting the For

M000236681

ALSO BY LISA M. MUNDEY

*American Militarism and Anti-Militarism
in Popular Media, 1945–1970* (McFarland, 2012)

Fighting the Forever War

The U.S. Service Member Experience in Afghanistan, 2001–2014

LISA M. MUNDEY

McFarland & Company, Inc., Publishers
Jefferson, North Carolina

ISBN (print) 978–1–4766–8889–3
ISBN (ebook) 978–1–4766–4682–4

LIBRARY OF CONGRESS AND BRITISH LIBRARY
CATALOGUING DATA ARE AVAILABLE

Library of Congress Control Number 2022002062

© 2022 Lisa M. Mundey. All rights reserved

*No part of this book may be reproduced or transmitted in any form
or by any means, electronic or mechanical, including photocopying
or recording, or by any information storage and retrieval system,
without permission in writing from the publisher.*

Front cover image: Soldiers of A Company, Special Troops Battalion, hand out snacks
to children at a local bazaar in Afghanistan, July 19, 2009. The snacks are used
to thank the community and their children for their cooperation.
Photo by Staff Sergeant Christopher Allison. (U.S. Department of Defense.)

The appearance of US Department of Defense (DoD) visual information
does not imply or constitute DoD endorsement.

Printed in the United States of America

*McFarland & Company, Inc., Publishers
Box 611, Jefferson, North Carolina 28640
www.mcfarlandpub.com*

Table of Contents

Acknowledgments

Without a doubt, I would not have been able to complete this book without support. Let me first thank Greg and Cheri Hartford, whose generous grant to the Department of History at the University of St. Thomas, Houston, financially supported the research for this work. Thank you to the helpful staff at the Army Heritage and Education Center at Carlisle Barracks. Thank you to my two research assistants, Haley Hewitt and Elysia "Ellie" Davila, whose leg work assisted me considerably. Thank you to my colleagues Robert Maberry and William Donnelly who read early versions of this manuscript and offered valuable insights. Any mistakes remaining here are mine alone.

My family gave up quality time with me so that I could work on this book. Thank you to my husband, Mike, whose love, support, and insight into military life proved invaluable along this journey. My daughter, Allison, did not quite understand why mommy was always reading and writing about Afghanistan instead of playing with her. One day, I hope she will understand. Thank you also to my extended family for their care, support, and love of history.

Preface

Given that my husband deployed twice to Iraq for Operation Iraqi Freedom (OIF), one could be forgiven for assuming that I would write about that conflict. Though I have published on OIF, I became interested in the "other war" of the Global War on Terror—Afghanistan—while a historian working for the US Army Center of Military History. While the nation focused on Iraq, I began to research and write about the US War in Afghanistan. In this volume, I rely on memoirs, blogs, oral history interviews, other published accounts, and available archival material to capture the experience of the troops who deployed to Afghanistan from the beginning of the war in 2001 through its transition to Resolute Support Mission/Operation Freedom's Sentinel in 2015. As of the fall of 2021, the United States and Coalition troops have left Afghanistan, and the Taliban have resumed control of the country. The nearly 20-year conflict came to a dramatic conclusion with the August 2021 evacuation of US citizens and Afghan allies by round-the-clock flights out of Kabul International Airport. The Taliban have reestablished their fundamentalist Islamic regime, much as it was before the Afghan War began in October 2001.

While there are many available sources for the earliest years of the war in Afghanistan, through the surge in 2010–2011, the primary source material for the period after the end of Operation Enduring Freedom in 2014 is not yet robust. Many of the oral history programs that captured service member voices did not continue past 2014. Much of the fighting has been done by Special Operations Forces in the years since then, which are difficult records to obtain. Additionally, most of the archival material for the wars in Iraq and Afghanistan remain classified and closed to civilian researchers. Despite these confines, this manuscript captures many voices from the years of the Afghan War, from those who served in combat to noncombat roles. It cannot relate every aspect of the war or every experience, though I have done the best I could with what is currently available to researchers. I hope that veterans of the war continue to publish their memoirs and conduct interviews. One interviewee has asked to remain anonymous, so I have given him a pseudonym, as indicated in the notes and bibliography. All other names are given as they appear in publications or in archival materials.

This book is chiefly organized thematically. The journey for most troops begins with pre-deployment training in the US, followed by the trip overseas and their first impressions of Afghanistan, covered in Chapter 1. While the troops lived in tents and temporary structures at first, the US went to considerable expense to build expansive forward operating bases with amenities such as fast food, salons, and coffee shops detailed in Chapter 2. An important part of the deployment for many troops was interacting with the locals, from purchasing goods at the local bazaar, interacting with their interpreters, to sharing cups of tea or meals with elders at meetings. These interactions are explored in Chapter 3.

Chapter 4 deals with patrols and combat. Some deployments were fairly quiet, with patrols rarely finding enemy fighters. As the Taliban regrouped and launched an insurgency, the troops encountered more frequent and deadly ambushes and roadside bombs, particularly in the eastern and southern provinces. Given the limited number of troops in Afghanistan for much of the conflict, coupled with the vast distances between the big bases and far flung combat outposts, American and Coalition forces relied extensively on air power for transport, supply, and to counter numerically superior enemy forces. Chapter 5 explores the air war both from the perspective of the aircrews and the troops on the ground.

American Special Operations Forces, and later conventional forces, trained Afghan soldiers for the Afghan National Army. The US created Embedded Training Teams to mentor Afghan officers and units in the field. The US military also took on the responsibility of training various Afghan police forces. These efforts are outlined in Chapter 6. Meanwhile, Civil Affairs teams provided humanitarian aid to the Afghans and began small-scale construction projects. The early successes of these Civil Affairs teams led to the creation of Provincial Reconstruction Teams, which spearheaded much of the construction projects as well as mentoring Afghans on governance. These topics are charted in Chapter 7.

Chapter 8 deals with the troop surge and subsequent draw-down of those troops. With the Taliban strong in their traditional southern heartland of Kandahar and Helmand provinces, American, Canadian, and British forces launched offensives to take back that territory. The offensives coincided with a surge in American and Coalition troops. With the intent for Operation Enduring Freedom to end in 2014, the Coalition began withdrawing troops in 2012 and turning over bases to Afghan control. The Taliban did not stop fighting in 2014, so the United States continued operations into 2015 and then extended them further. Final troop withdrawal came in July 2021. Was the war worth it? This question features in Chapter 9 about the meaning and memory of the Afghan War thus far from the perspective of the service members and from Hollywood. It includes reactions to the Biden administration's withdrawal of US troops to end the war.

This is a work from the ground-up perspective of those Americans who served in Afghanistan, not from the top-down levels of strategy and policy. I do not grapple specifically with what went wrong or give prescriptions concerning what could have been done differently. Rather, the war is viewed through the eyes of American troops. Though undeniably valuable, I do not include the voices of Coalition partners here or of the Afghans. These voices deserve their own volumes. For the Americans who deployed, the war looks different depending on time and location. It looks different in 2002 than 2006 or 2010. It looks different in the Korengal Valley than it does in Helmand Province. It looks different from the forward operating bases than the far-flung combat outposts. My aim here is to give readers some insight into each of these experiences. Where it is relevant, I also point out elements of the Afghan deployments that echo America's earlier twentieth-century wars, particularly the one in Vietnam.

Introduction

On an otherwise quiet night in Afghanistan, a rocket-propelled grenade suddenly slams into a metal structure at the corner of an American base. The blast "penetrates outward as a deafening boom that envelops the quiet tranquil sounds of night for miles in all directions like a vacuum sucking in all the extraneous sound," recounted an American soldier. The enemy began to shoot at them with small arms fire, which made a "crackle snap" sound like a Fourth of July firecracker. From which direction was the fire coming, though? No one could track the direction of enemy fire, even as its volume increased until it seemed as the bullets "rain as in a typhoon." Slipping and sliding over rocks and jagged terrain, the soldiers climbed the hill outside of their base in the dark. It seemed as though the troops took on the "form of an antiquated army charging the enemy flank." They are too late. The enemy has already disappeared into the ravine on the other side of the hill that borders the American base.[1] The insurgents slip away into the rugged terrain where it was difficult for the troops to follow. A surprise attack and a shadowy enemy characterized many of the assaults on US forces in Afghanistan. This action occurred when most of the public had already turned their attention toward another war.

As the United States ramped up for the invasion of Iraq in 2003, the original War on Terror—Afghanistan—slid into the background. "We are fighting the forgotten war," complains Corporal Kevin Clifford in 2004, a year after the US invaded Iraq.[2] Even those outside of the military thought Afghanistan was drifting out of view. In 2008, PBS filmed a spot about the Marine Corps in Helmand Province in Afghanistan titled "Afghanistan: The Forgotten War."[3] Marine Gil Barndollar, who deployed to Afghanistan twice between 2009 and 2016, echoes the same sentiment.[4] Collectively, the American people failed to notice much about the fighting in Afghanistan by the end of Operation Enduring Freedom in 2014 and the transition to the continuing operations, Resolute Support Mission/Operation Freedom's Sentinel, in 2015.[5]

Because the wars in Iraq and Afghanistan occurred simultaneously, many Americans—and even trainers in the military—conflated them. Though both Iraq and Afghanistan are Muslim countries, they are quite different in terms of their peoples, languages, cultures, and environments. Fighting in Afghanistan, though similar in some ways with fighting in Iraq and even the Vietnam War, proved unique. Troops who served in both theaters of operation note numerous differences between them.

Overall, US troops deployed to Afghanistan with good intentions to eliminate the threat from al-Qaeda and the Taliban, secure the country, and assist in rebuilding efforts. Although they sometimes felt alienated from the environment and culture, those troops who worked directly with the Afghan security forces or with the population proved well-meaning, even if the outcome of training or nation-building projects proved uneven. In their blog posts, emails home, memoirs, and oral histories, the service members revealed many of the problems conducting the war in Afghanistan that are highlighted in the *Washington Post's* "Afghanistan Papers" series in December 2019, particularly with respect to what Americans perceived as widespread corruption and difficulties training the Afghan security forces.[6] Constant turnover of troops also proved disruptive to building relationships with the Afghans, as each new rotation had to learn anew the terrain, the local politics, and enemy presence in the area. New troops met with the same elders over cups of tea and discussed the same issues the previous rotation discussed with them, and the rotation before them, too.

This work examines how American service members described the sights, sounds, tastes, people, and mental and physical environments in Afghanistan to friends and family and—if published—the public as well. As the troops encountered a foreign land, culture, and way of life, they drew on familiar images and associations, particularly from popular culture, to make their experiences understandable to themselves and to those back home. Given the popularity of television shows and Hollywood movies, it is not surprising that the troops made frequent references to them to describe activities and events overseas. They also invoked imagery from technology, nature, and more to explain their experiences. As with an earlier war in Vietnam, American troops brought US consumer culture with them overseas. Though many of the troops recounted difficulties, frustrations, and sometimes outright failures during their deployments, service members nonetheless felt pride in their service in Afghanistan. Though there are few examples of the war in Afghanistan in popular culture, most of them depict the American effort as heroic and honorable. Even though veterans are divided on the ultimate meaning of the war in Afghanistan, they often view the war through the lens of serving with fellow service members.

Included here are voices from those in battle, those who provide immediate support to those fighting, and those who provide the logistical backbone of any deployment. It captures experiences of combatants as well as service members serving in relatively safe forward operating bases, trainers embedded with the Afghan National Army and Afghan police forces, civil affairs, and military personnel operating with Provincial Reconstruction Teams. Though it is not possible to represent perfectly the demographics of the service members who have deployed, the source material draws from all the services and include a variety of ranks of military operational specialties. As is the case with many war memoirs, combatants are over-represented in the sources.[7]

The time and location of a service member's deployment varied drastically in the activity of the insurgency, from relatively quiet to sharply violent. As it is sometimes stated that the US did not fight for 10 years in Vietnam "rather it fought a one-year war 10 times in a row." Others have given variations on this theme, all describing it as a one-year war fought repeatedly. Indeed, knowledge of the locals, threats, and terrain was lost each time a new unit arrived.[8] In many ways, there were multiple Afghan wars depending on the timeframe and location of the deployment. Like the Vietnam War, there is no single dominant service member experience in Afghanistan.[9] The service member voices here give readers a sense of what life was like for deployed troops in Afghanistan in different locations over the time of the conflict. Additionally, the US military re-created, to the best of its ability and at considerable expense, stateside accommodations on its forward operating bases. Technology allowed service members to watch television, binge watch shows and movies, and communicate with home regularly, as well as rain down terror from helicopters, aircraft, and drones on enemy lines.

In order to appreciate the experiences of service members in Afghanistan, it is important to have a general understanding of what happened in the Afghan War over the duration of the conflict. While most Americans are likely familiar with the beginning of the war, once the US invaded Iraq, attention shifted to that theater of operation. Media coverage of the war ebbed over the years, spiking during particular events, such as the surge of troops ordered by President Barack

Afghanistan, which is about the size of Texas, is located in Central Asia, bordered on the west by Iran and on the east by Pakistan. Kabul is the capital, and the US held major bases at Bagram and Kandahar.

Obama in 2009. What follows is a general background of the history of Afghanistan and an overview of the main events in the war.

Though most Americans could not point reliably to Afghanistan on a map, the territory long held historical significance as part of the famed Silk Road trade route between the Middle East and Asia. Alexander the Great famously invaded in 330 BCE and failed to conquer it. In the nineteenth century, Afghanistan became part of the political and diplomatic "Great Game" between Britain and Russia, each vying for influence there. Britain fought three wars in Afghanistan in the nineteenth and early twentieth centuries. Indeed, the border between Afghanistan and Pakistan is an artifact of the nineteenth century, ignoring the ethnic diversity of the country. There are numerous ethnic groups including the Pashtun, Tajik, Uzbek, Hazara, and many more. The two main languages are Dari and Pashtu, though other dialects are also spoken. The majority practice Sunni Islam.

The people of Afghanistan had seen decades of war in the twentieth century before the events that led to Operation Enduring Freedom. The Soviet Union invaded in 1979 and quickly became mired in a civil war between those who supported the ruling communist regime and Islamic fundamentalists. The United States covertly funded and assisted the Islamic *Mujahedeen*, Muslim religious fighters. Neighboring Pakistan sponsored fundamentalist Islamic religious schools, or *madrassas,* which trained many ethnic Pashtun Afghan men. Upon returning to Afghanistan, they dubbed themselves Taliban. When the Soviets withdrew, various *Mujahedeen* militia groups, the Taliban, and Uzbek and Tajik warlords from the northern provinces fought for control over the state. With military and intelligence assistance from Pakistan, the Taliban successfully captured the capital Kabul in 1996 and established a regime under the leadership of Mullah Mohammad Omar. They governed all but a small segment of the northern provinces, which were controlled by the Tajik and Uzbek warlords who had come together to form the Northern Alliance. The Taliban allowed the international terrorist organization al-Qaeda to train in their country. It is where the terrorists prepared for the September 11, 2001, terrorist attacks on the United States.[10]

In response to the terrorist attacks, the US launched its war against al-Qaeda and the Taliban, who refused to turn over the terrorists to the US, on October 7, 2001, with airstrikes against training camps and al-Qaeda camps. They targeted Kabul, the capital city; Kandahar, the southern stronghold of the Taliban; and Jalalabad, the location of al-Qaeda training camps. Airstrikes against other Taliban-held territories, such as Bagram, an old Soviet air base, and a key northern city, Mazar-e-Sharif, followed the initial attacks. The air war established US air superiority by destroying the limited Taliban air force and air defense systems. Already on the ground, Central Intelligence Agency teams gathered intelligence and contacted local Afghans to coordinate with Special Operations Forces, which soon began combat operations.[11]

By October 19, 2001, Special Forces linked up with the Northern Alliance warlords, the most logical ally on the ground to overthrow the Taliban. Even the well-trained Special Forces soldiers found the steep mountainous terrain and sharp drop-offs challenging ground to navigate.[12] As a result of these conditions, the American and Northern Alliance forces operated on foot, on horseback, and by pickup truck. One of the service members, Staff Sergeant Stephen Tomat, explains that the horses were "like large dogs" with saddles that comprised "two-by-fours covered with a piece of carpet." The saddles also had short stirrups "so we were sitting on [these horses], our asses were sore, our knees were literally up to our chests," Tomat recollects.[13]

Though traveling by horseback, Special Forces soldiers carried state-of-the-art communications equipment, which brought down precision guided munitions on enemy targets. One team accompanied the Northern Alliance Uzbek warlord General Abdul Rashid Dostum to assault Mazar-e-Sharif, which fell on November 9, 2001. Other teams supported Northern Alliance Tajik warlord Ismail Khan to attack Herat and Northern Alliance Generals Fahim Khan and Bismullah Khan to capture Kabul. The Taliban fell back to positions in the south, around Kandahar, part of the traditional Taliban heartland.[14]

Meanwhile, Special Forces soldiers linked up with Hamid Karzai, a leader in one of the influential Pashtun tribes in Afghanistan, in the province of Oruzgan, near the city of Tarin Kowt. The small force, numbering 60 men, encountered a Taliban convoy of 100 vehicles, which could easily have ended their mission. Air strikes provided the firepower the Americans needed to decimate the enemy force before the Americans were overrun. The object of the American-Karzai force was to attack Kandahar. Likely recognizing the futility of holding the city, Taliban leader Mullah Omar disappeared on the night of December 6. Without their leader, Kandahar fell the next day.[15]

US air power focused next on the Tora Bora area near Jalalabad in eastern Afghanistan. Taliban and al-Qaeda forces had found refuge in a series of caves in the mountains there where they had stockpiled weapons and supplies. In early 2002, intelligence sources indicated a concentration of al-Qaeda and Taliban forces around the Shah-i-Kot Valley and surrounding mountains east of Gardiz. Starting on March 2, 2002, and lasting until the 16th, American and Coalition troops launched Operation Anaconda against the mountain holdout in the hopes of eliminating the last of the al-Qaeda terrorists in Afghanistan. They assaulted up rocky mountain terrain as al-Qaeda forces rained down machine gun and mortar fire. Despite efforts by Pakistani troops to block nearby border crossings, the remnants of the Taliban and al-Qaeda managed to escape Afghanistan into Pakistan.[16]

By early 2002, conventional forces had joined the Special Operations Forces in Afghanistan. Though US forces continued to hunt down Taliban and al-Qaeda leadership, US Secretary of Defense Donald H. Rumsfeld declared the end of major combat operations on May 1, 2003. The United States intended to have a "light footprint" so as to avoid perceptions by the local population that it was an occupying force, which US officials believed had contributed to the failure of the Afghan-Soviet War in the 1980s. As a result of this "light footprint," US troops began redeploying out of Afghanistan early in 2002. For a country the size of Texas with a population around 30 million people, there were only 7,000 troops deployed there. For comparison, 54,000 North Atlantic Treaty Organization

(NATO) troops deployed to Bosnia in 1996, which had a population around 3.76 million at the time and is considerably smaller in terms of geography. The light footprint became the norm for Afghanistan as most US troops deployed to Iraq after 2003. The few troops in Afghanistan could not effectively establish security in the country or prevent the infiltration of the Taliban from Pakistan. Additionally, the theater in Afghanistan became secondary after the US invasion of Iraq in March 2003. This effort in Afghanistan was called "economy-of-force," which meant the minimum effective force was being used there.[17]

After the fall of the Taliban regime, Northern Alliance warlords established themselves in various areas in Afghanistan. Tajik warlord Ismail Khan dominated in western Herat Province, Uzbek General Abdul Rashid Dostum controlled the north-western provinces, and Tajik warlord Mohammad Qasim Fahim led the north-eastern provinces. Enemy forces which opposed the establishment of a Western-sponsored Afghan state situated themselves along roughly three fronts. In the northern provinces of Nuristan, Konar, Laghman, and Nangarhar, as well as across the border in Pakistan, Gulbuddin Hekmatyar and his Hezb-e-Islami faction established its presence. Khowst, Paktia, and Paktika in Afghanistan and the corresponding provinces in Pakistan constituted the central front, where another splinter insurgent group, the Haqqani network, operated. The Taliban dominated the southern front Helmand, Kandahar, Oruzgan, Zabol, and Paktika as well as Baluchistan in neighboring Pakistan.[18]

Initially, US goals for Afghanistan rested on removing the Taliban, destroying al-Qaeda, and denying Afghanistan as a base for terrorist operations. The US State Department favored a peacekeeping force, while the Pentagon dismissed nation-building. Later, US policy slowly shifted toward the very kind of state-building the military opposed. Most American troops deployed to the eastern provinces due to their proximity to Pakistan, from where the Taliban were infiltrating back into Afghanistan.[19] At different times, US strategy focused on counterterrorism operations, or those targeting the terrorist leadership, and counterinsurgency operations, which protected the population from insurgent forces.

The international community cooperated in the rebuilding of Afghanistan with the NATO taking an active military role. The NATO command in Afghanistan was designated the International Security Assistance Force (ISAF). Initially, ISAF supported security operations inside Kabul only. When the United States supported ISAF expansion into other areas of Afghanistan, Coalition partners were less willing to cooperate because of their opposition to the US invasion of Iraq. Nevertheless, international troop deployments did increase to 10,000 by October 2004, while US deployments reached 20,000. Some of these troops began support and reconstruction activities through Provincial Reconstruction Teams that were established in the secure provinces of Afghanistan. Coalition troops also provided security for the first Afghan national presidential election in 2004.

Indeed, the low levels of insurgent activity led the US to announce a 3,000 troop withdrawal for 2006. In lieu of US troops, NATO expanded its footprint across greater areas of Afghanistan, which had started in the northern provinces in 2004 and included western, eastern, and southern provinces by mid–2006. US forces focused their operations on the eastern provinces, while Canadian, British, Romanian, and Dutch troops deployed to the southern provinces. At this point, US officials expected to remain in Afghanistan only for another three to five years, not anticipating the protracted insurgency which developed there.[20]

The Taliban interpreted the US troop withdrawal from Afghanistan as a sign that the US was pulling out of the country completely rather than a shift in strategy. At this time, the US strategy focused narrowly on the counterterrorism mission to kill or capture al-Qaeda or Taliban leadership. The Taliban who had regrouped and rearmed in Pakistan planned to return to Afghanistan and launch offensive operations, targeting Kandahar in southern Afghanistan. The Taliban assumed that NATO troops were less committed than US forces and did not expect the NATO forces to fight effectively.[21]

The Taliban pursued a strategy to undermine popular support for the Western-sponsored central government. They began to use car bombs and roadside bombs as well as sending "night letters" to locals promising violence and murder to intimidate villagers from cooperating with the Afghan government and Coalition forces. The Taliban started assassinating senior clerics, doctors, teachers, and policemen. They targeted schools, particularly those for girls. Adopting tactics from the insurgents in Iraq, the Taliban began suicide bombings in 2005. They created shadow governments in the villages to undermine the central government. The Taliban set up road blocks and checkpoints along the roads. The relatively small number of Afghan security personnel could not successfully defend against this more aggressive Taliban insurgency or protect the population from them.[22]

When Lieutenant General David Barno took command in Afghanistan, in late 2003, US strategy shifted from counterterrorism operations, which focused on targeting insurgents, to counterinsurgency operations, which focused on protecting the population from the enemy. The US goal was to turn security over to Afghanistan, so the US emphasized the training of the Afghan National Army (ANA) and later added the mission of also training the Afghan police forces. The US did not consider long-term commitment to Afghanistan, expecting to scale up the training of the ANA and police to hand over operations to them. The US expectations for a quick exit proved inaccurate. Historically, counterinsurgency operations last an average of 14 years with about a quarter of them spanning over 20 years.[23] Little did US officials realize that the American experience would fall neatly into the range. American forces were split between Afghanistan and the rising insurgency in Iraq. The conflict in Iraq garnered more attention and resources. As American troops in Afghanistan noted at the time, "If you're in Iraq and you need something, you ask for it. If you're in Afghanistan and you need something, you learn how to do it without it."[24]

In May 2006, the Taliban launched an offensive against British troops in Helmand Province. Expecting a peacekeeping mission, the British were surprised by the strength of the Taliban forces. At times, the British forces ran low on supplies as it became increasingly dangerous for helicopters to fly into Helmand. The British fought from secure bases, as they did not have enough troops to mount their own offensive against the Taliban. British troops in Helmand and Canadian troops in neighboring Kandahar Province experienced fierce fighting against a well-armed and full-blown Taliban insurgency, facing increasingly large enemy units. Fighting through the summer of 2006, the NATO troops caused enough casualties to force the Taliban back into refuge in Pakistan, but the Coalition never had enough troops to secure Afghan territory in Helmand and Kandahar permanently.[25]

The war in Afghanistan became increasingly violent and deadly. Between 2005 and 2006, suicide bombings in Afghanistan skyrocketed by 400 percent at the same time that improvised explosive devices doubled. The use of suicide bombers and improvised explosive devices by the Taliban came from the influence of al-Qaeda and Iraqi militants. Coalition forces were no longer fighting the remnants of the Taliban and al-Qaeda, but a reconstituted insurgency. In June 2006, the Pentagon reported that Taliban units increased from small units, to 100-strong units, to units numbering near 400. By late 2007, the insurgency had reached the capital city, Kabul. The Taliban appeared to control roughly one-third of the country, mostly in rural areas, while the national government retained control in more populated areas. In addition to a reconstituted Taliban, Coalition forces continued to fight Gulbuddin Hekmatyar's militant group as well as the one led by Jalaluddin Haqqani, both of whom had refuge in Pakistan. By 2008, the United Nations prohibited its personnel from working in 20 percent of Afghanistan's districts because of security concerns. Indeed, Afghanistan experienced more roadside bombs in 2008 than did the neighboring conflict in Iraq.[26]

While the British and Canadians fought in Helmand and Kandahar, attacks across the border from Pakistan into the eastern provinces increased as well. In order to prevent the movement of troops and supplies from Pakistan, the US set up forward operating bases, smaller combat outposts, and Provincial Reconstruction Teams in the eastern provinces of Konar and Nuristan, particularly in the Pech River Valley, as well as the Waygal and Watpur Valleys. The population proved hostile to the occupying forces, and the outposts were dangerously exposed and vulnerable to attack. In July 2008, insurgents mounted an attack on an American combat outpost in Wanat, which resulted in 9 deaths and 27 wounded. A similar attack happened in neighboring Kamdesh, when insurgents nearly overran Combat Outpost Keating in October 2009. In both cases, close air support saved the outposts. Ultimately, the United States was forced to abandon several of these exposed bases in Nuristan and Konar to the enemy after suffering unsustainable losses in near daily ambushes.[27]

Troop numbers slowly increased in Afghanistan. About 30,000 service members deployed to Afghanistan in 2008, up from fewer than 20,000 in mid–2005. When Barack Obama took office in January 2009, conditions on the ground in Afghanistan had deteriorated to the point where the President sent 17,000 additional troops to the country. This increased number of troops proved insufficient to prevent the Taliban from gaining control over large swaths of the country in the spring and summer of 2009. The crisis convinced the President to send a further surge of 30,000 troops, which arrived by August 2010. As a result, February 2011 marked the largest number of troops from the US, NATO, and other Coalition partners with about 100,000 Americans and just under 42,000 allied forces in-country.

The surge troops accompanied a renewed population-centric counterinsurgency strategy led by General Stanley McChrystal. His strategy focused on securing the population, contributing to reconstruction efforts, and promoting good governance through the local, provincial, and national government. At the same time, the US planned offensives in the heartland of the Taliban and attacked Taliban and al-Qaeda sanctuaries by drone across the Pakistani border. Kill or capture operations also increased. The renewed focus on protecting the population included more restrictive rules of engagement. The more restrictive operational rules caused some resentment among the troops, though it successfully caused civilian casualties to fall. Insurgents had no qualms about killing civilians through their use of suicide bombers or improvised explosive devices.[28]

McChrystal used the additional troops to bolster US forces in contested frontier provinces in the south and east and to help the US marines fighting the Taliban in Helmand Province. In February 2010 McChrystal launched the largest military campaign of the entire war, operation *Moshtarak* ("Together"). The goal of this operation was to seize the Taliban-controlled town of Marjah in Helmand Province. It had become the de facto Taliban capital inside Afghanistan. Once the operation started, the Taliban withdrew many of their forces but left some scattered around the town to harass the invading allies. The Taliban fought back sporadically with sniper fire and landmines, but the allies nonetheless succeeded in seizing the town in a short time. The Taliban melted away rather than allow themselves to be killed or captured by Coalition forces. The Coalition then flew in what became known as a government in a box. This consisted of a governor, administrative officials, and policemen. Taliban insurgents remained scattered among the people and killed those who cooperated with the Coalition troops and government. The Taliban threatened the population against working with the Afghan government or foreign forces. Afghan district officials had to take the precaution of traveling to work via armed convoys.[29]

In neighboring Kandahar, US forces moved into the districts, establishing combat outposts. The US intended to train Afghan security forces to take over these bases once the area had been secured. When US forces went on the offensive in the summer of 2010, the Taliban reacted the same way as they did in Marjah by disappearing before the marines swept through the districts. This time, though, the marines had to contend with improvised explosive devices as well as the booby-trapped houses, doors, gateways, and outhouses. Even the orchards hid explosive devices. Meanwhile, Special Operations Forces killed, captured, or forced across the Pakistani border a number of Taliban commanders, weakening the Taliban offensives over the next two years.[30]

In response to the surge and strengthened Afghan security forces, the Taliban turned to a new tactic: insider attacks or "green-on-blue" attacks of

province of Nuristan to the beauty of Colorado's Rocky Mountain National Park, and marine Ross Schellhaas compares parts of Helmand Province to Twentynine Palms, California.[73]

Despite their efforts to make the unfamiliar a bit more familiar, the rugged Afghan terrain often proved unsettling. Flying over the desert, Major James Powell remembers, "you look down and there's nothing, miles and miles of nothing."[74] One soldier complains about how the steep drop-offs and sparse vegetation were simply "horrendous."[75] Areas proved so rugged that vehicular patrols could only move at 15 or 20 mph. It wreaked havoc on vehicles, requiring constant maintenance and repair.[76] Rusty Bradley sums it up when he writes, "Afghanistan is murder on trucks. Busted axles, blown tires, and punctured hoses are common on the rock-strewn landscape."[77] Wallace remembers, "you learned a couple of hard lessons early on with wheels coming off." In order to avoid problems, "we stopped, you give a guy a wrench, he is under the vehicle, and he tightens everything up,

The Konar River Valley is seen out the crew chief's window of a 10th Combat Aviation Brigade UH-60 Black Hawk helicopter on January 2, 2014, over Konar Province, Afghanistan (US Army photograph by Staff Sergeant Matthew Clark).

then it doesn't happen. We figured that out and our vehicles would stop breaking," he adds.[78]

The terrain proved so rugged that Lieutenant Craig Mullaney muses, "NASA would have difficulty building a rover to maneuver in the Afghan countryside."[79] Traveling on "roads so rutted and bumpy" Special Operations Forces officer Michael Waltz says that "we felt like our guts were in a blender." During another ride in a dried out riverbed, called a wadi, he writes, "My spine felt like someone had beaten on it with a hammer."[80] Unsurprisingly, no one described the terrain as anything like off-roading for fun back home.

Much like their predecessors in World War II responded with "heighten[ed] emotional reaction[s] to natural settings," troops felt particularly awestruck by the mountains.[81] About half of Afghanistan sits at a height of 6500 feet, and the elevation rises dramatically in the Hindu Kush Mountains.[82] As Lieutenant Colonel Steve Truax recalls thinking as he flew over the mountains the first time, "My God, this is the trail that stopped Alexander the Great and the British Army."[83] Invoking the name Alexander the Great—one of the greatest military leaders in history—and the British Army, another great power in military history, suggests how intimidating the terrain had to be to stop such notable historical figures.

Shah Wali Kot District, Kandahar Province, Afghanistan. A view of the way ahead, taken from the gunner's turret on an M-ATV, shows the difficult terrain that the column had to move through. July 26, 2012 (photograph by Sergeant First Class Gary Malkin).

Afghan terrain appeared just as intimidating to a modern-day military service member, who had access to state-of-the-art technology. Major Mike Langley seems at a loss for words when he observes, "You just can't really explain how dark and how rugged and how bleak everything is there."[84] Rusty Bradley echoes the disquiet when he describes a mountain as "a rotten, jagged brown tooth sticking out of the sand."[85] Mixing his movie metaphors, Parnell references *Lord of the Rings* (2001) when he writes, "looks like we're at the gates of Mordor out here," looking at the mountains, and the shadows, he thinks, are like scary, soul-sucking Dementors from the *Harry Potter* films.[86] Major Robert Reed perceives the mountain passes as among the most beautiful—if scary—sights he had ever seen. He thought "it would become a climber's dream" if it were not in the middle of a war zone.[87]

One popular culture reference for Afghanistan makes sense only for a particular generation at a particular place and time. For some Americans who grew up in the US in the 1980s, one geographical feature in Afghanistan reminded them of Castle Greyskull from the children's cartoon *He-Man and the Masters of the Universe* (1983–1985).[88] The ruins of Bala Hissar, or High Fortress, date back to the fifth century CE and sit to the south of the capital, Kabul. British troops, for example, might associate the ruins with their history lessons from their Afghan wars.[89]

A Humvee from the 782nd Brigade Support Battalion, 4th Brigade Combat Team, 82nd Airborne Division Market Garden Combat Logistic Patrol navigates a difficult stretch of terrain on route to Forward Operating Base Orgun-E in Paktika Province, Afghanistan, on October 11, 2007 (photograph by Specialist Micah Clare).

Bagram Airfield, Afghanistan. After a day of rain, the beautiful Afghan mountains gleam in the sunlight on November 9, 2009. The high altitude of the Hindu Kush mountain range creates a harsh climate ranging from more than 100 degrees Fahrenheit in the summer to below-freezing temperatures in the winter (photograph by Captain David Faggard).

American troops immersed in pop culture gravitated to what proved familiar to them: Saturday morning cartoons.

For human bodies unaccustomed to the altitude, the first experiences in Afghanistan left the troops winded. Specialist Andrew Stock likens breathing thin mountain air as "breathing through a straw."[90] Mullaney writes that his "head felt like cotton candy" as a result of the altitude and lack of sleep.[91] Staff Sergeant Jason Thompson considers himself fit, but admits he had difficulty carrying his rucksack when he first arrived in Afghanistan.[92] Before his body acclimated to the elevation, even a short walk proved exhausting. "I feel like a gladiator entering the arena for the first time," Rico remarks. The Afghans laughed while watching the newly arrived troops struggle with the altitude and terrain, and Rico felt embarrassed.[93] After a while, troops became accustomed to their surroundings. As Anders reflects, nothing in the actual terrain had changed but his attitude toward the environment had improved. He describes the feeling as "less foreboding" and ascribes it to being more familiar with the landscape.[94]

American troops frequently commented on the weather extremes they experienced in Afghanistan. Seasonal winds caused havoc and discomfort for US troops. "The wind on the plains was vicious," observes Anders, describing the seasonal winds of 120 days. Just as predicted, the winds caused severe brownouts and "monstrous dust devils."[95] The wind kicked up sandstorms that affected flight operations, equipment, and physical comfort. Port-a-Potty latrines had to be secured lest they topple over. Dust worked its way into computers. It caused vehicles to break down and prompted soldiers to clean their weapons frequently. Troops could not keep clean once they stepped out of the shower.[96] "Just walking from the shower to the tent, I get dirty again," a soldier complains. Wind gusted into the chow tents, overturning plates. It caused physical discomfort. "I hate it," grouses Senior Airman Matt Berger. "It makes your nose bleed and your skin dry."[97]

Dust storms in Afghanistan proved so immense that they appeared on weather satellites. From the air, dust storms look like something out of a movie, according to Captain Curtis Garrett. "You could just see this wall of dust, almost up at your altitude, marching its way across the terrain," he describes.[98] The walls of dust towers proved high enough to prevent aircraft from landing safely. "On the roads, the effect can be similar to a whiteout, with oncoming traffic and secured behind a wall of beige powder," describes a journalist in Kandahar.[99] One service member remembers being caught in a dust storm with what he describes as a "towering wall of just dirt." It was so dense that service members only 10 feet away from their tents could get turned around and lost. Walking in the haze, troops became encrusted in the dust; "Their pockets were filled up with sand; their goggles and everything."[100] Whirling dust felt like "having your body rubbed with coarse sandpaper," observes Rusty Bradley.[101]

A dust storm rolls through the Kajaki Bazaar outside of Forward Operating Base Zeebruge, Helmand Province, Afghanistan, on June 3, 2013 (photograph by Lance Corporal William M. Kresse).

Even without the winds, the dust proved ever present. "It had the consistency of flour and seemed to defy gravity once it was disturbed," Anders writes. He adds that that the simple act of breathing in Afghanistan seemed like it was lining his lungs with dust.[102] Reflecting the common imagery of "alien" conditions in Afghanistan, Colonel Terry Sellers likens the dust to the moon. "You literally walked out, no joke, at least shin deep in a fine brown talcum powder dust," he explains, and "the soldiers were the same color as their uniforms." He concludes, "you felt like you were on the surface of the moon."[103] The dust proved so pervasive that Mullaney believes "I swallowed my own body weight in Afghan dust."[104] The dust invaded every crevice and opening in the human body. "It gets into your nose, it gets into your mouth it gets into your food," says Major Arthur Lyons. "I've had a sore throat ever since I got here," remarks Sergeant Ron Isola. "It's pretty brutal on your sinuses. Your eyes get dried out and your lips get pretty beat up," echoes Staff Sergeant Edward Smith.[105]

Afghanistan is hot and dry in the summer, and the troops found a variety of ways to describe it to friends and family back home, frequently invoking baking ovens and hair dryers to describe it. For a Special Forces soldier who served in both Iraq and Afghanistan, he felt the summers in Sangin in southern Afghanistan were hotter than Iraq.[106] Rico reports the temperature as "over 115 degrees in the shade," while Sergeant José Githens feels that it reached "150 degrees."[107] Major Chris Wells remembers fighting in 115 degree Fahrenheit heat and some of the soldiers had to stop engaging because of heat exhaustion. Combatants suffering heat exhaustion often have symptoms of cramping and vomiting.[108] Rico told his mother that he had "heard a hissing sound coming from my gear and realized it was my water boiling inside my canteen!"[109]

In the heat, Rusty Bradley "felt like a cookie slowly baking in the oven."[110] Lance Corporal Carlie Duggan, Jr., imagines it is "like when you open up the oven when you're cooking a pizza and you want to see if it's done, you get that blast of hot air."[111] Not even the breeze could penetrate the suffocating heat. Githens describes the breeze in the heat as "like a hair dryer blowing finely powdered dirt at close range into my eyes, nose, ears, mouth, and even under my clothes."[112] Rusty Bradley also used the comparison of the hair dryer to explain the environment in Afghanistan to a college student who asked him about it. He told her that fighting in 120 degree heat was like putting "a salon-sized hair dryer in your face at full blast" for days on end. While enduring the heat, he adds, "try to stay hydrated by drinking warm bathwater while stepping into and out of the bathtub while holding a radio, trying not to get killed."[113]

Troops' gear amplified the effects of the heat. A fully geared soldier, Tupper explains, "resemble[s] someone properly suited for winter climates, not extreme heat."[114] For example, soldiers wear about 33 pounds of body armor on top of the long sleeves, pants, thick socks, heavy boots, and gloves of the Army Combat Uniform. "Within minutes," Tupper describes, "your complete torso is soaked through with sweat," making it "a 100 percent effective heat-retaining and heat-maximizing uniform."[115] Rusty Bradley notes the heat rash that he and his men suffered from as a result of the extreme heat, sweaty uniforms, and chafing gear. The heat and sweat clogged skin pores with salt, oil, and dirt, which meant "dragging my body armor on and off felt like having glass ground into my skin."[116] Air conditioning proved nonexistent in rural forward operating bases.

Service members who served in Iraq also suffered through the intense heat of summer, but troops in Afghanistan also endured subarctic winters and snow. Indeed, troops could find themselves in hundred degree temperatures in the desert, then have a mission in snowcapped mountains the next day, experiencing wild temperature swings.[117] Major Christy Erwin admits, "I wasn't ready for the snow." She expected it to be hot like Iraq, so she was unprepared for the sub-zero temperatures found in Afghan winters. "That was a big shock for me," she adds.[118]

Corporal Jason Hazelwood, an artilleryman with Headquarters and Headquarters Battery, 3rd Battalion, 16th Field Artillery Regiment, 2nd Brigade Combat Team, 4th Infantry Division, builds a snowman on November 10, 2011. The small combat outpost in Qadis received six inches of snow within a 12-hour period (photograph by Sergeant Ruth Pagan).

The first winter storms often bring snowball fights and snowmen—some with vests and turbans—but then the snow and cold lost their fascination. Troops pulled out cold weather gear and strapped snow chains on the tires of their vehicles. Troops still had to patrol and conduct missions, even as enemy activity slowed.[119] As Tupper explained, snow drove the insurgents away. He recalls, "cold, bitter winds, slippery surfaces, and frozen extremities was like an army of white that had arrived to rout the enemy from these hilly hiding places."[120] Snow storms brought down snow measured in feet. As one soldier remembers, "nine feet of snow had fallen in the past six weeks" where he was stationed.[121]

Cold weather proved dangerous for troops, just as it had been for troops in World War II and the Korean War.[122] Anders remembers that it got so cold that frost coated their weapons and breathing became more difficult. When his nose hairs began to freeze, he thought, "Hell, it seems, had actually frozen over." The men looked out for cold weather injuries and moved around to keep blood circulation going. Even so, Anders' feet, hands, and faced ached from the cold by the end of one patrol.[123] For Stock, he admits that "these Texas toes have never felt such mountain cold."[124] Similarly, Logan Lewis describes how "I could slowly feel the cold seep through my clothes. I went from a mild cold to freezing in less than a minute." The cold affected his extremities, making it "excruciating" to stand on his cold feet.[125] Flying in the mountains proved just as bitterly cold. Helicopter pilot Amber Smith remembers that "the frigid air that came in the cockpit made exposed skin feel as if it were being stabbed with a thousand needles."[126]

A paratrooper from 2nd Platoon, Able Company, 2nd Battalion, 503rd Infantry Regiment (Airborne), navigates a steep incline during a patrol to Omar in Konar Province, Afghanistan, on January 11, 2008 (photograph by Staff Sergeant Brandon Aird).

Spring thaws turned the terrain into mud, where the dust became like clay or cement in the wet weather. The clay did not allow the water to drain properly, so the entire surface remained wet and muddy. Mud made the roads nearly impassable. Convoys and local Afghan trucks became stuck in the mire, tangling up traffic. Anders remembers one mission where the Humvees got stuck in shin-deep mud a mere two kilometers from base. It took them two hours to maneuver through the sludge as the soldiers' frustration mounted and they became covered in mud.[127]

Torrential downpours blighted the landscape. One service member recalls how it rained three inches in six hours, flooding the base two feet deep in places. The rain swept away Afghan villages, prompting US troops to provide humanitarian assistance.[128] Rico remembers a time when it rained for days on end at Kandahar, creating pools of water knee-deep. Service members had laid out wooden pallets, planks, and tires so that one could jump from one to the other to navigate the base.[129]

In addition to the mountains, wind, dust, heat, cold, and rain, American troops encountered creatures alien to the United States. Service members saw rhesus monkeys, leopards, giant porcupines, and lizards as long as six feet. The insects drew much attention from the troops, such as centipedes which grew longer than a foot.[130] Rico exclaims, "The ants down here are ferocious! And huge! The size of spiders! And they bite and they are everywhere!"[131] Similarly, Romesha recalls a spider-like ant that they dubbed "crack ants." The spiders, as he

Soldiers from C Company, 26th Field Artillery Regiment recover a stuck Humvee that attempted to cross a muddy road in the Khowst Province, Afghanistan. March 25, 2007 (US Army photograph by Staff Sergeant Isaac A. Graham).

remembers them, "were enormous, the yellow gray bodies the size of hot dogs that looked big enough to kill and eat birds."[132] These camel spiders, as they were called, grew larger than a man's hand and were capable of eating lizards, scorpions, and birds. To quell boredom soldiers would sometimes put a camel spider and scorpion together to watch them fight, a pastime shared by veterans of the Iraq and Persian Gulf wars, too.[133]

More than one service member found a snake or giant spider in a cot, sleeping bag, or latrine. While many of the insects grew to larger than expected proportions, the most deadly creature troops encountered was probably the sand colored carpet viper. This snake commonly grows to two-feet in length, and its venom is particularly dangerous, causing blood clots or bleeding if not treated quickly. In addition, the Naja Naja cobra, also known as the Asiatic cobra, could be found in southern Afghanistan. A grown adult can reach eight feet in length and stand four feet before it strikes. With all the critters, troops made sure to check boots, uniforms, and sleeping bags carefully before use. The snakes and critters proved more worrisome than the Taliban. Unlike troops in previous wars, service members in Afghanistan did not contend with lice, mosquitos, leeches, or other nuisances.[134]

Another way in which Afghanistan seemed different from home was the unpleasant smells American troops encountered. Afghanistan did not smell good to American noses, reminding most of them of human or animal waste. Staff Sergeant Thompson recalled it took two to three weeks to acclimate to the air quality in Afghanistan. He describes the smell in Kabul as "like breathing pure feces."[135] Similarly, in another city, Ghazni, "the streets are open sewers, and piles of garbage litter the intersection," Rico observes. As for its odor, "the ripe smell of rotten fruit and feces reminds me of the monkey cage at the zoo," he adds.[136] Stationed on the border with Pakistan, another service member recalls that "it smelled of urine, crap, and unwashed humanity."[137] In another area, Parnell describes "a combination of BO, rotting hay, feces, and mildew overpowering our noses" in one of the places he patrolled.[138] Rusty Bradley claims "Afghanistan smells like an open sewer running past a pine wood fire."[139]

Even American bases sometimes smelled awful. Back in 2002, Kandahar Air Field smelled like "raw sewage, spiced with the odor of disinfectant from the latrines outside the tent, not to mention occasional gusts of diesel fuel flowing off the line of helicopters on a nearby runway," according to one source.[140] Unbathed troops built up body odor. Some troops even made a game of it, "holding competitions to see who could build up the most impressive stink." Quarters sometimes reeked of "a layered mix of corn chips, body funk, and ass." As many of the troops worked out at the gym and took dietary supplements to build muscle, the supplements caused the men to be very gassy, "filling the air with noxious fumes," according to Romesha.[141]

Though American troops could find some familiarity in Afghanistan, such as landscapes that looked like Colorado or the American Southwest, most of the place proved unfamiliar. For many troops, it appeared as a step back in time or a completely alien environment. Even the creatures appeared alien. The weather

Old Ghazni City, located in Ghazni Province, Afghanistan. April 18, 2020 (photograph by Technical Sergeant James May).

extremes, altitude, and dust made deployments to Afghanistan physically uncomfortable. Once it became clear that American troops would be in-country for some time, the US military turned its attention to bringing parts of America to Afghanistan by building expansive, and very Western, forward operating bases.

•• 2 ••

Living Spaces

Living conditions for service members in Afghanistan varied considerably from austere observation posts, firebases or Combat Outposts (COPs) to fully supplied, almost stateside-like Forward Operating Bases (FOBs). Without a firm commitment to stay in Afghanistan for any length of time at the beginning of the war, the initial bases used by US personnel remained sparse. As it became clear that troops would remain in-country for the foreseeable future, the US began to build up large FOBs in Bagram and in Kandahar that included many of the amenities one would find stateside.

In other words, American consumerism came with the troops to Afghanistan. Units deployed to other areas of Afghanistan contended with more limited resources with the most remote outposts having the least amenities. Large, fully-supplied FOBs coexisted alongside the austere outposts so that a service member's location governed living conditions. Some service members spent their entire deployments on the large FOBs, while others courted danger in remote locations, recreating a traditional schism between the rear troops and the combatants.

In many ways, the American experiences in both Iraq and Afghanistan parallel the living conditions provided to US military personnel in Vietnam. As historian Meredith Lair argues, in Vietnam "the U.S. military built an Americanized world for its soldiers to inhabit, while the high-tech nature of American warfare and a sophisticated logistics effort to care for the troops guaranteed that a majority of soldiers ... labored in supporting roles, out of danger and in relative comfort."[1] Much the same can be said for the large FOBs created for the troops in Iraq and Afghanistan. Bases in Vietnam as well as Iraq and Afghanistan "were comparable to cities in the United States" and had a host of service personnel to keep the places running smoothly.[2] Both wars brought American consumerism to large, overseas bases.

From start to end, deployment created a different daily rhythm, starting with the time zone. Troops followed Zulu time while deployed to Afghanistan, which is Greenwich Mean Time (GMT), rather than local time. Afghanistan is 4 hours and 30 minutes ahead of GMT. As a result of the time shift, dawn comes around 12:30 a.m. Zulu and the sun sets at 1400 (2:00 p.m.) Zulu. Lights out comes around 1800 (6:00 p.m.) Zulu.[3] The difference between local time and Zulu, plus the time lag arriving from the US, required initial adjustments.

In the early years of the war, on the way to Afghanistan, many troops traveled through Karshi-Khanabad Air Base in Uzbekistan, nicknamed K2. The old Soviet air base was transformed into a modern American establishment with a rewired control tower, new hospital, and communications arrays. C-17 transport planes lifted in tons of supplies. In a couple of short months after the start of hostilities in October 2001, "thousands of soldiers and aircraft in vehicles closed along paved and graveled streets with names like Broadway, Maine, and Lexington, all marked with road signs."[4] The old Soviet air base had become a mini–American city. Later, Uzbekistan cancelled the agreement, and the Americans left K2.[5]

Inside Afghanistan, Americans took over the old Soviet air base, Bagram, outside of the capital city, Kabul. The place was scattered with wreckage of old Soviet equipment, planes and vehicles, and surrounded by mine fields. Air National Guardsman Staff Sergeant Scott Kauffman, recalls that in his tent he had "a heater about the size of a soda can." Given that the temperature fell below freezing, he kept on his jacket and gloves to stay warm, even in the tent. Describing Bagram at the time, he states "we woke up the next morning, opened the tent door, and it was like waking up in the middle of a Russian junk yard." At first, security proved minimal—a single chain-linked fence.[6] Air Force personnel began to

The 416th Air Expeditionary Group's aerial port flight at Karshi-Khanabad Air Base, Uzbekistan, takes care of soldiers who need transportation to forward-deployed locations on February 4, 2004 (photograph by Colonel Tim Vining).

transform Bagram into a functioning base. They set up tents, sinks, and showers. Concertina wire kept troops away from the uncleared mine fields.[7]

Staff Sergeant Antuan Ray explains that cleaning up Bagram came as extra duty after his regular 10- to 12-hour days. As they cleaned, the service members came across "all kinds of snakes and vipers, unexploded ordnance in the porta-potties, rats in the MREs [Meals Ready to Eat]."[8] In addition to cleaning, the troops constructed a makeshift hospital in the old airfield control tower. They had to cover broken windows, patch bullet holes in the walls, and install electricity.[9] It was an exhausting job cleaning and modernizing the base. Taking in the decrepit state of his surroundings, Private Drew Alan Ramm muses, "these people here must like fighting for fighting's sake because there sure isn't anything here worth fighting for."[10]

Within months, thanks to the hard work of the service personnel at Bagram, the base began to resemble a stateside post. As Sergeant Major C.J. Costello discovered upon arrival at Bagram, her living quarters consisted of a wooden-framed tent with fluorescent lighting with a foam mattress atop her cot. She even had a coffee pot. The tent was located near the showers, which had hot running water. By this time, Bagram sported a new electrical system and a new hospital. A Post Exchange, or PX, opened for service members to purchase snacks, toiletries, and DVDs to watch. Tellingly, troops began to follow military courtesies, such

A sign welcomes troops to Bagram Air Base. Note the flags of the other International Security Assistance Force member nations. October 6, 2002. P-0493. Civil Affairs & Psychological Operations, Operation Enduring Freedom: Historical Collection, 126th Military History Detachment, 2003, US Army Heritage and Education Center.

as saluting, common to a stateside posting, not a combat zone. Just outside the Bagram's gates, local Afghans set up a weekly bazaar to tempt service members to purchase pirated movies and music as well as local goods.[11]

Modern technology enabled the military to oversee the war from inside the main bases. Computers hummed in the operations center at Bagram. Troops spread across the room in a semi-circle of tables and chairs, facing a large video monitor. It was staffed in two 12-hour shifts daily, overseen by the officer in charge, nicknamed "battle captains." Battle captains monitored troop locations, while others tracked communications. Intelligence officers updated information. Other service members watched over the air space, keeping track of aircraft. Additional personnel in the operations center included those tasked to forecast the weather, liaisons for the Afghan government as well as subordinate units, Judge Advocate General lawyers for questions concerning the rules of engagement and a nuclear, biological and chemical watch officer. Remarking on the weight of responsibility resting on the shoulders of the personnel in the operations center, Major Anthony Yando said, "we realize that if we make a mistake, people die."[12]

Farther south, the marines established another main base at Kandahar Air Field (KAF). Unlike Bagram, which was fairly secure from the beginning, KAF initially endured enemy attacks. When the 101st Airborne Division arrived there in January 2002, Taliban and al-Qaeda insurgents attacked the perimeter defenses,

DVDs sold at an Afghan bazaar. October 11, 2002. P-0662. Civil Affairs & Psychological Operations, Operation Enduring Freedom: Historical Collection, 126th Military History Detachment, 2003, US Army Heritage and Education Center.

US Army First Lieutenant Katherine Robinson fields a question from her work station. Robinson, executive officer for Headquarters and Headquarters Troop, Task Force Shooter, 10th Combat Aviation Brigade, 10th Mountain Division, TF Falcon, spent the majority of her time with the squadron as a battle captain in the tactical operations center. April 23, 2011 (photograph by US Army Sergeant First Class JR Williams).

and some soldiers stepped off the plane right into a firefight with insurgents. As Sean Naylor reported at the time, one brigade commander channeled remarks from the movie *Patton* (1970) to his troops, emphasizing the combat role they were playing in Afghanistan: "No matter what happens, in 30 years' time, when you got your grandchild on your knee, and he asks you what did you do in the great war on terrorism, you won't have to say, well, I shoveled shit in Louisiana." No doubt the commander meant to emphasize the importance of their mission, tying it to the Greatest Generation fighting in World War II.[13] It probably also helped that the pop culture reference resonated with troops who had grown up with Hollywood movies.

Conditions at KAF proved austere in the first months of its occupation. At first, the US expected to stay in Kandahar for a mere two to three months. Troops slept on the ground in freezing temperatures, ate MREs, and bathed in rudimentary, cold-water showers. For shaving and hair washing, warm water had to be heated by propane burners. Troops had to contend with tainted water, forcing them to boil it or use bottled water for drinking instead. A small luxury proved to be hot coffee, served in a tent that the 187th Airborne Infantry (nicknamed "Rakkasans") called the Hard Rak Café. Before the Post Exchange arrived, troops at KAF bartered and bought items from the locals. Afghans marked up prices considerably for the troops, who were eager to get their hands on Afghan scarves, gloves, and other items. At one point, cigarettes sold for $50 a carton because they were in such demand.[14]

One challenge in any location where troops were lodged was how to maintain sanitary conditions. As an observer notes, "one of the most striking aspects of infantrymen's life is the intimate relationships they are forced to maintain with shit."[15] It permeates the air, is a topic of conversation, and burning it stands as one of the most detested duties available. At first, troops used communal, wooden latrines, where the waste was collected and had to be eliminated. The "shit truck" detail entails taking the contents of the latrines, mixing it with fuel, and setting in on fire.[16]

"It sounds simple enough" describes one soldier, "but if you just stood there and watched it burn, the flames would incinerate only the top layer inside the barrel." If only the surface burned, that meant that the unfortunate soul on "shitter" detail had to stir the contents. As the flames consumed the fuel, smoke and "burning particles of poo wafted up into your face" as the soldier stirred. The odor proved revolting, and the process could take from one to three hours to complete.[17] The makeshift latrines were accompanied by "piss tubes" of six inch PVC pipes dug into the ground. Where even latrines were a luxury, troops had to use "wag bags" with a powder to absorb moisture. These, too, ended up in a burn pile.[18]

Sabari District, Afghanistan: A US soldier from the 4–320th Field Artillery Battalion of the 101st Airborne Division uses diesel fuel to burn feces from toilets used by personnel at the outpost on January 17, 2009, in Sabari District, Khowst Province, Afghanistan. The method of disposing of feces is common at combat outposts that lack basic facilities (photograph by Jonathan Saruk/Getty Images).

As the FOBs became established, the military installed porta-potties and outsourced their upkeep to local Afghans. On one outpost in Kandahar, the soldiers dubbed the local Afghan who came to vacuum out the porta-potties "Bob Vila," after the host of the home improvement series *This Old House*. This Afghan earned his nickname because "he had a very short, thick beard that made him look like, well, Bob Vila." The Afghan cleaned regularly until he failed to show one week. "Days went by," one soldier recalls, "you could start to notice the smell all over the outpost. Every time we went into a porta-potty, you could see the level of poop rising like a newly formed landmass after a volcano eruption." When the toilets reached capacity, the soldiers were forced back to using ammo cans to collect waste. Then "Bob Vila" returned. It turns out that he had been on vacation.[19]

Rough conditions and lack of hygiene caused troops to become ill. Dysentery running through the troops caused some troops to nickname the place "Ass-Crack-istan." Additionally, medics frequently treated service members complaining of nausea and stomach problems. At Kandahar, troops nicknamed a flu-like ailment "Kandahar crud."[20]

Following sanitation guidelines proved only a small fraction of the rules and regulations which governed service members in Afghanistan. Unlike US troops in earlier wars, who had access to alcohol and local women, for soldiers deployed overseas in Iraq and Afghanistan, General Order (GO) 1 prohibited drinking alcohol and engaging in sexual relations. Unsurprisingly, violations of GO 1 occurred in Afghanistan. Service members managed to acquire alcohol and got drunk. Sometimes family members sent alcohol in care packages. Other times, the Americans managed to procure it from other NATO members who shared their bases. Those NATO troops did not have the same restrictions on alcohol.[21] When authorities cracked down on unauthorized alcohol, one battalion commander "found cases and cases of booze hidden behind a false wall in the company headquarters" in one example.[22]

Service members deployed to Afghanistan pursued sexual relations as well, though they tended to be with other American personnel rather than with the local population. "If anyone thinks there's no sex, [they're] kidding themselves," one female soldier reports.[23] Married personnel sometimes had affairs with others in their units. Female service members, who were vastly outnumbered by their male colleagues, attracted attention from males, sometimes accepted and other times not. Sometimes service members would drive off to a secluded location on base for a tryst. Occasionally, these sexual encounters resulted in pregnancies. When pregnancy was discovered, service women were ordered home as military regulation bars deployment for pregnant service members. Troops caught violating GO 1 were sometimes punished with a reduction in rank, though there was wide discretion afforded to commanders in terms of applying disciplinary measures.[24]

Illicit drug use also proved a problem for some service members. One way to get high was by "huffing," or inhaling vapors from aerosol cans. Some friends and family members sent brownies baked with pot to their loved ones. Service members also procured hashish to smoke.[25] One Army investigation of the 5th Stryker Brigade Combat Team concluded that soldiers from 2nd Battalion, 1st Infantry

Regiment regularly smoked hashish during their 2009 deployment.[26] Drug tests are not administered during deployments, so the scope of the problem remains unknown. Other government reports conclude that illicit drug use is fairly low among active duty service members compared to the US population as a whole when they are stateside.[27]

Another unauthorized activity that many service members took up was keeping pets. In one example, in a unit at Camp Phoenix, at least four dogs and two cats had been adopted by lonely service members, kept hidden from command. Often commanders turned a blind eye to such pets. If someone got hurt because of an animal, commanders had to crack down on the practice. The soldiers at Camp Phoenix had to give up their pets when a stray dog had been rumored to have rabies. Commanders rounded up the pets, and the soldiers never found out what happened to them, though they suspected they had all been euthanized.[28]

Other regulations required troops to wear their combat gear, even on base, though it varied by service and nation. Soldiers in the US Army faced the most onerous requirements to wear their full battle gear of helmet, bulletproof vest, and weapon at all times, whereas airmen and marines merely wore their uniforms with personal weapon while walking on post. The Canadian Army similarly required body armor and helmets for its troops. The Special Forces soldiers took the most relaxed attitude toward military formalities, as they wore uniforms comprised partly of Army desert uniforms, partly of Afghan clothing such as hats, scarves, or blankets, and partly civilian clothing, such as jeans. Unless going out on a mission, the operators eschewed wearing body armor.[29]

By spring 2002, the physical infrastructure at KAF had improved. There were showers, though one had to wait up to 90 minutes to use one. They operated only for a couple hours a day for the female troops deployed there. Still, it was an improvement. The wooden latrines had been replaced by portable ones. Some hot meals served in tents replaced the steady diet of MREs, though troops still lacked fresh fruit and vegetables, relying on pre-packaged tray-rations. A small PX, which popped up in a tent adjoined to one of the buildings, proved so popular that troops lined up three hours before it opened. A Morale, Welfare, and Recreation (MWR) tent opened up, screening movies, sports, and news. Computers and Internet access allowed troops to contact home. The KAF also hosted the first live concert for the troops, the band Mink. Even surrounded by concertina wire and guard posts, KAF came under rocket and mortar attack.[30] It was a reminder that despite the touches of home with shopping, movies, and computers, Kandahar was still in a war zone.

As spring turned into summer, the temperature around Kandahar steadily rose, prompting the first air conditioning units to be installed. Showers with temperature controls came too. Fresh produce appeared in the chow hall. Even with these perks, improvements at Kandahar trailed behind the amenities at Bagram. One officer muses, "it just seems that we are behind because no one thought we would be here for very long," which was true. The length of America's commitment to Afghanistan kept getting extended beyond what had been initially expected. It was also more difficult to supply Kandahar, sitting in the middle of

Taliban territory, than it was to deliver goods to Bagram, safely ensconced in Northern Alliance territory.[31]

More stringent uniform standards arrived in Afghanistan by autumn. Confronted with media photos of Special Forces soldiers in beards and out of uniform, the Pentagon ordered increased grooming standards. The edict frustrated the Special Forces soldiers, who noted that Afghans assign wisdom and maturity to male facial hair. One soldier explains, "In this culture, men respect men who have the ability to grow facial hair, and the longer the better." Though the Special Forces troops dressed and ate like Afghans to blend in with the local population, Western civilian aid agencies criticized the behavior. As Robert Goodwin of Mercy Corps clarifies, "We were concerned that they were dressed as aid workers." These complaints reached the ears of military commanders, who subsequently "agreed that American soldiers in Afghanistan would wear at least the parts of the uniform with an American flag patch, and would not conceal their weapons" to avoid confusion with the aid organizations.[32]

Conditions at KAF steadily improved to resemble more closely a stateside post with many more touches of home. It gained gyms, beauty and barber shops, and a 24-hour theater to watch movies. The small PX expanded to sell televisions, mountain bikes, and video game consoles. A trip to the chow hall now featured T-bone steak, lobster, fresh salad and baked potatoes. Troops constructed a makeshift golf driving range at the edge of the base. Mid-afternoon, troops headed for the MWR tent to watch the big screen televisions or call home. Most importantly for the safety of the troops, enemy contact had all but ceased.[33] Over the next year, the MWR tent and gym expanded. A new PX mini-mall offered shops for jewelry, sporting goods, coffee, and uniform alteration. New, modular housing units with central air conditioning, toilets, and showers replaced tents. A Nathan's Hog Dog franchise opened along with Pizza Hut.

Six years into the war, Kandahar was home to around 10,000 people, including international troops.[34] The international troops from NATO brought their own shops to the FOB as well. The Italians built a pizzeria, while the French opened a café offering smoked salmon. Meanwhile, the Canadians brought over the Tim Horton's coffee franchise, and "it seemed as if at least a quarter of all the Canadians on the base were waiting in line for a beignet and a double-double (a coffee with two sugars and two shots of cream)." To gain the patronage of Americans under the General Order 1 restrictions, the Dutch served nonalcoholic beer at their bar. The Germans constructed a sporting goods store, which sold "all manner of tough-guy paraphernalia: long hunting knives, brass knuckles, and camouflage outfits" and more. The Canadians built a hockey rink, too.[35] Not only had American commercialism come to Afghanistan, but wholescale Western consumer culture as well.

The large-scale consumerism on the FOBs did not sit well with General Stanley McChrystal. When he took command in Afghanistan in 2009, he shut down some of the fast food franchises. Though Burger King went away, it was replaced by a sit-down TGI Friday's restaurant. The problem with the change was that "instead of wasting fifteen minutes at Burger King, troops began spending

Soldiers, other coalition members, and civilian contractors fill the aisles of the Post Exchange (PX) on April 9, 2012. It was the grand opening of the new Camp Marmal PX (photograph by Sergeant Richard Wrigley).

an hour waiting for a table at TGI Friday's and then another hour or two eating and gabbing," undermining the entire point of forcing out fast food.[36] Though the reform proved counterproductive in terms of time and efficiency, the troops clearly enjoyed the experience of eating out, just like at home. Consumer culture would not be easily dismissed as long as large numbers of troops continued to deploy. As one public affairs officer explains the logic behind lavish base amenities, "if the soldiers have a good quality of life on base, it means the morale is high when out on missions."[37]

All the Western goods brought to Afghanistan for the troops proved a temptation for theft by the locals to be resold later at the bazaar to American troops. "They collect a lot of stuff from the rubbish," one Afghan teenager admits. Another shopkeeper acknowledges, "we know most of it is stolen." Afghans set up a bazaar outside of KAF and sold electronic goods, military gear, Western foodstuffs, sleeping bags, military boots, and camouflage uniforms, even ones that were used. Some of the items appear to have come from the base, but given the low prices—$25 tee shirts went for $4—meant they were stolen goods.[38]

Bagram Air Base experienced a similar growth in size and amenities, enjoyed by service members stopping there temporarily before going elsewhere in-country. These troops stayed in transitional housing, a large tent with temporary floors sporting cots.[39] Service members made use of the showers, a fully equipped gym, and fresh fruit and made-to-order omelets in the chow hall. On Fridays, the chow hall offered steak and seafood. Supplementing the chow hall were a Green Beans Coffee shop, Burger King, and Subway. Troops visited the beauty salon and could get massages at the spa. They watched movies, listened to music, and played video games. Troops could take distance learning classes and dance lessons.

Outside the perimeter gate, troops could visit the Afghan bazaar where they could purchase everything from jewelry to pirated DVDs. They could even take pictures with a camel to send home. Female service members particularly liked to use the salon services to help them feel feminine in an overly monochromatic and male environment on the FOBs. Even with all the amenities built up in Bagram, Amber Smith thought that Bagram paled in comparison to the infrastructure built for troops deployed to Iraq.[40] Major Marvin Linson agreed. Afghanistan consistently came second in the two main theaters of the Global War on Terror. He deployed to Afghanistan in 2010 and notes, "I can relate it back to 2005 when I deployed; the infrastructure in Afghanistan was not even to the level we were at in Iraq in 2005 and there we were five years later in Afghanistan."[41]

Troops who left the luxuries of the big bases at Bagram or Kandahar had to adjust to more austere conditions in smaller bases. Camp Ghazni offered three hot meals at the chow hall and hot water for the showers. Still, troops had to launder their uniforms by hand in buckets. Troops adhered to 15-minute time limits on phones and the Internet. Sergeant Doug Cote says, "You wake up, exercise, eat, call home, do some training and maybe go out on a mission," and adds "you get excited about the ice cream and the soda. Just little things."[42] Michael Creedon

Sergeant First Class David Richey, Detachment 62, 95th Division, US Army Reserve, receives the first Pizza Hut pizza after a reopening ceremony on February 20, 2011, at Camp Phoenix in Kabul, Afghanistan. Richey, along with several other service members and civilians, came to eat and celebrate Pizza Hut's return (photograph by Sergeant Rebecca Linder).

remembers that his small FOB, Naray (later renamed Bostick), in Konar Province, sported a small gym, MWR tent, and chow hall. Though they had a few wood buildings on base, he spent his entire deployment in a tent.[43]

Camp Tiger in Ghazni had even fewer amenities. Troops encountered a makeshift chow hall, cold showers that cut off mid-stream, and no access to the Internet. They wore the same uniform for days on end. One soldier complains, "I'm gonna find some rocks and start beating my clothes" to launder the uniform, harkening back to the days before electricity and washing machines. "It's just like a prison, but I got a gun," gripes another soldier, clearly frustrated by the restrictions necessitated by a small base in a hostile environment. A third soldier took it all in stride singing "the Mr. Rogers' Neighborhood theme song. Only he was saying it was a beautiful day in Afghanistan, instead of a beautiful day in the neighborhood."[44]

Even in remote locations and austere conditions, the military came bristling with modern technology. One service member describes the operations center as "filled with the latest space age gear—satellite communications, computers, display screens, miles of wire, and hundreds of blinking lights," which generators powered.[45] Rusty Bradley likens the inside of the Tactical Operations Center (TOC) as "the bridge of a starship," with screens showing video feeds from Predator drones, others tracking unit movements. He compares the battle captain to "the conductor of the orchestra of war."[46]

A view of tents inside an American base in Afghanistan on October 29, 2002. P-1594. Civil Affairs & Psychological Operations, Operation Enduring Freedom: Historical Collection, 126th Military History Detachment, 2003, US Army Heritage and Education Center.

Soldiers of Charlie Company, 1st Battalion, 148th Infantry Regiment, 37th Infantry Brigade Combat Team, sort through incoming mail at their remote combat outpost, Ghormach, Afghanistan, February 20, 2012 (photograph by Sergeant Kimberly Derryberry).

Troops enjoyed the first July 4 holiday as well. They played basketball and soccer. For the celebration, the military had seven thousand T-bone steaks flown in from Nebraska, as well as crab legs, corn, and baked beans for the troops. The party was "a welcome relief from the military ration packs that make up the daily diet of the troops here."[137] Other troops threw together informal holiday parties, such as for St. Patrick's Day.[138] Troops celebrated Easter one year with a sunrise service on the roof of the motor pool building.[139]

Since before World War II, Thanksgiving has held a special place in military celebrations as the mess hall rolls out an entire traditional turkey feast served by the officers. For the 12,000 troops deployed to Afghanistan in 2002, the military secured "6400 pounds of turkey, 11,635 pounds of ham, 8200 pounds of beef ribeye, 1260 pounds of collard greens and 624 pumpkin pies." Even the troops scattered in outlying posts enjoyed the offerings as helicopters flew the food out to them.[140] One soldier fondly remembers Thanksgiving in 2004: "The DFAC [Dining Facility] personnel put on a very lavish spread[;] it was very nice," she wrote in her diary. "Even had an ice sculpture," she added.[141]

Sometimes the troops took holiday celebrations into their own hands. One year, the troops stationed in Barakai-Barak raised its own turkeys to eat on Thanksgiving. The soldiers took a 55-gallon drum and turned it into a smoker. They ate traditional fare along with Afghan flatbread and nonalcoholic beer.[142] Other troops decided to forgo the traditional turkey meal in favor of fresh grilled meat.[143]

Thanksgiving dinner, November 28, 2002. Feeding troops well is an Army tradition to keep morale high through the holidays when service members are separated from friends and family. P-3016. Civil Affairs & Psychological Operations, Operation Enduring Freedom: Historical Collection, 126th Military History Detachment, 2003, US Army Heritage and Education Center.

Christmas, too, came with a hearty feast. The first year of the war, the German government provided the holiday meal for the troops stationed at Bagram. The troops scrounged together materials to make a Christmas tree from mosquito netting and invented Christmas carols, singing "on the second day of Christmas, my sergeant gave to me, two hand grenades and a ride in a busted Humvee" to the tune of "The 12 Days of Christmas."[144] By the second year of the war, the troops decorated their bunks with Christmas lights and little Christmas trees. The chow hall provided turkey, mashed potatoes, gravy, cranberry sauce, salad, and more. There were interdenominational Christmas services and carols.[145] One year, the troops in Kandahar decided to stage a Christmas pageant reenacting the Three Wise Men arriving on camels.[146] Where there were pine trees, the troops cut one down for the Christmas tree. They decorated it with "spent shell casings, chemlights, grenade spoons, and an assortment of other military themed trinkets."[147] Helicopters delivered Christmas gifts to troops in remote outposts.[148] At COP Spera, a helicopter "delivered several trunks full of hot food fresh from Salerno," remembers Rickard.[149]

Living conditions in Afghanistan started out austere, as the United States had no intention of a long-term presence in the country. As the war continued

Soldiers from the 25th Signal Battalion decorate a Christmas tree for a Christmas tree lighting ceremony on Bagram Airfield, Afghanistan. December 17, 2011 (photograph by Sergeant Melisa Washington.

unabated and America's commitment to Afghanistan lengthened, Americans built up expansive FOBs, bringing in the comforts and luxuries of home and bringing American consumerism overseas. At the same time, the military maintained more austere COPs and firebases in remote areas. The experience of troops, therefore, depended on when and where they were stationed in-country—early in the war or in a remote location, conditions proved sparse. Additionally, the gap between frontline combatants and rear-echelon troops remained as stark as in previous wars. Modern communications allowed for almost constant contact with home, a new development for the wars in Iraq and Afghanistan. As always, troops found ways to entertain themselves, even as the routine became like *Groundhog Day*. Troops took the opportunity to break from the routine to celebrate holidays. Though America brought its culture to Afghanistan, many service members who had contact with the local population got to experience Afghan culture as well.

•• 3 ••

Getting to Know the Locals

"When we think of military occupation, we don't generally imagine it as a cultural immersion experience for young Americans," assert Marian Eide and Michael Gibler. "These men and women have the unusual experience of living in a war zone but also sharing in another culture's customs in a way that no tourist could."[1] During pre-deployment training, troops learned about Afghan culture and language. Yet, American troops did not regularly live, work, and interact with Afghans in their cities and villages. Troops patrolled and attended meetings, but for the most part stayed on their bases. When patrolling through villages, troops carried weapons, which created distance between the troops and the local villagers.

When Americans did interact with Afghans, many exhibited an attitude of cultural superiority, especially with respect to the treatment of women and the rule of law. American troops found aspects of Muslim culture's notion of *Inshallah*, or "as God wills," particularly frustrating as it seemed to be an excuse not to act as Americans believed the Afghans should. On the other hand, many service members appreciated the culture of hospitality, included in what is known as *Pashtunwali*, the traditional tribal code of many Pashtun Afghans. While service members might show gratitude or even affection for their interpreters, most did not trust or have faith in the capabilities of the locals. With over a decade of exposure, neither the Americans nor the Afghans learned to trust one another. Without trust and genuine cooperation, successfully winning over the population, creating effective government structures, and defeating the insurgency proved unachievable.

Afghans are divided by ethnicity, tribe, clan, family networks, and religion, though most Afghans are Sunni Muslims. Despite the fragmentation, "Afghans have a very clear, indeed often xenophobic, sense of the foreigner, resistance to outsiders who seek to impose their will," according to scholars.[2] One American observer notes that "the tribes tend to have 'stereotypes.' Tajiks are usually more passive and pay more attention to academics. The Pashtu fight more. The Hazara are more hospitable."[3] As with any generalization, these descriptions may not apply to particular individuals within the group. Afghan culture includes both hospitality and a deep sense of honor. If someone offends an Afghan's honor, he often reacts violently.[4]

American service members often felt the vast differences in culture and outlook between themselves and the Afghans, generating descriptions of alien worlds. "They looked at us like we were from another planet. We looked at them the same way," Captain Robert Anders remarks.[5] Similarly, Lieutenant Sean Parnell echoes the sentiment with his recollection that "they stared at us as we passed as if we had come from a different planet."[6] Special Forces officer Michael Waltz reflects, even after his training and preparation, "As I looked around at the villages dotting the countryside, I was seized by how little I really knew about the people here and what we were getting ourselves into." His soldiers knew little of the tribal make-up of the area of operations or what motivated them to support the insurgents—and this was four years into the war.[7]

Those service members who deployed both to Iraq and Afghanistan warned others not to confuse the two countries. From his perspective in 2007, when Iraq was in the midst of violent insurgency which captured news headlines, Lieutenant Colonel Michael Slusher declared the war in Afghanistan successful, crediting the people there: "If we have success in Afghanistan, is because the Afghans are different than the Arabs.... Don't think that whatever's working in Afghanistan will work in Iraq," he stresses.[8] The differences between Iraq and Afghanistan surprised Major Christy Erwin during her 2011–2012 deployment. She perceives the Afghans as "less educated and I would say less receptive" than Iraqis, but also "they seemed militarily smarter than the Iraqis were, which is odd," she thought.[9] Though Erwin did not explain her comment further, one surmises that she perceived Iraqis as more educated or advanced than Afghans, which would make Afghan superiority in soldiering unexpected.

Compared to Western standards of living, Afghans failed to measure up in various ways. For example, Afghans often lacked basic infrastructure Westerners take for granted such as electricity, plumbing, and water sanitation. Some places had small generators to provide power. Many areas lacked proper sanitation with latrines that were "really just pits that frequently empty into streams." Special Forces assessments of central Afghanistan in 2002 observed the need for humanitarian assistance because "the people lack extreme cold weather gear. Most homes are in need of windows, doors, and roofs due to destruction by the Taliban or lack of materials." The population also suffered from poor nutrition and hygiene compared to the West.[10]

Afghans were so poor in some cases that they barely had enough clothing. Special Forces soldiers note that clothing was often dirty and partially unserviceable, but "seems to be enough to get by, but not truly what is needed." Additionally, "the entire populace is in need of socks and better footwear," they observe.[11] Afghan men wear the *shalwar kamiz*, a long, loose fitting shirt worn over pants. Some wear turbans, while those from the mountains wore a roll-brimmed wool hat called a *pakul.* Men also kept a cotton or woolen shawl that could be used as a blanket, prayer mat, or cushion. It was the cultural norm for men to grow beards.[12]

Troops regularly commented on the Afghans' appearance. To Anders the male villagers looked identical, all wearing beards and the *shalwar kamiz*, or

Afghan women retrieving water from a well. Many homes in Afghanistan lacked running water and electricity, among other modern conveniences. October 15, 2002. P-0835. Civil Affairs & Psychological Operations, Operation Enduring Freedom: Historical Collection, 126th Military History Detachment, 2003, US Army Heritage and Education Center.

what the Americans dubbed the "man dress," a rather emasculating term. Anders describes, "their faces all shared the same rugged Pashtun features, weathered by a heritage of hardship," and "most wore tattered leather sandals that clung to their gnarly, calloused feet."[13] Major Paul Darling observes the Afghans wore colorful clothing, even the men. Unlike Western gendered color association, he explains, Afghan men routinely wore pink and purple. The colorful clothing reminded James Christ of gypsies. Young girls also donned colorful outfits. Even traditional burkas the women wore were often a light blue color.[14]

Colorful and eye-catching also describe the local "jingle trucks" ubiquitous in Afghanistan. Some had geographic designs, while others sported faces. They often had tassels of various colors hanging from side mirrors and headlights. The "jingling" sound came from chains hanging from the body of the trucks. Though they grabbed attention, American attitudes proved quite dismissive of the vehicles. Anders gripes, "They were all creatively different and completely ridiculous in the ostentatious tastelessness."[15] Lieutenant Colonel Forsyth states the jingle trucks "are so ridiculous looking with their murals and pictures painted all over them and the ubiquitous jangling chains."[16] One soldier learned the significance of the noisy chains—to ward off evil spirits. In addition to their colorful decoration, the trucks were often in terrible driving condition with bad tires, missing mirrors, and excessive loads.[17] Of course, most vehicles in Afghanistan were older

An elder speaks during a *shura* at the government center on May 22, 2010, Marjah, Afghanistan. Notice that the elder is wearing the traditional *shalwar kamiz* (photograph by Corporal James Clark).

Note the colorful clothing worn by these Afghan girls at school. October 28, 2002. P-1554. Civil Affairs & Psychological Operations, Operation Enduring Freedom: Historical Collection, 126th Military History Detachment, 2003, US Army Heritage and Education Center.

with numerous mechanical or aesthetic issues, another consequence of the country's overall poverty.

Most Afghans are Sunni Muslims with the exception of the Hazara ethnic group, which are predominantly Shia Muslims. Given that the Muslim holy day is Friday, the pattern of activity in Afghanistan differs from the American norm. Afghans do not conduct meetings or work on Fridays. The US monitored the Friday calls to prayer, as some mullahs promoted anti–American messages during their services. Troops noticed that enemy activity dropped off on Friday and resumed on Saturday. All activities were curtailed during the holy month of Ramadan, called "Ramazan" in one local dialect.[18] Americans felt frustration at the lack of activity exhibited by Afghans during the Ramadan holiday. As one officer explained, "this meant that there would be almost no government activities, including security operations, due to the religious observances. Everything comes to a screeching halt during this month."[19]

Though the US is a predominantly Christian nation, work and business is rarely curtailed for Christian holy seasons, with the exception of Christmas and Easter. As American troops did not observe the Ramadan holiday, they continued operations without Afghan assistance. Troops had a choice about how they reacted. Brown remarks, "This whole month of Ramadan nothing is going to happen. You can let that make you angry or just accept it."[20]

Afghan truck drivers pause after unloading bags of grain from a jingle truck during Operation Buffalo Thunder II at the 5th Kandak headquarters in Shorabak, Afghanistan, on June 30, 2012. Specialist Nathan Smith (lower left), an infantryman with 1st Battalion, 17th Infantry Regiment, 2nd Infantry Division, provides security during the unloading (photograph by Staff Sergeant Brendan Mackie).

Ramadan offered an opportunity for American troops to foster good relations with the Afghan people. Lieutenant Colonel Forsyth chose to celebrate Ramadan with the locals. He decided to "provide gifts for the poor for *Zakat* (gift offering in Islam) and express our respect in order to build those good relationships needed for security cooperation." The local Provincial Reconstruction Team put together gift baskets of food and clothing for the poor. "Some of the mullahs responded positively to our effort, others were clearly keeping us at arm's length," Forsyth remembers. The troops prepared an *Iftar*, the large meal that breaks the Ramadan fast, for local Afghan government officials as well.[21]

Perhaps the most frustrating aspect of Islam for American troops was the concept of *Inshallah*, or "as God wills" or "if God willed it." The concept comes from the belief in predestination, that every event is known by God and is part of God's will. As one scholar explains the concept, God has "calculated out the span of every person's life, their lot of good or ill fortune, and the fruits of their efforts. God's omnipotent to intervene, quite inexplicably and suddenly, whenever He wants."[22] The pervasiveness of this concept differs considerably from the pattern in American society. Captain Benjamin Tupper observes, "In a nutshell, it's how Afghans, as well as other Muslims, use religion to deal with the hardships, violence, and chaos of life around them." While Americans are also influenced by religion, "none of them compare to the degree that Inshallah shapes an Afghan's

Helmand Provincial Governor Haji Mohammad Gulab Mangal speaks to the gathering of US and British personnel with Regional Command Southwest, Afghan National Security Forces (ANSF) leadership, and members of the Government of the Islamic Republic of Afghanistan during an *Iftar* at the Cultural Center on Camp Leatherneck, Helmand Province, Afghanistan, on August 7, 2012 (photograph by Staff Sergeant Raul Gonzales).

daily life."[23] It proved a cultural obstacle that many American service members never overcame.

American troops almost universally attributed the Afghans' lack of initiative to *Inshallah*. Major Ronald Walck describes the "*Inshallah* mindset," as this: "If God wanted me out of this mud hole I'm sitting in, he'd miracle me out of this mud hole." If Americans assisted the Afghan out of the predicament, the Afghan interpreted it as God's intervention. Walck adds, "Whatever else he needs now, he'll ask you for because he thinks you can give it to him." Walck thought this mindset created a culture of dependency, where the Afghans turned to Americans to solve all of their problems.[24] Many service members believed it contributed to a lack of an American-style work ethic.[25] *Inshallah* also governed the battlefield. Most Afghan soldiers believe that if God "wanted me to hit the target, I would have hit the target," Christ asserts.[26] Colonel Walter Herd agrees: "If Allah wants the bullet to hit, then it will hit so I don't need to waste my time aiming."[27] Since God directed the bullets on the battlefield, it proved difficult to get Afghan soldiers to practice shooting. "Getting the ANA [Afghan National Army] to the rifle range is harder than herding cats," comments Tupper.[28]

As frustrating as *Inshallah* proved to US troops most of the time, Tupper remembers one incident when it worked in his favor. One day, Tupper and his soldiers found themselves in the middle of a massive traffic jam. "In America, horns would have been honking, people would have been swearing, fistfights would have broken out," Tupper notes. "But here, among the sunny, snowy panorama, our crowd of interrupted travelers play the role of curious onlookers—the whole event, how it originated, how it would be solved, was all just *Inshallah*." In other words, God had intended for the traffic jam to happen as part of his master plan. Therefore, "There was no point in getting angry about it. The delay was serving some heavenly purpose, even if this purpose remained unknown to all who were present."[29] Even though it was a positive experience, it clearly demonstrated a deep cultural difference between the American troops and the local population.

American troops found the Pashtun moral and ethical code, *Pashtunwali*, much easier to accept, at least as far as it pertained to hospitality. *Pashtunwali* includes hospitality, taking visitors under one's protection, as well as defending honor and exacting revenge.[30] Most troops encountered *Pashtunwali* as hospitality and occasionally protection. As Lieutenant Colonel Anthony Hunter understood it, *Pashtunwali* meant that Afghans "accepted you into their homes. They fed you. The lodged you for the evening. They provided security for you."[31] As part of their culture of hospitality, Afghans "were always inviting us into their houses" remembers Colonel Eugene Augustine.[32] Rico notices that even the poorest Afghans offered food and tea, even if they did not have much for themselves.[33]

"I tell you, these are very hospitable people," observes Colonel Dominic Cariello.[34] Navy Commander Kimberly Evans recollects arriving at a village where the troops were the first Americans the locals had ever encountered. Immediately, "they were trying to pull us into their houses." She had to explain to the Afghans that they had brought their own food, so "you don't have to cook us anything."[35] Not only would the Afghans "give you the shirt off their backs," they also "provided you with information on what was going on, not just telling you what you wanted to hear," Hunter observes.[36]

Anders describes an incident where he and his soldiers benefited from *Pashtunwali*. They were out on patrol when one of the tires came off of a Humvee. It was the middle of winter, so the soldiers had to sleep on the snow in sleeping bags while rotating guard duty through the night. As the troops were making their camp, two young Afghans came up to them. The Afghans brought out supplies, including a plastic tarp and a small propane tank with a burner. The locals also carried out to the soldiers a pot of chai tea, seasoned rice, and flatbread.[37] "It was such a humbling experience to have them visit us like that and bring us hot food and tea," recalls Anders. "I really didn't know how to tell them that, but I think they somehow understood our sincere gratitude," he hoped.[38]

Pashtunwali sometimes required a leap of faith on the part of the Americans. When coming into an Afghan's home, one comes under the protection of the host.[39] Major Edward Croot remembers how he inadvertently disrespected the Afghans by coming into a home fully geared up and with his weapon out. His interpreter explained to him that coming into the Afghan's home with weapons suggested that the Americans did not trust the Afghans to provide for their security and safety while under the protection of *Pashtunwali*. "So, we went back in and just decided to tell him that we didn't understand *Pashtunwali* to its fullest and that we were sorry," Croot explains. "We didn't mean to offend him in any way. We took off our flak vests and put our guns down, told him that we understood he could provide security in his home. From then on we had a good 15-minute discussion on culture."[40]

Pashtunwali conflicted with the Coalition mission to search homes and led to cultural clashes between Western troops and Afghans. First, no one should enter a home without an invitation to do so, and Coalition troops did not always ask permission to enter. Secondly, it is not permitted for unrelated men to search Afghan women. When troops methodically searched compounds, they inevitably searched the women's quarters as well, upsetting both Afghan men and women. Afghan men interpreted this inadvertent cultural faux pas as dishonoring them and their imperative to protect their female relations.[41]

For those under its protection, *Pashtunwali* could provide goodwill from the population. When not under its imperatives, one was vulnerable. One Special Forces soldier explained that "the same Afghan that will give you his last grain of rice and die protecting you because of *Pashtunwali* could be the same Afghan that rapes (even though you are a guy) and tortures you to death and then mutilates your body afterwards" in revenge. He also warns, "They can offer it [*Pashtunwali*] to you and then turn on you later so you cannot be sure if it will be in full effect."[42]

One area of Afghan culture which universally clashed with American cultural and societal norms was the treatment of women. In order to maintain family honor, Afghan culture separated men from women, keeping women away from unrelated men. The separation, or "practice of seclusion, called *purdah*, was preserved symbolically through the Burka," explains one scholar. Women were not permitted to leave their homes without permission and then only in the company of a male blood relative.[43] As a result of this separation, American troops rarely saw Afghan women. As Herd observes, "I never even saw an Afghan woman of childbearing years. The only Afghan females I saw were small children or old women." He found the practice distasteful, commenting, "any culture that arbitrarily writes off half of their intellectual capital has limited the potential for progress."[44] Forsyth echoes Herd's criticism by writing, "when they see women they act like animals who can't control themselves. They think an uncovered woman causes them to sin. It never enters their minds that they have to exhibit self-control. The solution to temptation is to cover up the woman."[45]

Anders likens the way Afghan women were treated to livestock or other property. Another soldier thought the Afghans valued their goats more than their daughters.[46] Amber Smith agrees that Afghan women were treated as property, and further states "baby girls were often unwanted, especially if the family already had a daughter. Lots of families decided they couldn't afford extra girls, for that they would be worthless, or for whatever reason decided to literally toss them out. It was a disgusting reality of Afghan 'culture.'"[47] Even more disturbing to American sensibilities was when troops stumbled upon a room filled with cut clitorises off infant girls, removed so that they could not enjoy sex when they matured.[48]

Doherty relates a story that illustrates the low value Afghan men placed on their female relatives compared to Western society. A grandmother brought her granddaughter to an Afghan hospital because she was in pain. The father had dropped off the grandmother, mother, and daughter because he wanted to go home to eat. "A short while later the doctor kicked them out of the hospital because he wanted to go

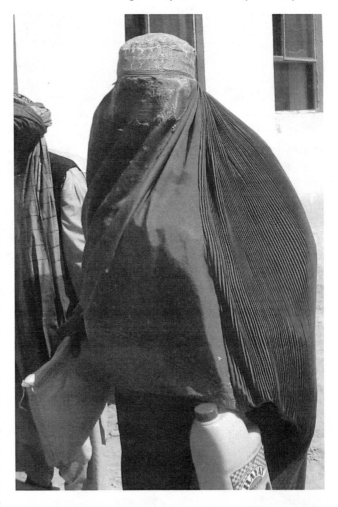

Qalat, Afghanistan. An Afghan woman clad in a traditional burka accepts gifts on Saturday, March 8, 2008, at an International Women's Day celebration (photograph by US Air Forces Central Command Public Affairs).

home and eat also," Doherty relates. "Since it was a girl she was not worth anyone's time," he explains. The American troops medically evacuated her to a US hospital, but they later learned that she had died there, likely from appendicitis that had not been treated in time.[49]

As a result of the cultural seclusion of Afghan women from unrelated men, female service members came to conduct searches of Afghan women. Female Engagement Teams (FET) evolved out of this need. The Army began to use female service members in this role in 2003 in Iraq, dubbing it the Lioness program. In Afghanistan, at first, female Military Police personnel or females in other military operational specialties searched the Afghan women.

The Marine Corps began the FET program in 2009, and they were attached to all-male infantry units.[50] According to the Pentagon, the service women were trained in "Pashtu language qualification, seven-mile rucksack marches, night weapons qualification, tactical combat casualty care, combat training and other mission essential courses." They also had to learn how to conduct a patrol, react to enemy contact, and determine what to do in case of a roadside bomb.[51] The Army created a parallel program. Army FET members similarly trained in infantry individual soldier skills.[52]

Additionally, the teams were trained how to be culturally sensitive. They always sought permission from the male head of the household to talk to their female relatives. The FET members of brought items such as school supplies or medicine and sat down to talk to the Afghan women over cups of tea. If all went well, the FET would "get information about the village, local grievances and the Taliban."[53] As the program developed, FET members expanded the scope of the mission to include hygiene, baby care, medical exams for children, and other women's needs.[54] The Army differentiated FETs into tactical and operational teams. Tactical teams operated with maneuver units searching women who might have contraband or intelligence hidden on them, while operational teams helped Afghan women "build and maintain a self-sustaining political, economic, and social support structure" in their villages.[55] Other NATO partners also deployed female engagement teams so that 14 countries fielded 149 different teams in 2011.[56]

When the FET team entered a compound, they generally removed their helmets and wore headscarves to make the Afghan women feel more comfortable. "The general perception has been ranging from positive to dumbfounded," says Second Lieutenant Carly E. Towers, one of the team members. "We just tried to sit down, talk to them, and get to know them a bit. We hear a lot of things from the women that we wouldn't hear from the men or that would be said in a different way," Towers notes.[57] Members of FET were able to gather intelligence from the Afghan women that proved impossible to get from male-only interactions. For example, based on her conversations with the women in one household, Major Maria Rodriguez determined that the Taliban had been recruiting the women's teenaged sons. At times, the men hid items with their women in hopes of evading searches. The FET discovered and confiscated these items. The presence of the FET helped keep Afghan women and children calm during searches since they were not being searched by non-related men.[58]

Qalat, Afghanistan. Captain Iajaira Perez, Combined Team Zabul Female Engagement Team (FET) officer in charge, engages with an Afghan woman during the FET's visit to a local village in Zabul Province, Afghanistan. July 15, 2011 (photograph by Staff Sergeant Rebecca Petrie).

The FET members had more access to Afghan households than male service members alone. As women, "We got to go into their kitchens and bedrooms; usually guests are only allowed in their living rooms. It was definitely a rewarding experience," recalls Sergeant Melinda Crosby.[59] Afghan women reacted more warmly to the FET team members because, unlike men, "we're not the ones kicking down their doors," adds another team member.[60] The FETs also participated in community-building activities such as radio broadcasts, gardening projects, and career days.[61]

Despite their efforts the FET teams recognized the limits of what they could accomplish. "I think we had the right idea: We would win hearts and minds. I thought we were going to make an impact and, woman-to-woman, be able to get on their level and help them understand they are worthy of living a normal life" according to Western norms, remembers Sonja Childers, but at the end of the day, "they didn't want to change," she admits.[62] A few positive encounters with women could not fundamentally change Afghan culture.

Troops came in most frequent contact with their Afghan interpreters, and many established positive relationships with them. The military had different levels of interpreters. The highest rated ones had security clearances and were contracted from the United States. Most troops encountered the Category 1, or local, interpreter.[63] Major Stuart Farris remembers that his interpreters were Hazaras, who did not get along well with the Pashtun population. They were young men between the ages of 18 and 24.[64] Major Eric Lanham recalls the names of his interpreters—Shafik and Haroun. He thinks highly of them, stating, "They were very intelligent. They spoke perfect English. They spoke probably five languages—Urdu, Pashtu, Arabic, English, and I was teaching them French. They were worth their weight in gold."[65]

David Thompson relied heavily on his interpreter to convey to him not only the translated words but the cultural context as well. He praised the dedication of his interpreter as well. "While engaged in major combat operations he was right there in my Humvee with me, ready to go," Thompson explains. "He was as much of a dedicated human being as anyone could ask for." Even though it was his interpreter's job to be there, Thomson recognized that he acted above and beyond expectations. He referenced his interpreter's actions as "selfless service." He adds, "they were right there with us; engaged in operations and supporting us."[66] Farris' interpreter's name was Safi. He understood both American and Afghan culture. He had been born in Afghanistan but moved to the US at age 14. Farris recalls, "Because Safi was a little older than some of the others, he commanded a lot of respect from the village elders in the local people be dealt with" since Afghan culture placed a lot of weight on age.[67]

"I had a great relationship with the interpreters that I was with," Major John Tabb relates. "Just the camaraderie that we built on our team—I'm still in contact with them and always will be."[68] Anders remembers that when it was time for his redeployment home, one of his interpreters said he would be sad when Anders left. "He even told me that he was going to cry, and I laughed until I realized he was serious," Anders recollects. "He said that crying at the loss of his brother was what they did in his culture," underscoring the deep and positive connections between some Afghans and the troops.[69]

Many interpreters spoke both Pashtu and Dari, the two most prominent languages in the country.[70] Even with both

Staff Sergeant Robert Ham (right) poses with Afghan interpreter Saifullah Haqmal. Six years later, Haqmal and his family finally secured American visas with the help of Ham and many others. February 6, 2010 (photograph courtesy of Staff Sergeant Robert Ham).

languages covered by translators, the troops would sometimes come across local Afghans who spoke different dialects. "We would have to have multiple translators with us on missions just to communicate in provinces," Plummer remembers, and even that was no guarantee that they spoke the specific local dialect.[71] "The translating was shaky at best," Woodring admits. "And don't ask them to write anything down in English," he adds, as writing proved a different skill set.[72] If no interpreter were present, then the troops relied on "pointing and gesturing," which they dubbed "pointy-talky."[73] The lack of an ability to communicate with Afghans without a translator suggests the inadequacy of pre-deployment language training, particularly early in the war.

Some troops made a special effort to get to know the Afghans. Major Diego Davila recalls, "Almost every night we sit down with the interpreter and talk about their religion and our religion; the differences between our armies." He tried to talk with as many different Afghans as he could each night and included the Afghan commander as well.[74] Major Robert Reed sought out his Afghan counterpart, Captain Haseem, to eat breakfast each day. They would drink chai tea and talk.[75] Others made an effort to learn some of the language, such as the Pashtu greeting, "singeh, jureh, pachaitai."[76]

Other troops preferred to maintain distance between themselves and the Afghans. Anders relates a conversation between himself and an officer from the unit that was replacing his in Afghanistan. This officer admitted that he had come to Afghanistan to kill enemy combatants, not to help the locals. The effect of the words on Anders was that they "slammed into me like a freight train.... Just the thought of it literally made my muscles tense up."[77] By this point in his deployment, Anders and his unit had come become friendly with the local Afghans. To the incoming unit, that relationship was *too* friendly. The officer explains to Anders that the incoming first sergeant and company commander did not like the location of the American troops inside the village next to the police and governor's compounds. They planned instead to move to the outskirts of town to maintain distance between themselves and the locals.

Anders believed it was a terrible idea, but the officer defended it. Anders feared, "There was a real danger that these guys were going to systematically dismantle what we built."[78] Indeed, the continuous rotation of troops through the districts disrupted any relationship a given unit had with the local population. At most, a unit deployed for over a year before they were replaced. The turnover meant that long-term relationships with the Afghans were impossible to maintain, which undermined the efforts to create security and stability.

American troops often encountered Afghan children when they went on patrol and visited area villages. Children, especially boys, followed the troops when they came through the towns. "The children swarmed around us, giggling and laughing," Anders observes.[79] They often asked for candy or other handouts.[80] When Leo Jenkins brought out candy to distribute to the children, "I instantly became the most popular person in the province," he recalls. He relates a story about giving candy to one particular Afghan girl. He remembers kneeling down and offering candy to her. "She was an absolutely adorable little girl who was maybe 4 or 5 years old. Her brown hair was matted and wild. Her facial expression was that of great curiosity," he noticed. The girl hesitantly reached out and took the candy from his hand, then ran back into the safety of the group of other children in the room.[81]

Little girls did not fare well in Afghan society, so troops took extra care to make sure that girls received handouts just as well as the boys. Parnell felt horrified to see the boys beat up and steal candy from the girls, right in front of their parents. "After that, we always made sure the girls had ample time to escape before we left," he explains.[82] The children were attentive to the US troops who came through their villages. In one area, some of the kids picked up the "hang loose" gesture—a fist wave with thumb and pinky extended outwards—from the 25th Infantry Division soldiers from Hawaii who had rotated through their village.[83]

One aspect of Afghan culture which often shocked American troops was the cultural norm for male affection. Afghan men often held hands and touched one another a great deal more often than in American culture.[84] Sergeant Michael Mormino writes, "It was a culture shock when I first got there. It was hard seeing grown men walking around holding hands and kissing on each other."[85] Afghan men sometimes reached out to hold the hands of American service members. Anderson admits "it was definitely uncomfortable" when Afghan men would take his hand.[86] Colonel Terry Sellers remembers the governor of Ghazni's militia commander "reached out and grabbed a hold of my hand and held my hand the

Soldiers of A Company, Special Troops Battalion hand out snacks to children at a local bazaar in Afghanistan, July 19, 2009. The snacks are used to thank the community and their children for their cooperation (photograph by Staff Sergeant Christopher Allison).

way I hold hands with my wife, as we walked around inspecting his compound." He was relieved when only a few soldiers saw him, as he did not want to become an object of ridicule among his own troops.[87] Some service members proved more open to the experience. Reed understood the cultural significance when his counterpart took his hand, that it "shows that he respects me and it shows his soldiers, this guy is going to be okay."[88]

Adult Afghan men sometimes had what Americans considered inappropriate relations with young boys. The practice is known as *bacha baazi* or *bacha baz*, "boy play," in the Dari language. Boys as young as nine years old were kept by Afghan commanders for sexual gratification.[89] Additionally, young Afghan army soldiers, dubbed "chai boys," sometimes "would wear make-up and act as feminine servants to their senior leaders," recalls one soldier. For some American service members, such behavior proved a huge obstacle to creating productive relationships. Some troops who raised concerns about these practices had their careers ruined as the chain of command largely ignored the issue.[90] Troops also joked about bestiality among Afghan men. The joke went, "Show me an Afghan soldier who hasn't screwed a donkey and I'll show you a liar."[91]

Afghans did not share American standards of hygiene, which also caused discomfort for American troops. Parnell remembers his shock when "an Afghan border policeman stopped and dropped his trousers. Right there in the open, he squatted and relieved himself. He wiped himself with his left hand, and continued on his way. That was an unexpected cultural moment." Now that he noticed

Skhin, Paktika Province, Afghanistan. Afghan men are more comfortable with physical contact than Western men. August 10, 2010 (photograph by Sergeant Justin Morelli).

the way Afghans went to the bathroom in open areas, he saw "shit mines everywhere."[92] Christ noted that the recruits for the Afghan National Army needed to learn how to use porta potties. "The Westerners were appalled that the recruits thought nothing of just squatting anywhere in the training grounds when they felt the need to defecate," he recalls.[93]

Service members noticed that Afghans did not share Western concepts of abstraction or the passage of time. Captain Mike Toomer is convinced they are "a society of people who, for the most part, cannot think abstractly."[94] Sergeant Neil Arrieta explains that the Afghans "don't read, don't write, and can't think linearly."[95] Captain Andrew Boissonneau agrees, stating, "the idea of an abstract representation of concrete items isn't a concept that comes easy to them because they don't do it."[96] Anders echoes the sentiment when he wrote about one local: "Like many Afghans, he had an enormous difficulty creating three-dimensional relationships onto a two-dimensional surface. Distances and directions we received from locals are grossly distorted." He also observes that most Afghans "did not even know their own age."[97]

Woodring notes that Afghans do not share the same perception of time as Westerners. He did not think they could even tell time or owned watches. So, it proved challenging to get the Afghans to leave for a mission at a particular hour since the Afghans did not see it as important.[98] Doherty suggests that the Afghans are "not stupid, mind you, just literally ignorant. They just are not aware of as many 'worldly things'" as we are, a reflection of the country's low literacy and lack of education.[99]

Food proved to be another difference between American and Afghan culture. Afghan food often revolved around goat meat. While it is not a common meat in the United States, it is a staple in rural Afghanistan. Like many others, Augustine recalls eating "a lot of goat" during his deployment.[100] Afghans commonly ate rice pilaf, soup, naan, and kebobs.[101] An Afghan translator treated his American unit to a meal of lamb kebab, "*kafta* (ground meat mixed with parsley and onions), and *kabuli* (rice cooked with carrots, raisons, cabbage, and beef)."[102] Some Afghan hosts offered raisins and pistachios to their American guests.[103] Staff Sergeant Clint Douglass remembers eating lamb and chicken kebabs with jasmine rice. "It was delicious," he declares.[104] "The food was phenomenal," Reed gushes.[105]

A number of troops recall slaughtering goats, lambs, or other animals to eat while deployed. First Lieutenant Will Mangham notes, "If you want meat in Afghanistan, chances are you're going to have to kill something. There are no grocery stores in the mountains."[106] Major Steven Wallace agrees. "We buy a goat and we kill it, butcher it, and it makes do for the whole company. We all eat a goat or lamb stew," he notes.[107] Reed remembers having to choose between a goat and a cow when visiting one village. "The cow looked like it had mad cow disease for ten years," he laughs. "It's sitting there with his head down going, 'Please kill me! Please kill me!' I was like, 'I'm not going to have the cow.'" He ate so much lamb while deployed, "I can't even stand looking at it" now.[108]

Unless one grew up on or near farms, most Americans are unfamiliar with killing animals for food. Anders observes that when the Afghans slaughtered an

Traditional Afghan food, including rice, naan, and pomegranates. October 30, 2002. P-1806. Civil Affairs & Psychological Operations, Operation Enduring Freedom: Historical Collection, 126th Military History Detachment, 2003, US Army Heritage and Education Center.

Goats, a staple source of meat for Afghans, outside an Afghan compound. November 19, 2002. P-2548. Civil Affairs & Psychological Operations, Operation Enduring Freedom: Historical Collection, 126th Military History Detachment, 2003, US Army Heritage and Education Center.

animal, they lay it facing Mecca. Anders describes how the Afghan used a knife in the neck to kill the goat. The sight was so unfamiliar and disturbing to Anders and some of his soldiers that they turned away from watching it. He writes that some of the soldiers lost their appetite after watching the slaughter. He liked the resulting meal that came from the goat, but not all of the soldiers did. Some complained it tasted "gamey."[109]

Afghan flatbread proved popular with the troops, though not necessarily the way it was made. The soldiers dubbed it "foot bread" because "the bakers pounded the dough with their bare feet before hurling them into the oven." They particularly liked it when the flatbread was covered in sugar.[110] Flatbread was used as a utensil to scoop up meat or stew to eat.[111]

Afghans traditionally serve food from a common plate. The Afghans set out a large tablecloth or blanket to place the food. Large platters, perhaps two feet in width, hold staples, such as rice, meat, and vegetables. They are placed in the middle of the eating area for easy access by everyone.[112] The Afghans use their hands, rather than utensils, to eat. Major Dave Tukdarian recalls a meal of rice, stewed meat, and beans. There were no utensils to eat it. "Out of the corner of my eye I am watching the interpreter and doing what he does," Tukdarian remembers. He followed the example to "grab the bread, scoop the rice, and tear off a piece of meat." He ends with the thought, "Oh well. When in Rome...."[113] One had to watch which hand one used to eat as well, as the left hand is considered unclean in Muslim culture. Therefore, US troops were advised never to eat with one's left hand. Herd observes that the Afghans "either put their left hands behind their backs or in their pockets and [ate] with the right hands." So, he followed their lead.[114]

In one instance, an American proved more open to eating raw goat liver than his Afghan interpreter did. When Lieutenant Mangham and the other members of his platoon were visiting with the local population, his host slaughtered a goat for them. "The old man cut off a rectangle of goat liver and threw it back like it was candy," then he handed out pieces to the others. When the Afghan offered a piece to Mangham, he remembers that "it had the same texture as raw fish— somewhere between that and a gummy bear." To his surprise, he liked the flavor. "The only thing that threw me off was the warmth," he writes, as the goat had not been dead long enough to cool.[115]

While some American service members loved Afghan food, others found it less than palatable. Sergeant First Class Gregory Strong complains about the Afghan curry he ate because it still had the bone in the meat, and he found the lamb "tough as shoe leather and you get one bite per lamb chop." He found the food so unappetizing that he lost a lot of weight while deployed.[116] Alvin Tilley turned down eating sheep one time.[117]

Afghans frequently offered and drank tea as well. Afghan chai often consisted of green tea with cardamom seeds.[118] "I lost track of the cups of chai I [drank and] the number of biscuits I ate," Anders states.[119] "Tea all the time," agrees Augustine.[120] "In fact, I miss chai," Colonel Dominic Cariello admits. "I had chai withdrawals when I got back [home]."[121]

Sometimes eating the local food made the troops sick, even when they took measures to prevent illness. "I always made sure my tea was extra hot," remembers Tilley, even though he took medicine to avoid dysentery.[122] "A lot of guys on the team got sick," Reed acknowledges, though he did not. "You just have to be sure you're not eating their vegetables because they wash their vegetables in their water," which was how the service members contracted dysentery.[123] Farris made the mistake of eating fruit washed in local water once, and "about 12 hours later, I felt like I was on death's door."[124] Undercooked food also posed a danger. "I had to eat a goat that was undercooked on a mission once to please the village elder. I got dysentery really fast, literally within a couple hours," Major Christopher Plummer admits.[125] Some soldiers called this inevitable food poisoning "Intestinal Jihad," a play on the Muslim term.[126]

American troops complained almost universally about what they perceived as a culture of corruption among the Afghans. Plummer generalized the culture of corruption to all Muslims: "It's a vast difference between a US mindset and that of the Muslim. Theirs is a culture of dishonesty and corruption that seems prevalent in Muslim cultures going back thousands of years." He criticizes their lack of urgency and propensity to lie to save face.[127] Parnell agrees that for Afghans "lying is part of their culture. There's no stigma to it. It is expected."[128] Similarly, Doherty asserts that Afghans "lie like a five year old."[129] Acknowledging the culture of corruption, Arrieta ascribed it as a cultural norm. The system of bribes

To avoid sickness, one early restriction on US troops prohibited them from eating local food. October 8, 2002. P-0541. Civil Affairs & Psychological Operations, Operation Enduring Freedom: Historical Collection, 126th Military History Detachment, 2003, US Army Heritage and Education Center.

and kickbacks required to conduct business functioned almost as a system of taxation. It proved "mafia-like" in its operations, according to Arrieta.[130]

As part of this culture of corruption, American service members complained about Afghans hoarding and stealing supplies. Cariello observes, "The hoarding philosophy is that you never know when you're going to get it again, you get it when you can, if you can get more, you do that."[131] Master Sergeant José Medina criticizes the Afghans for selling fuel, noting that the drivers regularly sold off a portion of their load.[132] Major Christy Erwin also notes the Afghan penchant for siphoning off fuel. "Fuel was corrupt the entire way up and down," she remembers. She explained it as a hoarding mentality among the Afghans. "If you have stuff, you were good. If you didn't have stuff, that was bad," she notes. Erwin tried to be understanding of the cultural differences, though. "I think that we need to be a little bit more accepting of other people's opinions, and other people's standards, essentially," she concludes.[133] Afghans simply did not operate according to American norms.

Americans often questioned Afghan motives. Herd repeated a saying they had, "While you cannot *buy* Afghan loyalty, you can *rent* it, which is better than not having it at all."[134] Mormino thought Afghans were trying to milk as much

US Civil Affairs soldiers and Afghans drinking chai together. October 30, 2002. P-1815. Civil Affairs & Psychological Operations, Operation Enduring Freedom: Historical Collection, 126th Military History Detachment, 2003, US Army Heritage and Education Center.

money as they could "from us dumb Americans."[135] Walck agrees: "I think a lot of the people I interacted with were seeing the presence of the Americans as an opportunity for individuals to make money or get something off of the Americans." Unlike most American service members, Walck exhibited some sympathy for the Afghans. He adds, "I can't really fault them for that way of thinking when you realize that these are people who have been living hand to mouth since 1979." Indeed, generations of Afghans were raised that way.[136] He acknowledges that the near constant state of warfare in Afghanistan since the Soviet invasion and subsequent fighting to control the country after the Soviet withdrawal profoundly affected the people.

Americans also found it difficult to discern which side—government or Taliban—many Afghans supported. Insurgents, of course, did not wear uniforms or advertise their allegiance. Christ revealed that he suspected Afghan soldiers of "playing both sides of the fence—working for and getting paid for being in the ANA [Afghan National Army] and yet providing Intel for the anti-coalition militia and Taliban."[137] In fact, one elderly Afghan man admitted to Michael Golembesky, "When Americans are around, I am not Taliban. But when they are not here, I am Taliban."[138] Hunter concurs, stating, "You could tell one day they were Taliban, and one day there were pro-government, depending on who was arriving at their doorstep and who was putting pressure on them."[139] Arrieta discovered that the local workers he employed on civil affairs projects all considered themselves Taliban.[140] The inability to know which side the locals supported affected service member perceptions of local loyalties and whether their actions in Afghanistan were worthwhile. In a survey of one marine platoon in 2011, about 36 percent believed the Afghan people supported the Taliban, 58 percent thought the people were okay but were intimated by the Taliban, and just 6 percent believed the people were worth fighting for.[141]

Cultural interaction goes both ways, so Afghans also reacted to the obvious cultural differences between themselves and the Americans. At first, Afghan men stared at American service women. Dietra Korando noticed that some of the men looked at her "like, ooh, tasty" or the men had the look "this is so wrong" since she was acting outside of the norm for Afghan women. She attracted the attention of Afghan children too. Overall, she thinks, "people were very, very curious—not necessarily all disapproving, but just looking at me like, wow, it never occurred to me that a woman could walk around like that."[142] With continuous deployments of American service women to Afghanistan, the people became increasingly used to seeing women in uniform. By the time Christy Erwin deployed, she found there was little controversy in being female. "Most of the senior leaders over there, again, had been dealing with us for 12 years," she states. "They're used to it now and they've accepted it. So, I don't think that it was a disadvantage anymore."[143]

Similarly, many Afghans had never seen a person with black skin color before. Alvin Tilley recalls going to villages where he was the first African American the villagers had ever seen. He noticed the children rubbing their faces, so he asked his interpreter about it. The interpreter said, "Oh, they think your color comes off." Tilley was dumbfounded by that response.[144]

Afghan reactions to American troops varied widely, from friendly and welcoming to overtly hostile. The longer the US remained in Afghanistan, typically the more hostile the local reaction became. In 2002, a farmer by the name of Ahmed Khan, said, "Right now, people are glad the Americans are here, and so am I. I think they will help us rebuild our country and bring stability." He wanted the Americans to continue to pursue al-Qaeda and the Taliban to prevent future problems.[145] At the same time, another Afghan, a guard for the Oruzgan provincial governor, asserted, "We don't know why they stay here. They should go."[146] Anders noticed resentment building in some of the villages where he patrolled. His interpreter told him the villagers thought Americans were getting drunk and raping women. Other Afghans complained Westerners brought prostitution, vice, and alcohol to their country.[147]

Afghans universally denounced civilian deaths attributed to American and NATO operations.[148] As reported at the time, "No matter which Western soldier fires a fatal gunshot, and even if the numbers pale in comparison to civilian deaths caused by the Taliban, Afghan anger is often turned on NATO." After an incident in June 2007 when a US soldier fired into a crowd, one Afghan stated, "they are against us. They are against Afghans."[149] Afghans also protested acts of cultural insensitivity such as reported burning of Korans at a US military base and a video of US soldiers urinating on Taliban corpses.[150]

In many ways, American reactions to Afghans, and their reactions to Americans, paralleled the experiences of US troops in Vietnam. As historian Peter Kindsvatter argues, "American culture shock at the poverty of the Vietnamese added to the fading expectations. Were these poor, dirty 'gooks' worth saving?"[151] Vietnamese villagers did not act the ways Americans expected them to act. Moreover, Americans in Vietnam perceived that the population actively disliked them and were corrupt. Indeed, it appeared the Vietnamese did not even want the Americans there, much like the Afghans increasingly resented the presence of American and NATO forces.[152]

Despite the years of contact between the American troops and Afghans, they were never able to bridge completely the cultural gaps between them. In these reactions, service members did not differ much from their Vietnam-era counterparts, who often felt resentment that the "local people did not appreciate the sacrifices American soldiers made on their behalf."[153] Americans disliked many aspects of Afghan culture and outright rejected Afghan attitudes toward women and corruption, though some had close relationships with their interpreters. While Afghans learned to tolerate the presence of the NATO troops, the longer the war dragged on, the more resentment built, particularly as civilians became casualties. These casualties were an unintentional consequence of combat operations against al-Qaeda, the Taliban, and other insurgent groups in Afghanistan.

•• 4 ••

Patrols and Combat

Over the years of the Afghan War, the size of the force, the operational tempo, and type of fighting changed. In the earliest part of the war, there were only about two thousand troops deployed, while at the height of the surge in 2010 there were over 100,000. Those who served in direct combat with the enemy constituted the smallest number of those deployed, as support personnel outnumbered those in combat.[1] Special Operations Forces conducted night raids to capture or kill high value al-Qaeda and Taliban leaders, while conventional forces patrolled villages, provided humanitarian aid, and engaged insurgents in combat. Starting in late 2003, combat operations shifted from a counterterrorism focus on killing or capturing enemy insurgents to conducing counterinsurgency operations focused on securing the population.

As US and NATO forces pushed out into even more remote locations, the enemy unsuccessfully attempted to overrun a few isolated combat outposts. Some troops hardly encountered any violence during their deployments, while others endured frequent firefights. No two deployments were exactly alike, so this chapter attempts to capture the variety of experience throughout the conflict, including patrols, ambushes, IEDs, and other types of violence, as well as the sights, sounds, and physical sensations of combat. Combat experiences in Afghanistan differed from those in Iraq, even if some of the same types of events happened.

Though combat is the defining characteristic of warfare, most service members, even combatants, find that the uneventful outweighs the action. "Contrary to what Hollywood would have you believe," Major Chad Rickard explains, "not every mission contains a lot of excitement and a spectacular gunfight." For anyone familiar with the military, they will tell you "it's ordinarily 99% boredom, 1% sheer terror and excitement," he notes.[2] As a predictable outcome, most combat memoirs tell readers about the one percent of intense combat and devote far fewer pages to the more mundane tasks. It is, after all, the one percent that captures readers' attention. In the same way that Hollywood skews civilian perceptions toward combat, war memoirs emphasize action over tedium.[3]

Though both Afghanistan and Iraq experienced insurgencies, those troops who had deployed to Iraq before deploying to Afghanistan brought with them a different type of combat experience. When he deployed to Afghanistan after three combat tours in Iraq, a sergeant first class advised Sergeant Rickard, "to forget everything I knew about Iraq," since none of it applied to Afghanistan.[4] Captain Robert Anders believes that the Iraq experience was a detriment to troops deployed to Afghanistan. He thinks that Afghanistan is so different that "their experience in Iraq was really going to be no help to them. In fact, it might be worse than having no combat experience at all."

In a conversation Anders had with a soldier who was replacing him, the soldier explains that in Iraq, they assumed everyone was hostile until proven otherwise. "Well, sergeant, that's exactly the opposite of what's going on here" in Afghanistan Anders replies sternly. "You've got to consider that everyone here is a noncombatant unless they convince you they are hostile."[5] Captain Dan Kearney, deployed in the Korengal in eastern Afghanistan, realized quickly that Afghanistan differed tremendously from Iraq. He noted two differences: one, the Taliban were a distinct enemy, and "number two—the terrain offered some kind of advantage that I'd never seen or read or heard about in my entire life."[6] Comparing the Afghanistan deployment to a previous one in Iraq, another soldier observes that "Baghdad was pretty much all urban, all flat. Here there's been a lot of walking the mountains, a lot of looking for these guys."[7]

The earliest fighting in Afghanistan consisted of Special Operations Forces linking up with Northern Alliance warlords and their militias to coordinate air strikes on Taliban and al-Qaeda encampments. They traveled on horseback or in Toyota pickup trucks with their modern equipment, bringing down precision munitions on the enemy forces. At this time, troop numbered below 1,000 with only a small number of Special Forces soldiers in direct combat.[8] As the Taliban government toppled, conventional forces deployed to Afghanistan to deal with the remnants of al-Qaeda and the Taliban.

Among the official assessments of enemy forces is one completed by Special Forces Operational Detachment Alpha (ODA) 553. It notes that the typical Taliban fighter is armed with the AK-47 or other Soviet small arms weapon, generally old and well-used. It states, "Basically they are equipped with whatever weapons and ammo they can piece together." The Taliban commonly use RPG-7s [rocket-propelled grenades], which were designed to be used against armored vehicles or strongholds. Instead, the Taliban adapted them to use at maximum range so that the rounds burst over a target area, allowing them to attack from a greater distance. The Taliban had some battered Soviet DShK machine guns as well.

Instead of military vehicles, the enemy utilize civilian vehicles, particularly diesel Toyota Hilux pickup trucks, which were difficult to differentiate from ones used by the local population. Since vehicles proved scarce, the Taliban fit as many as possible into each truck. At the beginning of the war, the Special Forces soldiers believe the Taliban soldiers they were facing had "very little, if any, formal military training. Soldiers know how to operate their assigned weapons, but little else." Lack of training meant that the enemy did not fire accurately. Additionally, Afghans, the soldiers perceive, are more willing to surrender than foreign-born al-Qaeda combatants, such as Arabs and Pakistanis.[9] American forces faced these foreign al-Qaeda fighters during Operation Anaconda.

So, the patrol waits twenty-five minutes to see what happens next. The radio comes alive again with the Taliban commander asking, "Okay, are you in position?" "Yes, I'm in position."

"Are you ready?" "Well, why don't we ambush them after lunch?"

The Taliban really did take a lunch break. So, after a time, the Taliban commander comes back on the radio,

"Well, you ready?" "Well, I think we should pray first."

After all the chatter and delays, the Taliban never got around to hitting Fontes and her team at that time, but they did ambush the Americans with rockets two weeks later. Fontes admits, "the lunch and prayer breaks at the time were pretty hilarious."[52]

In addition to ambushes, improvised explosive devices (IEDs) proved a danger to troops in Afghanistan. At first, the IED was a weapon used in the Iraq War. Shortly thereafter, insurgents in Afghanistan adopted it, and IEDs became an increasing danger there as well.[53] Waltz explains the difference between IEDs in Iraq and Afghanistan—mainly the presence of paved roads. Since Iraq had paved roads, insurgents buried their bombs along the curbs, causing explosions to hit vehicles from the side. Afghanistan had dirt roads, allowing insurgents to set IEDs in the middle of the road to detonate directly underneath vehicles. Though there were fewer IED attacks in Afghanistan compared to Iraq in 2006, for example, the explosions in Afghanistan proved more deadly. The blasts hit the vulnerable undercarriage of vehicles rather than the armored sides.[54]

Once again, troops use a variety of everyday comparisons to make the experience of encountering IEDs understandable to civilians. Parnell describes the explosions from an IED as a "bubble of orange flames" on the right side of the Humvee ahead of his. It was followed by a "flame ball boil[ing] underneath" the vehicle, and a third explosion was a "bloom of fire" between the two Humvees. Then, "My truck trembled, and suddenly it sounded as if somebody was making popcorn." The popcorn noise was shrapnel from the IED hitting the armored plates on his Humvee.[55] When Christ faced an IED explosion, "All he could see was a dark, reddish wall of dirt rising up like a living being. The front of the Humvee was lifted into the air like it was a weightless toy." Then the vehicle reappeared, off road, sliding down the embankment toward the river below.[56] American troops tried to mitigate the deadly effects of IEDs by modifying their vehicles. Major Rusty Bradley observes that a number of the trucks sported plating that looked like it came out of a *Mad Max* movie in order to protect them from the IEDs.[57]

Over time, the enemy created ever more sophisticated weapons. Specialist Daniel Baker remembers when his teammate thought he had disarmed an IED buried in the road. When the Afghan National Police went to remove the bomb from the road, it exploded.[58] Insurgents learned to booby trap the bombs so that a secondary explosion would detonate, hitting the troops responding to the first explosion. The insurgents also innovated with the placement of the IEDs. They would "deploy them at canalizing terrain points—meaning they place them in areas where if one vehicle was hit, it left no room for another vehicle to maneuver

Afghan National Army soldiers from 205th Corps found an improvised explosive device (IED) in a village in the Sangin District of Afghanistan's Helmand Province, on December 29, 2007. The soldiers found the IED only 50 meters in front of the village mosque while conducting a security patrol in the area (photograph by Office of the Secretary of Defense, Public Affairs).

around it," explains one marine. They also laid IEDs in clusters to cause multiple injuries.[59] The insurgents would place IEDs in a "daisy chain," where "the enemy set off one IED and back it up with another IED fifty meters back and another fifty meters back from that" to hit all the vehicles on a patrol or in a convoy, Christ describes.[60]

The IEDs created a cycle of countermeasure and enemy adaptation. In order to counter the threat of remotely detonated IEDs, the US developed jammers to prevent the signal from reaching the bomb. In response, the insurgents switched to pressure plates that detonated when a vehicle rolled over it. The US countered the pressure-plate IED by developing a mine roller to detonate the explosive before the vehicles passed above it. The insurgents then offset the mine roller by placing the explosives a distance from the pressure plate so it would still explode under a vehicle. Sometimes the insurgents reverted to simple measures, just running a wire from the bomb to a triggerman waiting to detonate it.[61]

The US developed a new vehicle to counter the IED threat, the Mine-Resistant Ambush Protected vehicle (MRAP), first for the war in Iraq. As the IED threat in Afghanistan increased, the military deployed the MRAPs there as well. Though the V-shaped hull did disperse the energy from the explosions, the vehicle did not work nearly as well in Afghanistan's difficult terrain as it did in more flat, urbanized Iraq. Major Mark Melson notes that the MRAPs performed well on highways, but not off-road. He observes, "The MRAP was very susceptible to certain things like rocks. They were extremely heavy, you could not self-recover." He recalls that an MRAP had a rollover during his deployment. One of the four passengers had been injured. The accident happened, in part, because of deep ruts in the road.[62]

A newer MRAP all-terrain vehicle (M-ATV) solved the rollover issue, but both the MRAP and M-ATV proved too large to navigate the narrow and mountainous roads through much of Afghanistan's villages, limiting their usefulness. Additionally, the US military emphasized force protection, that is, protecting the lives of service members. Waltz argues that this weight on force protection made the US more reliant on vehicles like the MRAP, which, given their limitations, resulted in ceding the initiative and terrain to the insurgents.[63]

Taliban insurgents also booby-trapped their compounds to injure and kill service members during raids. They secured antipersonnel mines to doorways and set them up with trip wires to detonate as troops entered the compounds. In one case, the Taliban filled several rooms with C-4 explosives meant to bring down the roof on the troops inside. Fortunately, the explosives did not detonate that time.[64]

These booby traps proved deadly to personnel walking on patrol or maneuvering through compounds or villages on foot. During one operation, a marine platoon started clearing a portion of a town. As the platoon systematically cleared

Mine-protected, ambush-protected vehicles sit on Forward Operating Base Tagab, Kapisa Province, Afghanistan, on March 18, 2013. These vehicles replaced the Humvees, which were more vulnerable to roadside bombs (photograph by Specialist Andrew Claire Baker).

building after building, they heard two explosions. Two marines had stepped on IEDs at the same time. One lost a leg, while the other lost both legs. Then they heard yet another explosion. This time, "The armored vehicle leading the way for the CASEVAC [casualty evacuation] vehicle struck an IED en route to the platoon casualty collection area. The driver and vehicle commander were both knocked unconscious," the company commander recalls. Once the two marines were attended to, the others resumed their mission to clear buildings in the compound. At the point where they came to an open area in the middle of town, the men covered each other as they bounded across the danger zone. "I moved to the edge of the opening and tapped the marine in front of me on the helmet; a nonverbal gesture letting him know I was ready to cover his move," the commander explains. The marine began to move across the compound, then "just as he reached the other side, he disappeared in an explosion in the cloud of dust. He would be the third marine to lose a leg in just over an hour" that day.[65]

At this point, with three wounded men, the company commander decided "I was done dealing with all this IED bullshit." Instead, the marines would move through the farmland and ignore the abandoned buildings. As soon as they pushed out into the open area, the marines received enemy machine gun and mortar fire. They called in airstrikes. By this time, the marines were more than ten hours into the mission. Temperatures rose to over 100 degrees, and the men were starting to feel the effects of the heat. Even though the marines could see their objective, the commander estimated it would take another four to five hours of fighting to reach it. "We were so close, but I knew it wasn't the right time," he remembers. "I called the mission. We withdrew under mortar suppression so that our movement was covered." Despite the obstacles in their way and the casualties, the commander still felt the sting of disappointment. "I was a Marine company commander who had failed to reach his objective," he said in regret.[66] In the feelings of helplessness against the hidden explosive devices, the troops in Afghanistan (and Iraq) paralleled the experience of their predecessors who felt vulnerable in the face of landmines and booby-traps in World War II and Vietnam.[67]

Insurgents also packed vehicles with explosives to create Vehicle-Borne IEDs, or VBIEDs. One example occurred in September 2011, when a VBIED detonated outside the main gate of COP Sayed Abad in Logar Province. The massive explosion collapsed several buildings. "I was getting ready to go eat when I heard the boom," Georgia Army National Guard Specialist Robert Schrader recalls. "Initially I thought one of the [field artillery Howitzers] had malfunctioned, but, when I stepped out and saw the mushroom cloud of dust I knew that was not the case." After accounting for his teammates, Schrader assisted with moving the wounded to the casualty collection point and later onto the medevac helicopters.[68] Specialist Jason Tully remembers a VBIED attack on his outpost. After a soldier shouted the warning over the radio, "VBIED, VBIED, VBIED," Tully looked up "and saw [the bomber] get out of the car, running." Then the car exploded. Tully recalls, "I got bounced around inside my vehicle" from the force of the detonation. He then exited his truck and provided covering fire, as the insurgents were also attacking the outpost with small arms fire at the time.[69]

Fighting in Afghanistan generally followed a pattern governed by the weather. Winter placed most combat on hold, but after the spring thaw, the campaigning season resumed.[70] Captain Benjamin Tupper describes it as a "cat-and-mouse game."[71] Naturally, the Americans were the hunters and the Taliban the hunted. It would not be surprising if the Taliban thought of themselves as the hunters, given that they were fighting in their own territory. At one point, when the deployment began to weigh on his mind, Captain Craig Mullaney admits, "We didn't want to hunt *or* be hunted; we wanted to go home."[72]

Each passing year, the Taliban grew in strength and ability to fight the Coalition. According to a report released in June 2006 by retired US Army General, Barry R. McCaffrey, "The Taliban operated in small units three years ago; last year, they grew to company size units of 100 plus men; and for this year's summer fighting season they are maneuvering in 400-hundred strong battalion-sized units." In addition, "They appear to have received excellent tactical, camouflage and marksmanship training, and they are very aggressive and smart in their tactics."[73]

Soldiers noticed the changes in local engagements. Major Brandon Griffin, who deployed as part of a Special Forces operational detachment, recalls that during his first tour of duty, US troops engaged with three to five men, then it increased to eight to ten. During the second rotation, the Taliban were fighting in strength up to 100 men, but the losses became so heavy that the Taliban started engaging in lower numbers again.[74] Foreign fighters introduced new tactics to the Taliban, including kidnappings, assassinations, suicide attacks, and remote-controlled bombings, particularly against so-called "soft" targets, such as non-governmental organization personnel.[75] The Taliban increased its use of suicide bombings between 2005 and 2006; they had been used rarely until that point.

In 2006, it was the British and Canadian forces who took the brunt of the insurgency. In the summer, "British and Canadian troops deployed to Helmand and Kandahar confronted a well-armed and full-blown insurgency by reinvigorated Taliban." While the British and Canadians were able to push much of the insurgency back into Pakistan, the Taliban had not been defeated. Coalition troop levels remained too low to secure the country.[76] Waltz reflects, "for everyone serving in Afghanistan in 2006, it was obvious that the insurgency had turned a corner for the worse" for the Coalition but the focus in Washington remained on the Iraq War.[77]

Troops observed the Taliban improving their military skills, such as building sophisticated field works and camouflaged dugouts. The Taliban figured out that covering dugouts with logs, dirt, and pine needles rendered thermal sights used by Coalition forces useless. Exhibiting good military tactics, the Taliban often timed their attacks to be just before dawn because limited visibility covers movement. Since pre-dawn attacks were expected, the troops woke an hour before sunrise for "stand-to," which meant standing ready in firing positions. In order to keep the Taliban from planting roadside bombs or ambushing them, the Americans started moving their checkpoints every two to three hours. Keeping up that pace for days outside the wire, "all of us were smoked, filthy, and reeking," admits Parnell.[78]

The Taliban paid local men to plant roadside bombs, fire rockets, and harass troops with machine gun fire then disappear into the population. Harassment attacks often did not result in casualties, but they kept up the stress on American and Coalition forces.[79] More trained fighters formed cells that attacked US and Coalition forces. The highest ranking Taliban, "received training in Pakistan or Iran and carried the best weapons and gear," Golembesky noticed.[80] In the first couple of years of the war, the Taliban fighters often engaged American forces only until air support arrived on station. After 2004, they tended to stay and fight even with the presence of air power overhead.[81] In other words, the enemy adapted to the environment.

Even though Coalition casualty numbers remained relatively low in comparison to many of America's other twentieth-century wars, American troops lived in fear that dead and wounded combatants would fall into enemy hands and become enemy propaganda. Partly as a result of this fear, troops took risks to recover the fallen from the battlefield, even if this meant that more service members lost their lives in the effort.[82] If US troops went missing, a declaration of "personal [sic] recovery" or "DUSTWUN (duty status whereabouts unknown)" could be called. In one declaration, "the [theater] Special Operations Command responded immediately by dispatching Apache attack helicopters and Air Force helicopters with pararescue jumpers, or PJs," Meyer remembers.[83] Considerable time and effort went into finding missing service members.

Given that the enemy insurgents in Afghanistan did not wear uniforms, American troops became increasingly frustrated about their inability to identify the enemy. The same proved true of the insurgency in Iraq.[84] Sergeant Christopher Norton notes that "unless you catch somebody red-handed in a place like this, it is next to impossible. Because there's no telltale signs that they're bad or good. Everybody looks the same." Staff Sergeant Emmitt Adkins asserts, "This land is cursed by God. There's no intelligence on them. All we can do is react to them—reaction to contact. It kind of feels helpless sometimes." Because the insurgents melt into the population "they could be right in front of you and you wouldn't know it," he adds. Meanwhile, the Americans stood as easily identifiable targets. "These chickenshits won't stand and fight," grumbles Sergeant First Class Michael Torano. Staff Sergeant Philip Velasquez observes, "they hit and run. Which is a smart tactic, 'cause we ain't catching 'em" because they blend in with the population.[85]

In addition, the increasing intensity of the Taliban insurgency took its toll on the troops. Parnell recounts the relentless missions, where the troops only made quick stops inside the base to resupply, refuel, and rearm. Then they were back outside the wire on missions. Parnell notes that the "frantic pace wore us out and degraded morale." He and his soldiers patrolled the entire area around Bermel, extending 50 miles out in each direction. "We drove the wadis, discovered goat tracks that could handle our Humvees, and use them as shortcuts to get around potential roadside bombs. Signs of the enemy abounded" even as capturing them proved elusive.[86]

In order to wrest the initiative away from the enemy, American and NATO forces conducted offensive operations against the Taliban. One campaign was Operation Mountain Thrust in summer 2006. It aimed to deny sanctuary to insurgents in Kandahar, Helmand, Zabol, and Oruzgan provinces. As explained by the US commander, Major General Benjamin Freakley, "This is our approach— to put simultaneous pressure on the enemy's networks, to cause their leaders to make mistakes, and to attack those leaders." The Coalition effort included about 2300 Americans, 3300 Britons, 2200 Canadians and 3500 Afghans.[87]

American troops who fought in the operation had to contend not only with enemy mortars and small arms, but with heat and rugged terrain. "I am hungry, thirsty and dirty. Welcome to my world," says Sergeant First Class Gonzalo Lassally. In summer temperatures and lugging gear, the men sweated as they scrambled over rocky terrain. Dehydration proved such a concern that the troops used intravenous drips to keep hydrated. "I'm pissing orange," Staff Sergeant Brian Rice complains, indicating that he was severely dehydrated. "I hate this place. You can drop the devil here and he'd hate it," he gripes.

Echoing Vietnam War veterans who said the same thing, Captain Jared Wilson notes that the reality of military duty did not match romantic, glorified images seen in the action movies he grew up watching. "They don't show that in Hollywood," he grumbles, "they don't show you getting dehydrated." Others took the situation in stride. "As much as the Army sucks, I still love it," Lassally states.[88]

Offensive operations were not always as effective as envisioned. In 2008, the marines were given the mission to patrol in Now Zad in Helmand Province, an area controlled by the Taliban. As one company commander remembers, "These villages we're stuck in are, no shit, held by the fucking Taliban. With full complements of enemy troops, fortifications, and bunkers." The Taliban had infested the area with IEDs, which led to near daily explosions and casualties. As one would expect, it had a negative effect on morale. In the commander's words, "The daily dose of amputees and IED's inflicted a festering wound to our morale."[89]

Another type of operation in Afghanistan was clearing and securing polling sites for elections. One example of this type was Operation Determined Resolve, part of which occurred in the Deh Chopan District, Zabol Province. American troops engaged in a small arms firefight with insurgents, calling in air support. They had been engaged for over two hours when the Chinook helicopters arrived, but the landing zone was too "hot" to land. "You can't imagine how scary it is to be in a firefight like this and after two and a half hours of fighting, to see the support leave," relates Sergeant Michael Ortiz. As the troops began to clear the village, they found "high walls and locked doors everywhere," describes First Lieutenant Les Craig. The Taliban trapped the soldiers in the village by locking the doors and gates throughout the compounds, making it difficult to advance and secure. The tenacity of the Taliban fighters surprised the Americans, who had anticipated more hit-and-run tactics.[90]

At times, the intensity of the fighting called to mind images from America's other wars, particularly Vietnam. One soldier exclaims, "We are no-shit laying down suppressive fire just to exfil, are we in fucking 'Nam?" He and his fellow soldiers were firing from a ditch, and he notes "the amount of gunfire was indescribable. It was a wall of hot lead." He felt the ground shake from explosions, thinking this was "one of the most unbelievable experiences I've ever been a part of."[91] It is not exactly clear why heavy fire reminded this soldier of Vietnam, but he clearly tried to place what he was experiencing in a framework to understand it. He chose Vietnam to make it relatable. When COP Keating was being overrun by the Taliban, Romesha recollects that a soldier said something that "none of us had ever expected to hear, except maybe in a movie: 'Charlie in the wire!' He yelled. 'Charlie in the wire!'" The soldier invoked "a phrase lifted from the jungles of Vietnam and appl[ied] the thing to a firefight in the mountains of Afghanistan," when the insurgents breached the outer perimeter of the combat outpost.[92]

For those fighting in the most remote locations in Afghanistan, troops were connected to headquarters, support, and reinforcements by modern communications technology. The military invented its own internal-use Internet chat system, "mIRC," known as "merc chat," Romesha explains. It works like an instant messenger application that multiple users could exploit at the same time. "During the heat of battle, this form of tactical chatting or tac-chat was more efficient than phone lines or even radios," Romesha adds. The system connected remote outposts in Afghanistan through satellite connections to United States Air Force personnel operating drones in Nevada and New Mexico. The Air Force pilots read the tac-chat messages and responded with armed Predator and Reaper drones that were already on station over the battlefield.[93] Thanks to modern communications technology, pilots in the US maneuvered and fired drones thousands of miles away in Afghanistan.

Similarly, when COP Keating was under assault, Lieutenant Andrew Bundermann communicated with US bases at Bostick and Jalalabad as well as monitoring five radio channels, or nets, to maintain contact with his soldiers. The force Pro net allowed the commander and the platoon section leaders to talk inside the perimeter. Platoon leaders used the Platoon net. In order to contact Outpost Fritsche, the commander jumped on the Troop net, while the mortar crews utilized the Fires net. Another channel connected Bundermann with the pilots of any aircraft or helicopters within range.[94]

As troops engaged the enemy, the battle captain became like a "conductor" who "kept the whole orchestra of death going."[95] One soldier recounts how surreal it felt to watch a firefight on video screens from the Joint Operations Center (JOC), a level higher than a Tactical Operations Center (TOC). "There is action; movement, flashes of light, a white flicker on the screen when a large explosion happens. But there is no sound, at least not from the video." Without the corresponding sounds to accompany the gunfire and explosions, "it makes the battle seem less ... real for those watching."[96]

Perhaps the experience of watching combat from inside an operations center is captured best in a poem by Charlie Sherpa, "Quiet as TOC-Rats." He starts out by commenting that the place resembles a church in its quiet. Then he likens the TOC as the "nervous system" of the operation rather than its brains. Sherpa comments on the communications running through the center from radios to mICR-chat, while noting the buzz of the air conditioning under the fluorescent overhead lights. The story boards that track the operation are "Houston"—a reference to NASA's Johnson Space Center—to the commander's "Mars"-like mission. Sherpa hopes the information can cut through the "fog of war," a term lifted from the military theoretician Carl von Clausewitz. The purpose and focus of the TOC is to "track the battle," a phrase he repeats three times for emphasis. In the TOC, the soldiers listen to the battle on the radio rather than fighting in it, fearing to hear static on the other end—an indication they lost service members.[97]

More than any other experience, combat sets troops apart from the sights, sounds, smells, and touches of home. As World War II soldier Laurence Critchell describes it, "combat is foreign to all other experience; nothing in ordinary life reminds me of it."[98] Translating that experience to friends and family proved challenging, as combatants already felt separated from their fellow "Fobbit" comrades in uniform. Indeed, even service members who participated in the same firefight could not always agree on what they had experienced.

As Grant McGarry explains, "anyone who has been in combat knows that everyone involved in the firefight remembers certain incidents with no recollection of details from someone else's account."[99] Mullaney agrees, adding, "what were facts to me conflicted with the certainty of others' recollections. Distances and directions were jumbled. The sequence was out of order." He concludes, "the only thing that was clear was that none of us had been in the same battle."[100] Unsurprisingly, combatants struggled to find language that could at least hint toward the sights, sounds, smells, and physical experience of battle.

One common misperception is that Hollywood accurately portrays combat. "Most combat is a lot less dramatic than most war movies," observes Doherty. "It is often slower paced with peaks of action. Combat gets intense and then dies down then gets intense again," he adds.[101] Firefights often follow a rhythm. "Bedlam isn't unusual in the first seconds of an attack," explains Meyer. The enemy fires through several magazines while American troops "go flat and scramble for position." In a short time, the troops get into a rhythm where a senior service member directs radio calls and the forward observer calls in close air support. Once artillery and air support start firing, the enemy's rate of fire subsides. "Firefights were often like that—a sudden, violent spasm lasting 10 or 15 minutes at most before things quiet down" followed by "a steady, sustained exchange of fire as everyone settled into a rhythm," Golembesky describes. "Seeing you[r] enemy outright is a blessing," Doherty notes. "You are often shooting at movements and gun flashes or areas you received fire from," he clarifies.[102]

Soldiers employ many associations familiar to civilians to describe the sights of battle. These images range from fireworks to thunderstorms to movies. Many visualize combat as fireworks. Rico describes "momentary microsecond daylight and speckles of Fourth-of-July sparklers." At a distance, the battle is a pretty "fireworks display," he muses. Rico also observes a rocket propelled grenade flying overhead "like a Fourth of July celebration where you lie out in the grass on a blanket and watch the fireworks explode in the sky." Kingsley thinks a firefight "looks like a Fourth of July celebration and laser light show were both going on at the same time." Logan Lewis sees "tracers ricochet off the rocks and into the air, which gave the same appearance as fireworks."

Other light displays feature in combatants' descriptions. The exchange of fire below his position appears as a "symphony of blinking Christmas lights" according to Rico. He continues with another analogy, likening them to lightning bugs like he remembers from summers growing up in Iowa. Lieutenant Nathaniel Fick prefers the image of a rainstorm with lightning and thunder: "After sunset, the eastern horizon flashed as if with distant lightning ... low rumbling followed the biggest flashes." Other combatants describe the visual battle in terms of Hollywood. With rockets and tracer fire coming from all directions, Specialist Andrew Stock explains, it has a *Star Wars* effect," another reference to the popular film. Parnell describes the same scene as having "an almost sci-fi appearance."[103]

Bullets flying through the air were observed through tracer fire, which combatants describe with a variety of images. McGarry perceives the tracer rounds as "a ball of fire ripping and popping over us and leaving the fire trail as the round passed over." Another soldier depicts the same tracer rounds as "glowing like tiny green champagne bubbles on my NODs" (night observation device). Sergeant First Class James Taylor Grimes asks, "Do you know how you can tell if the tracer is going to hit near you? If you see a tracer and it looks like a line, it's going to go either left or right of you or both. If it's a dot, it's coming straight at you," he concludes helpfully to those who lacked any similar experience.[104]

Combatants pull from a number of familiar civilian sources to explain other visual images of combat. Night vision goggles made "chem lights bend and bow like neon tiki torches over the convoy." Illumination rounds that light up the battlefield "hung in the sky like a string of full moons." An RPG resembled "a flaming football" for one combatant. Another description of an RPG is "a speeding orange oval that was on fire," much like a flaming football.[105]

Just as their predecessors in earlier wars quickly learned the sounds of the battlefield to determine danger, so too did the combatants in Afghanistan learn the sounds of battle. Service members proved creative in describing the sound of bullets to civilians. Rico thinks bullets make a crackle snap sound like firecrackers. McGarry describes bullets has having a "popping noise" as they went overhead. Waltz uses the same language to describe multiple machine guns firing: "It suddenly sounds like I had stuck my head into a popcorn machine." Invoking another pop culture reference, Parnell believes they sounded like the whip used by Indiana Jones in the movies. Against the door of a Humvee, bullets could sound like a "ping" or they could sound "like thuds from a sledgehammer" or "jackhammer."

Another soldier remarks that a bullet hitting armor makes a "flat tunk" and, at a loss for words, "nothing in the world sounds remotely like it." Christ writes that "he could hear the tink tink tink as bullets slammed into his Humvee turned and ricocheted off." Similarly, in another passage, a soldier "could hear the tink tink and plink plink as the rounds struck his Humvee." Specialist Timothy Bates, notices that "you could hear the rounds popping overhead, you could hear them smacking the sandbags." Rounds from a PKM Soviet machine gun sound as a "heavier thwak thwak thwak" against the side of a Humvee.[106]

As Westerners familiar with machinery and modern technology, troops use mechanical analogies to describe the sounds made by various types of machine guns. The 30 mm Gatling cannon from an A-10 Warthog sounded like "a wood chipper grinding thick logs." Another soldier thinks the metallic whir sounds like "a high speed circular saw." The Gatling machine guns on the Chinook helicopter made "BRMMMMMMMMMMMMMMMPH! BRMMMMMMMMMMMMMMMMPH!" noises. The soldier comments, "their extreme rates of fire made them not even sound like guns, but some sort of power tool." Similarly, the .50 caliber machine gun is "a noise that resembled a chainsaw tearing through steel metal." The M240 machine gun "sounded like a giant zipper being ripped open." The Russian B-10 recoilless rifle "sounded like a freight train was dropping down on top of us."[107]

Sound can orient a combatant to danger on the battlefield. Meyer points out that bullets make different sounds depending on their proximity. If the bullet cracking sound breaks the sound barrier, "they're high, maybe five or ten feet over your head. The bullets that snap close by your ears are the real killers," he explains. The ones that are slowing down and losing power make "a low buzzing sound" Meyer adds. Lieutenant Beau Cleland agrees, noting that "guns make a distinctly different sound when they are pointed at you—sharper and higher pitched. Bullets make a zip noise that's tough to describe." He relates, "you can sort of judge how close they get by the sound and intensity of that noise." Meyer also corrects a misperception created by the movies: when a bullet strikes a body, it does not fall back. Instead, the person either "stumbles on or he falls dead."[108]

Parnell explains that the rate and direction of gunfire gave it its own language. "Suppressing fire, the purpose of which is to pin you down, sounds undisciplined; it wanders back and forth over you without much aim," he explains. That kind of fire was random, so it did not appear as deadly to Parnell. Fire that is accurate and directed on target sounds different. According to Parnell, these shots "come with a rapid fire focus that underscores their murderous intent. Somebody is shooting at you. It becomes intimate and fear inducing."[109] In addition, machine guns could "speak" to one another. It refers to when "one gun shoots a burst and then is answered by the other gun shooting a burst, going back and forth until they finished firing."[110]

Unsurprisingly, combatants state that the noise of battle proved deafening. "Think of the loudest war movie sequence you've ever seen," Cleland writes, "and multiply that until it would make your ears bleed." It made Golembesky's ears ring. Aerial bombardment was like "every pot and pan in your kitchen hitting the floor simultaneously and then stopping," relates Cleland. An RPG sent "concussive echoing blasts through the valley." Mortars make a "whoomp" sound when they are fired. Sailing overhead, mortars make "a high pitched whistle." Inventing a word to describe the noise, rockets sound like "sssssSHHHIIIIIIEEEEWWWWWW! SHHCKWAAAAM!" according to Anders. Grenades make "a dull thump every few seconds," states Golembesky, or they made a "pffft ... buh-wham!" sound, according to Romesha.[111]

Romesha imagines the cacophony of a firefight as a composer might describe a symphony with the sounds of each instrument making a separate contribution to the whole. He mentions that "each of their guns had a distinctive sound. The sharp piercing percussion of the M240 was underplayed with the bass growl of the slower and heavier .50 cal. Beneath all of that, you could also hear the chug chug chug" of the Mark 19. Inside the tactical operations center, there are voices, radios, incoming fire, outgoing fire, all with different pitches and intensity. It made perfect sense to himself and the commander, though a civilian might find it confusing and chaotic.[112]

Insurgent voices add to the discordance of battle. "Howling like banshees, they poured over the tops of the eastern ridges down the tree covered slopes toward the valley floor" describes Parnell. They made "one terrifying undulating sound. li-li-li-li-li!"[113] The motion "reminded me of the zombie apocalypse movies filmed back in my hometown in Pennsylvania. *Dawn of the Dead* meets Afghanistan." The cries of the wounded became part of the aural landscape of battle. As one soldier describes it, "Someone who is seriously hurt screams like a wounded animal, like their mind has left them."[114]

When the battle was over, the silence leaves ears ringing. It is "like the peaceful respite in sound that comes after a long-running lawn mower or wood chipper has suddenly been turned off," according to Rico.[115] On long deployments where the troops were under constant harassment, ears eventually acclimated to the sounds. "Having at one time flinched at every pop, bang, or boom," Captain Matt Smenos recalls, "we now hardly blinked an eye at explosions or smoke."[116]

The sounds of the battlefield included music that the troops played through speaker systems in their vehicles. One soldier describes chasing insurgents across the Afghan desert in what he dubs a "classic movie style car chase." As the Humvee accelerated in pursuit, the compact-disc player started playing heavy-metal band Metallica's "Enter Sandman." The soldier found the music appropriate to the setting with "the ferocious tempo of the heavy-metal [keeping] pace with their speed across the desert. The song itself was ironic too, as it blared about the Sandman, a mysterious ghost in Never Never Land." He believes the music and lyrics "added a lot to the atmosphere of everything we did."[117] Rusty Bradley's fellow soldiers hooked up an Apple iPod to speakers and blasted techno and country music.[118]

Combat also creates physical sensations that combatants attempted to describe to civilians back home. The physical responses are related to stress and "magnifies and intensifies every human emotional response," explains Golembesky. Fear, Cleland explains, "is very uncomfortable, like you had lead pancakes for breakfast." Christ observes that "the younger soldiers, who had never been in firefights before, were in shock. [A soldier's] body was physically shaking to where he could not stop it." Jimmy Settle describes how "the hair stood up on my skin, prickling like porcupine quills, and I broke out in an instant cold sweat." At another time, he notes, "I didn't just have butterflies in my stomach; my guts were writhing like a ball of water moccasins." On the other hand, the expectation of combat could make one's heart pound with adrenaline. Rico recalls that his knees were "wobbly and shaky" when he raised himself to return fire. Mullaney remembers after one battle "I wanted to piss in my boots." A person bounces from emotion to emotion, "one minute, we are cheering and exultant. The next ... tormented by what we witness," writes Golembesky.[119]

Adrenaline gave combatants a physical and emotional boost to get through combat. Parnell describes, "my exhaustion gone, my legs grew light. The burn in my lungs vanished. Euphoria drove me forward." The effects of adrenaline could mask a wound. "You get so amped up on adrenaline that you tend to focus on everything but yourself," explains Romesha. Bradley recounts a combination of adrenaline and emotional rage he felt during combat. He acknowledges it is a feeling that probably only soldiers understand, not civilians. He defines it as "the physical combination of adrenaline, testosterone, exhaustion, and emotion" that caused him to feel a primal rage.[120]

When the firefight was over and the adrenaline drained away, combatants were left with "sudden exhaustion," writes Parnell. It left McGarry losing fine motor skills. Constant exposure to adrenaline built up resistance to its effects. Parnell recalls that with daily patrols, "The adrenaline rushes no longer gave us the euphoric high we had experienced in the spring." The experience was not as intense and did not last as long; "our bodies were getting used to that chemical surge, and its effects were diminishing with every injection."[121]

Combatants tried to explain to folks back home the physical sensations of coming into close proximity to explosions. Romesha explains, "What you feel, mostly, is a kind of fast pushing sensation, almost as if an ocean wave has struck you in the solar plexus and, through some strange trick of physics, is now passing through your tissue, your bones, your entire body." Located not too far away from the impact area of a large bomb, Golembesky exclaims, "Holy shit! I felt the heat of that one on my face!" Near the explosion of a fragmentation grenade, McGarry likens it "to being hit in the face by a baseball bat."

The concussion of a blast knocked Parnell down, "just as a furnace of heat stroke my side and back. I hit the ground and tumbled side over side until dirt, sky, trees, and rocks all vanished in that terrible dark void once again." Like McGarry, he likens it to someone hitting his head with a baseball bat. Hot brass coming off of a machine gun "felt like lava rocks being hurled into my face," according to Lewis. An RPG landed a few feet away from Air Force Technical Sergeant Kevin Wallace. When it detonated, "I was thrown into the front wall and saw nothing but sharp white light," he remembers. "I couldn't smell, feel, see, and couldn't comprehend what was going on for moments" as his body absorbed the shock of the round.[122]

Combat brought a number of unpleasant smells, particularly associated with the explosives used in ordnance. Exploding rockets left a smell of gunpowder. Blood added another odor. The smells left a taste of "sulfur and chalk and copper on my tongue. It made me feel like I was about to gag," Romesha describes. Kingsley also remembers "the sulfur smell of gunpowder." Rickard notes the "smell of cordite from explosions and gunfire" creating "an acrid smell in the air." Settle mentions the same smells: cordite and blood. Corbin Chesley, after two days of sweating in his Humvee, stood in the turret, firing at an enemy concealed 200 meters away. He recalls "the acrid smell of gunpowder mixed with the stench of unwashed men and diesel fumes." Settle, as a parajumper medic, describes the smells of combat and death: "That rich copper smell of blood. Smeared shit. Piss-soaked pants. Sweat, bile, filth, and fear." He adds how the odors "permeated my uniform, my flesh, and dug deep into my being."[123]

Perceptions of time lost all meaning during combat. As combatants in previous wars discovered, "time, playing other tricks on men under fire, alternately compressed and extended its movement." Rico asks himself, "How long have we been firing? Hours, it seems. A quick glimpse at my watch reveals it to have only been six or so minutes." First Sergeant Troy Steward remembers "time slows to a crawl as your mind works in overdrive." Cleland exhibits the opposite reaction. "I looked at my watch," he recalls, "and six hours had passed in what seemed like the longest five minutes of my life." Parnell wonders, "how much time had passed? Five minutes? Five seconds? In such moments, time has no traction." The same was true for air personnel as well. Staff Sergeant Antonio Delvecchio, a helicopter flight engineer, felt five minutes had passed during a medevac mission, "but in reality looking back and going through the tapes it's 45 seconds." For Settle, memories of combat blurred, disconnected "like a pile of snapshots" rather than a logical, linear timeline.[124]

Troops who have experienced combat before have reactions on the battlefield different from those who have not. Major Mark O'Neill reflects on the distinction: "You could see the stark contrast between those folks that has spent a year in combat and those that were inexperienced. You saw those who had been there for a while jumping the action and you saw all the others just frozen." He notes that the inexperienced troops were not necessarily scared, they just wondered "What do we do? This is our first time under fire. What's the protocol?" O'Neill mentions that these troops needed additional guidance compared to those who had already been in combat.[125] Kingsley observes that everyone felt lost during their first combat experience. He admits that it took several missions before he started to feel comfortable.[126]

In the aftermath of combat, troops found themselves surrounded by shell casings and other debris. Rusty Bradley describes the interior of his Humvee after one firefight. First, the floor was littered with brass casings from the machine gun with all the empty rifle magazines tossed on top. Ammo cans and water bottles joined the debris tossed inside the truck. He notes how enemy fire had damaged both the windshield and headlights, while RPG detonations had torn away the Humvee's antennas, in addition to the shrapnel damage to the armor around the machine gun turret. He writes, "Blackened telephone-book-sized pieces of Kevlar on the hood and sides of the truck were shredded; bullet holes the size of a pinkie finger pockmarked the rest." Despite the damage to his vehicle, Bradley's dark sense of humor prompted him to take out a Sharpie marker and write "MISSED ME BITCH" on the hood with arrows pointing to bullet holes.[127]

Whether on patrol, in a firefight, caught in an ambush or other violence, American troops suffered casualties. In one ambush in the Korengal Valley, a bullet hit Specialist Carl Vandenberge in the arm. Private Misha Pemble-Belkin rushed to his aid. The bullet hit Vandenberge in an artery, so there was a danger he could bleed out. Pemble-Belkin stuffed gauze into the wound, but Vandenberge had lost a lot of blood by that time. Vandenberge lost so much color in his face that he started looking like a ghost. In addition, "his eyes started sinking into his head, he started to get real brown around the eyes." Vandenberge vocalized, "I'm getting really dizzy, I want to go to sleep." Pemble-Belkin reacted, "That's some rough shit to hear, coming from one of your best friends and you're watching him die right in front of you, that's some fucking shit."[128] Between Pemble-Belkin and the medic, who inserted an IV, Vandenberge stabilized, and he managed to climb down the mountain, propped up by soldiers on either side, to ride a medevac helicopter to a medical facility. He survived. Most casualties who are treated in the first "golden hour" survive, but not every service member did.[129]

One of the worst moments for troops in combat is the loss of a fellow service member. Since casualties remained fairly low in Afghanistan, individual losses hit hard emotionally. In comparison, Philip Caputo notes of the Vietnam War, "Experiencing heavy or constant losses tends to diminish the significance of on individual's death."[130] When Mullaney lost a soldier in combat, they followed tradition. The platoon came back to the base, still covered in muck and blood, to stand for company roll call. At the sound of the fallen soldier's name, there was a pause and a second call of his name. After another long pause, a soldier answered, that the named soldier was "no longer with us." To commemorate the fallen soldier, the men set out his combat boots, his rifle, bayonet in the ground, dog tags, and in this case, a wide-brimmed camouflage hat. Later, they had a formal memorial ceremony, where the roll call was read again. Seven soldiers fired a three-volley salute. Taps began to play. Everyone snapped to attention. Tears fell.[131]

When a service member died, it was the responsibility of the members of the unit to remove any weapons, unexploded ordnance, and classified information from the body. Other personal effects remained with the service member as they were brought into Mortuary Affairs and through the process of returning the body home. If the objects were covered in blood, they were often removed before going to the family. Separately, the unit inventoried the service member's equipment and personal effects left in his or her room.[132] When Meyer lost the members of his team, he personally tended to the bodies, removing their armor and personal items from pockets, noting which items would be sent back to the families. After taking off the fallen's field gear, Meyer and another service member moved the bodies into the black body bags. Meyer explains how they "mark the name at the head, drape an American flag over each bag, bow our heads in prayer, and drive them to the helo pad."[133] Mortuary Affairs prepares the deceased for return to their families.

An officer in Mortuary Affairs, Captain Brian Alexander, remembers the most difficult part of his deployment to Afghanistan, when a helicopter crashed with 22 casualties. He recalls that "most of the remains were burned beyond recognition, but not all." The team worked in two shifts for 12 hours straight to process the remains within 24 hours. There were too many bodies for the facility to hold, so they had to arrange for pallets of ice to refrigerate the remains. He relates, "all we do every day is death; and it is tough," which was why the service members have six month rotations rather than year-long deployments. Despite the difficulty of working in Mortuary Affairs, he believes that "being able to return loved ones home is an honorable and amazing responsibility."[134]

When the remains of the fallen were ready to be transported home, there was a ramp ceremony onto the aircraft. Amber Smith recollects that ramp ceremonies "are always solemn and gut wrenching." She participated in one procession, observing that "soldiers lined the streets as the Humvee that carries the American flag-draped transfer case—the military's term for caskets, a silver colored metal container—drives by. There is a moment of silence and then in unison every soldier gives a final salute." "Taps" plays as the transfer case was brought onto the aircraft. The body was transported as priority one. At this level, only medevac or the president of the United States flies with higher precedence.[135]

Given the extreme nature of combat, the military has found ways to recognize those who have experienced it through awards. For infantry, recognition for action in battle may result in a Combat Infantry Badge, or CIB. It is an award exclusive to infantry performing action in ground combat. It was first introduced in World War II, and awarded in the Korean and Vietnam Wars as well. As Anders explains, "a CIB, more than any other badge, represented the kind of intimate

Troops bow their heads during a chaplain's prayer during transfer of a fallen comrade at a ramp ceremony on Kandahar Airfield, Afghanistan. July 20, 2009 (photograph by the Office of the Secretary of Defense Public Affairs).

knowledge that only came with hard earned experience." For service members other than infantry who have experienced combat in Iraq or Afghanistan, the Army created the Combat Action Badge, or CAB. In areas of intense violence, soldiers earned their CABs quickly. One soldier relates how three civil affairs service members earned their CABs in the first month and a half of his deployment, notable since civil affairs personnel do not typically engage in combat. Even though women were barred from combat, given the lack of frontlines in the wars

Bagram Air Base, Afghanistan: In this handout image provided by the US Air Force, eight American flag-draped caskets line the floor of a C-17 Globemaster III from the 15th Airlift Squadron, Charleston Air Force Base, SC, awaiting transport home at Bagram Air Base on February 2, 2004, in Afghanistan. The soldiers were killed in an explosion at a weapons cache on January 29, 2004 (photograph by Brian Davidson/US Air Force via Getty Images).

in Afghanistan and Iraq, more than 9,000 women have been awarded the CAB as well as other awards.

The equivalent award for personnel from the Marine Corps, Navy, or Coast Guard (when operating under the Navy) is the Combat Action Ribbon, or CAR. The US Air Force created the Combat Action Medal, and there is also an equivalent award for medics attached to combat units, the Combat Medical Badge. Some service members engaged in "combat tourism," trying to get close enough to the action to be awarded the CAB without actually endangering themselves. So many CABs were awarded that one senior noncommissioned officer laments, the "badge had become the Army's equivalent of a participation trophy," losing its intended purpose to recognize soldiers who have engaged in combat with the enemy. Combatants in America's earlier wars, such as World War II and Vietnam, similarly complained about too many, mostly rear-echelon troops, being unfairly awarded in their opinion.[136]

Experiences of combat differed—sometimes dramatically—for troops serving in Afghanistan. It also differed from the combat experiences in Iraq. Some units encountered very little combat, while others suffered under constant threats of ambushes, IEDs, and firefights. Combatants tried to explain the visual, aural, and physical sensations of combat to those back home using analogies civilians would recognize, including references to pop culture. As the war progressed, the behavior of the enemy became bolder, as they appeared to fight in ever greater numbers. The Taliban introduced IEDs to combat in Afghanistan and began to use suicide bombers as well. Increasingly, American and Coalition troops relied on air power to thwart the emboldened enemy.

•• 5 ••

Air War

With few troops on the ground in Afghanistan in the opening weeks of the war, the US relied on air power to help topple the Taliban and al-Qaeda and then to support troops during the subsequent insurgency. A hallmark of the war in Afghanistan is the use of close air support (fixed-wing aircraft) and close combat aviation (helicopters) to provide fire superiority to US troops on the ground, even if the use of airpower angered the local population due to the civilian casualties it sometimes caused. As one officer described, the challenge was to "somehow mold extremely violent air power into a way of destroying the enemy without using excessive power or having any kind of unnecessary collateral damage and loss of civilian life, at the same time protecting the troops."[1]

Air power over Afghanistan comprised Navy aircraft carrier jets, Air Force fighters, bombers, and ground attack planes, and Army helicopters, as well as drones.[2] Aircraft also provided supplies, moved troops, and medically evacuated casualties. What follows are experiences from the crews flying in support of Operation Enduring Freedom and eyewitness accounts of the effects of air power from the ground. As with other descriptions of combat, the service members invoke common images and occasional pop culture references to make the experiences understandable to themselves and to civilians back home.

During the opening campaign, the first aircraft to support operations in the war came from overseas. Aircraft from US Navy aircraft carriers sailing in the Arabian Sea and US Air Force fighters and bombers stationed in the Middle East provided the initial air support for ground troops. In addition to bombing runs, the aircraft provided reconnaissance and boosted morale for US and Northern Alliance troops. Aircraft maintained tight rules of engagement (ROE) about when they could drop ordnance in order to avoid civilian casualties or upsetting the Afghan population.[3]

The first female navigator on an AC-130H Spectre gunship, Captain Allison Black, provided air support to the Special Forces detachment assisting Afghan General Dostum. After a successful mission, Dostum reportedly taunted the Taliban on the radio saying, "You're pathetic. American women are killing you. It's the angel of death raining fire upon you," whereupon Black earned the nickname "Angel of Death."[4]

Afghanistan proved dangerous to aircraft because of the mountainous terrain and frequent poor weather conditions. "The enemy are number eight on my list of threats," states one US Air Force helicopter pilot. He explains, "The biggest threat is Afghanistan itself—the altitude, heat, darkness, brown out [when high winds kick up dust that limits visibility] and weather."[5] Mountain valleys were particularly dangerous because of the lack of maneuverability. "A lot of the valleys that we fly in, you didn't have the area to maneuver," describes Major Michael Zendajas. "You've got 6000 or 10,000 foot mountains on either side of you."[6] With numerous aircraft in the air space, controllers defined altitudes for flying different types of aircraft. Fighter jets, for example, had to stay aloft at certain altitudes to prevent collisions with helicopters.[7]

One of the first tasks for US personnel in Afghanistan was to build or refurbish air fields. The US Air Force concentrated on building up Bagram and Kandahar airfields, while the British Royal Air Force worked on Kabul International Airport.[8] Once the airways were operational, military aviation units deployed to Bagram and Kandahar. The importance of supporting the ground troops in combat framed the aviators' mindset. On one tour at Bagram, the 335th Fighter Squadron posted a sign reading, "The mission is an 18-year-old with a rifle, everything else is support."[9]

From Bagram airfield in March 2002, helicopters supported Operation Anaconda in the Shah-i-kot mountains. Helicopters delivered troops to the area, attracting fire from the enemy. At first, the pilots did not even recognize that they were taking fire. In explaining the experience, one co-pilot recalls that "it sounded

Helicopter maneuverability was hampered by mountains. A Black Hawk helicopter assigned to the 1st Air Cavalry Brigade, 1st Cavalry Division flies over mountains in eastern Afghanistan during a cargo movement mission on October 18, 2013.

like somebody just took their bare hand and slapped the side of the aircraft." It never occurred to him that his helicopter would come under attack.[10] The helicopters suffered bullet holes through their rotor blades as well as all along the body, tires, and even the cockpit Plexiglass.[11]

Apache helicopter pilot Warrant Officer John Hamilton arrived within 10 minutes of the first assault in Operation Anaconda. The next hour proved chaotic. "It was very fluid and confusing, with all kinds of voices on the radio. It was hard to tell where the friendlies and enemies were on the ground." He remembers taking enemy fire, which hit his helicopter. Enemy fire proved so heavy that the wounded could not be evacuated until the following day.[12] For the next week, troops on the mountains called in airstrike after airstrike on enemy positions.[13] Without mortars or field artillery in the country, aircraft became "flying artillery."

Somewhere in the range of 150–175 airstrikes hit enemy positions in the first ten days of the operation. With so many aircraft flying missions, the airspace over the battlefield proved crowded. One pilot recollects that "an F-18 split right between me and my wingman. I have a Predator [drone] that almost bounces off the top of my canopy," then a bomber dropped its ordnance through his formation.[14] The troops on the ground appreciated the efforts of the supporting aircraft. One Special Forces staff sergeant expresses it when he says, air support is his "American Express card—I don't leave home without it," a play on the credit card advertisement.[15]

When awaiting a mission, bombers fly in a pattern 20 miles long and 10 miles across, dubbed a "race track."[16] When the ground troops contact the pilot, the speakers on the radio first identify their call signs. Then the ground controller gives the coordinates where he wants the ordnance to drop, which the pilot repeats to verify the information before typing the numbers into the bomb's GPS. Once the bomb is armed, the pilot announces, "pickle, pickle, pickle," the signal for "bombs away." Another push of a button, and the bomb drops from the plane. "Thirty seconds" the pilot warns the troops below, so they could prepare for the impact.[17]

One particular bomb, the Joint Direct Attack Munition (JDAM), "became the weapon of choice during the Afghan campaign because of its pinpoint accuracy and ability to be launched in bad weather," though it had not originally been designed for a role in close air support. Given the need for close air support, the tactics, techniques and procedures for that role were developed in real-time on the ground at the beginning of the Afghan War. The largest JDAM measures 12 feet in length and contains 1200 pounds of explosives.[18] With that amount of explosives, JDAMs made an impressive impact on the ground. It sounded like "a roaring phoooooossshhh," making an echo through the valley, explains Michael Golembesky. "To the uninitiated, it sounded like a jet making a low altitude pass," he adds. When one JDAM fell on a building, "the blast sent tentacles of smoke and flames shooting skyward as debris rained down for hundreds of meters," he describes. The bomb was so precise that even though the shockwave reverberated through the area, no other building sustained damage.[19]

A U.S. Air Force B-1B Lancer aircraft banks away after receiving fuel during a mission over Afghanistan on May 27, 2008 (photograph by Master Sergeant Andy Dunaway).

In addition to dropping bombs, aircraft ferried supplies and troops throughout Afghanistan. Given poor road conditions in many areas, the distance of some outposts, and the threat of enemy attacks, air drop proved the best solution to keep troops supplied in remote areas. In the first few years of the Afghan War, air crews delivered between six and eight million pounds of supplies each year. Those efforts ramped up considerably, so that by 2012 around 60 million pounds of supplies were air dropped. In areas with high threat to aircraft, the Joint Precision Airdrop System utilized GPS and other technologies to allow the planes to drop supplies safely from 20,000 to 30,000 feet in altitude.[20]

Aircraft faced the threat of enemy fire from the ground. In one example, a C-130 Hercules crew prepared for a 16-hour long mission flying out of Manas Air Base in Kyrgyzstan. They received a briefing on the mission with all the operational and intelligence updates. Given the threat of enemy fire to aircraft, the crew adopted blackout conditions to fly, turning off all lights. "The cover of darkness is our best protection against many of the threats we face daily," explains an airman. Often, the crews also wore body armor for additional protection.[21] With blackout conditions, crews relied on radar and GPS to navigate through the terrain. Major Chris "Mookie" Walker notes, "You could say, okay, we're in a valley now, you can descend. Or, there's a mountain ridge about three miles to the right." He adds, "when you're flying down with no lights into a totally pitch-dark valley, knowing where there are mountains all around, that can be really, really nerve-racking."[22] Major Mike Foley remembers using radar to navigate: "I would sit down and watch the radar for the terrain instead of looking visually" like the

A C-130 Hercules airdrops supplies for coalition forces in Sayed Abad District, Wardak Province, Afghanistan, on January 7, 2014 (photograph by Mass Communication Specialist 2nd Class William S. Parker).

old way of flying. He indicates it was safest flying with the crew monitoring both the radar and having some members look out of the window.[23]

On this particular night, the enemy shot at the C-130, causing the defense weapons system to activate. The pilot took the aircraft into a defensive maneuver, ascending as "flares shot out of the aircraft like a Fourth of July fireworks display," invoking a common visual image for combat. Having averted any damage, the crew completed their flight.[24] Without any lights, the pilot of a blacked-out aircraft donned night vision goggles in order to land safely.[25] Walker explains that using night vision goggles to land proved a common practice for pilots in Afghanistan since the crews tried to keep a low profile by routinely turning the lights off for both takeoff and landing. The precautions proved necessary. He indicates that ground personnel often sighted tracer rounds aimed at the aircraft as the planes took off and landed.[26]

Sometimes combat conditions required aircraft to perform an assault landing. Major Carla Riner, a pilot, describes an assault landing as "a procedure involving aggressive use of breaks and reverse thrust to get the airplane stopped on a short runway." She recalls one landing where both her and the flight engineer were working the throttles and yoke in blackout conditions to land the aircraft.[27] Thomas Young remembers another assault landing at FOB Salerno. The landing zone was "4000 feet of soft dirt and big rocks, with a runaway condition reading of God knows what. On the side of a mountain of loose shale, limestone, and scraggly evergreens." Just as Rainer had described, Young's plane descended rapidly, hit the dirt runway, and engaged the brakes and reverse on the propellers to stop safely. The aircraft landed roughly, sending dirt into the air and bouncing on the rough runway until it came to a full stop.[28] The human body felt tremendous pressure on such landings. "Your body feels like it's becoming squished down completely," describes one passenger.[29]

With the threat of enemy fire, aircraft had to ascend as quickly as they landed. Young explains that the pilot throttles the engine to maximum, while the flight engineer turns off all unnecessary systems to boost power. It means the air conditioning went off, even in the heat of summer. "Sweating in the vibrating, roaring machine," Young describes, "the pilot releases the brakes while the navigator times the acceleration with the stopwatch." The crew had to track acceleration to assure the plane reached the minimum flying speed. With the plane climbing in altitude, it avoids stalling out.[30] Amber Smith was on the ground watching as US Air Force F-16 fighter jets made quick afterburner takeoffs. She observes, "Essentially they flew straight up into the air to get to a safe altitude as soon as possible. It looked cool, and it even sounded cool—once." Unfortunately, with continuous air operations through the day and night, such takeoffs disturbed everyone's sleep. Smith complains, "it woke me up every two hours, so the novelty wore off fast."[31]

A key mission for aircraft in the Afghan War was providing close air support for troops on the ground. The military terminology for a firefight was TIC, or troops in contact. Rusty Bradley refers to close air support as "modern angels of the battlefield" and assumes they "would finally level the playing field."[32] Given that the enemy did not also rely on air support, it was not really leveling the playing field as much as dominating it. Air power gave the Coalition a definite advantage over al-Qaeda, the Taliban, and the other local insurgent groups. When ground troops required air support, they radioed in what was called a 9-line, which gives the flight crew the pertinent information for dropping ordnance, including the "location of the target, location of the nearest friendlies, the direction of flight the JTAC [Joint Tactical Air Controller] wants the aircraft to be going at the moment of release, and a number of other details," Golembesky explains.[33] Aircraft from around the entire country could be called to respond to a troops in contact situation. One pilot recalls, "You could end up anywhere in the country on any given day. I flew one mission up against the Iranian border [in the west], hit a tanker [for fuel], and then ended up on the Pakistani border [in the east] on the same sortie [mission]."[34] Another pilot describes providing close air support in Afghanistan as "playing whack-a-mole," as no one knew where the fight would be on any given day.[35]

Stringent rules of engagement governed when aircraft could fire on enemy fighters. The intent of the strict ROE was to avoid civilian casualties, which antagonized the population.[36] "Before we can shoot for the ground guys in combat," Smith explains, "they must give us clearance of fire." Clearance of fire entailed accounting for the position of all friendly forces in the area and assuring the pilots that the troops had a minimum safe distance from the target area. "As pilots we

an IR [infrared] laser. Friendlies marked with fireflies." Smith turned her Kiowa to find the enemy position. She spotted the American Humvees, which were pinned down by enemy fire. The soldiers had attached the infrared light to a cord and "swung overhead like a lasso—making a circle of light that was only visible through NVGs." In this way, Smith identified the friendly forces, so she turned her attention to finding the source of the enemy fire. When she did, her Kiowa and her partner's helicopter took turns targeting the enemy fire position.

"This is the dance of war," she writes, "two helicopters circling in a ring of fire. I've been to left, outbound cold, and Sammy [the pilot of the other Kiowa] came in hot. Two more rockets. And he is out, and on in. Two more rockets. It happened in seconds. It was beautiful." After they fired the rockets, Smith engaged her guns. "Dat! Dat! Dat! Our entire aircraft rattled as the gun fired. I clenched my jaw so I wouldn't bite my tongue. A stream of bullets landed perfectly on the target."[102] One way to locate an enemy's position was to observe the direction of the enemy's tracer fire. "Their muzzle flashes looked like blinking Christmas lights" as the pilots hit their targets. "Dirt and mud are flying up in the field from all our impacts," describes Captain Casey Blasingame.[103]

Given the lethal air power at the disposal of American troops, Taliban insurgents developed tactics to avoid it. Enemy fighters had several options. First, they could scatter into small groups and run away. Secondly, they could find cover and hide, which could work amid the rugged terrain. Another alternative was for the Taliban to attack close to American lines, which would mean air support dropping ordnance "danger close" to friendly troops.[104] Golembesky recognized some of these tactics as he fought against Taliban forces. The enemy fighters had studied and learned from their encounters with American troops, so the Taliban were familiar with US tactics he acknowledges. One lesson the enemy learned was how to get in close to American troops to negate close air support. He also noticed that the Taliban would fire, then immediately move into a different position so that aircraft on station could not pinpoint their location. On one mission, Golembesky observed the Taliban moving from building to building in two- and three-man teams, "shooting and scooting." As a result of these tactics, the Taliban "countered our airpower advantage with constant movement."[105] The Taliban proved an intelligent and capable enemy.

Casualties are inevitable in any war, and helicopters provided medical evacuation (Medevac) to take the injured and the dead off the battlefield. Medical evacuation followed the NATO standard procedure to stabilize a casualty and transport that person to the necessary level of care. Role 1 was the local medic providing the first and immediate care to the casualty. Role 2 consisted of the doctors who treat the casualty at the brigade level. If further medical attention was needed, Role 3 was provided by the medical personnel at the major airfields, such as Bagram or Kandahar. For the most severely wounded, Role 4 involved long-term medical care at a facility such as Walter Reed Medical Center in Washington, D.C. Given modern medical care, for most casualties, "if they make it to Role 2, they generally live," observes Darling.[106]

Just like a call for air support, ground troops used a standardized nine-line radio message to call for a medical evacuation. Darling relates one medevac call he placed. Following the instructions he had posted on the window of his Humvee, he calls into the radio:

> "Break, break, Zabol base, Crazy Bear 6, requesting immediate medevac, over." By calling "break," Darling gets the attention of the others on the radio.
>
> Line 1: "Uniform Alpha 300672," which tells the helicopter his location.
>
> Line 2: "56.125," which gives the air crew his radio frequency.
>
> Line 3: "1 Bravo, 3 Charlie," which explains the number and seriousness of the casualties. "Bravo—the most serious. Charlie is a priority patient, needs help, but will live for a while without it."
>
> Line 4. "Delta" requests the helicopter bring special equipment.
>
> Line 5. "Four Litter," which announces that all the casualties are on stretchers.
>
> Line 6. "Echo" describes the enemy activity in the area. In this case, the Taliban were not engaging, but most likely were observing the area.
>
> Line 7: "Red Smoke" describes the color of the flare the soldiers would use to mark the landing zone.
>
> Line 8: "4 Charlie" indicates that the wounded are not Americans.
>
> Line 9: "Open area," which meant there were no obstacles for the helicopter in the landing zone.[107]

Darling's soldiers had enough stretchers for the Afghan policemen who had been wounded on this particular mission, as each Humvee had a litter on the back and one in the trunk. When the helicopters arrived, the soldiers moved the first casualty. The flight medics secured the casualty in the helicopter, while the soldiers ran back to carry the next casualty. The process continued for all four of the wounded.[108]

The remoteness of some combat outposts, firebases, and combat missions made medical evacuation difficult in Afghanistan. In Iraq, helicopter medical evacuation tended to come quickly. Not so for Afghanistan. A medic "couldn't simply staunch a wounded man's bleeding and expect that the helicopter would appear from out of nowhere to whisk your patient off to hospital," Romesha explains. Given the distances in Afghanistan, often troops had to wait an hour and a half for medevac to arrive. Sometimes it took longer.[109]

Enemy fire or weather conditions could delay medevac operations. Captain Robert Anders remembers one incident when his call for medical assistance arrived too late to save the life of the wounded soldier. Dry conditions, plus dust and sand, prevented the Black Hawks from landing on their first attempt. Anders recalls the Black Hawk had descended to about 30 feet above ground when the rotors kicked up enough dust and sand to create brownout conditions. The pilot could no longer see the ground. Instead of landing, Anders heard the engine accelerate to lift off again. Anders retrieved his infrared laser pointer and marked the landing zone for the pilots who could see the IR light with night vision goggles. Unfortunately, by the time the helicopters retrieved the casualty, it was too late.[110]

Other medevac crews risked their safety to land in combat conditions to retrieve the wounded. When insurgents attempted to overrun American positions in Wanat, medevac crews flew through smoke and heavy fire to pick up the

An MH-60 Black Hawk helicopter during a medical evacuation in Shah Joy District, Zabol Province, Afghanistan, on January 27, 2012. Helicopters provide the fastest way to transport personnel with medical needs from rural areas of Afghanistan to medical facilities located at larger coalition bases (photograph by Petty Officer Second Class Jon Rasmussen).

wounded. One soldier recounts, "I've never seen anything like what they did. It was one of the most amazing things I've ever seen." He adds, "I couldn't believe the pilots landed where they did, that exposed" as Apaches were firing only 30 meters away.[111]

Staff Sergeant Antonio Delvecchio, a flight engineer from a US Air Force HH-60 Pave Hawk helicopter, a variation on the Black Hawk, recalls a mission where they took fire. The crew came to medevac a wounded marine. The ground troops popped smoke to signal their position. As the helicopter landed, "We start taking fire from our 11 o'clock. The marines that are covering start shooting across our nose. Then the enemy opens up at our 9 o'clock and our 2 o'clock." Delvecchio states, "that sound never leaves your mind. From that point on if you heard a pop or a crack you knew exactly what it was."[112]

Taking fire was but one danger for aircraft in the Afghan War. They also had to deal with terrain, weather, and, for helicopters, altitude as well. Ground troops relied on air power for transportation, resupply, close air support, and medical evacuation. Fixed-winged aircraft, helicopters, and drones provided essential fire power to keep enemy forces from overrunning Coalition forces in remote areas of Afghanistan. Aircraft crews experienced long hours in flight on their missions, adhering to strict rules of engagement when attacking enemy forces. Rules of engagement were put in place to prevent civilian casualties and avoid friendly fire incidents. Air power compensated for few troops on the ground, particularly during the time period when the US deployed forces both to Iraq and Afghanistan simultaneously. By the end of Operation Enduring Freedom, the air war gave way to Afghan security forces taking the lead based on years of training by embedded training personnel.

•• 6 ••

Embedded Trainers

A unique aspect of counterinsurgency operations is building the host nation military forces. Special Operations Forces generally take the lead in this mission, but with the strain on personnel with simultaneous wars in Iraq and Afghanistan, conventional troops assumed the role in Afghanistan. These Embedded Training Teams (ETTs) worked to build the Afghan National Army (ANA) and, later, the Afghan National Police (ANP) and additional auxiliary police forces. Most service members made a genuine effort to work with their Afghan counterparts. In the early part of the Afghan War, most trainers felt that they had achieved some improvement with the Afghans they worked with over the time of their deployments. As time wore on, trainers became increasingly frustrated with their efforts, convinced that a culture of corruption prevented the Afghans from succeeding.

Long before the revelations of *The Washington Post* "Afghanistan Papers" about the problems with the Afghan security forces, trainers and mentors expressed increasing exasperation with the lack of progress and corruption of the Afghan soldiers and police, and much of that frustration stemmed from differing cultural norms.[1]

Almost as soon as the Taliban regime had been toppled in December 2001, the international community began to plan for an Afghan National Army. The first members of the new national army were drawn from the Northern Alliance, which had helped to defeat the Taliban. The US Special Forces trained mid-level militia commanders to be company-grade officers, while the warlords became generals. Within the first year of development, the US abandoned the policy of recruiting militia and warlords for the ANA because Afghan militia proved ineffective in combat. Furthermore, the continuing influence of the warlords undermined the central government's authority in the provinces. This initial effort entailed creating a light infantry corps stationed in Kabul. The first ANA *Kandak*, or battalion, emerged as a result of this effort in May 2002. Given the numerous ethnic groups in the country, Coalition policymakers wanted the ANA to be multi-ethnic so as to appear as a legitimate national force. Hence, the ANA was deliberately constructed to mix ethnic and tribal groups, though Tajiks were overrepresented.[2]

At first, the US equipped the ANA with armaments donated by former Soviet bloc countries, since Afghans were familiar with these weapons. Since American trainers were not experienced with Soviet arms and equipment, trainers from these former Soviet nations led the initial training. For vehicles, the ANA used Toyota Hilux or Ford Ranger pickup trucks. It was difficult to keep them in repair as spare parts proved hard to find.[3] Since vehicles were at a premium, the ANA tended to fit as many soldiers in the trucks as possible. It prompted a joke among American troops, "How many Afghan soldiers can you get in a Ranger pickup truck?" The answer was "one more."[4]

Training for the ANA took place at the Kabul Military Training Center, which had been established in the summer of 2002. Initially, the physical infrastructure of the training center needed repair, and it even lacked heat during the first winter. To share in their counterparts' hardships and build camaraderie, the American Special Forces trainers went without heat until the Afghans had it as well.[5]

American trainers put the Afghan recruits through activities that were similar to basic military training in the US: physical fitness, marching, marksmanship and basic infantry tactics. Other lessons included human rights, the laws of war, and the necessity for civilian authority over the military, all Western concepts sometimes at odds with traditional Afghan tribal culture. Although most of the Afghan recruits were familiar with AK-47 rifles, they had to learn how to set and use the sights correctly.[6] One Special Forces sergeant asserts that "a lot of them had experience firing a weapon, but not necessarily in aiming a weapon." Another

A group of Afghan National Army soldiers, assigned to the 5th Kandak, enter Afghan Ford Rangers at the Maiwan Compound, Forward Operating Base Shank, Afghanistan, on June 11, 2012. A running joke among US troops is that you could always fit "one more" Afghan soldier in one of these trucks (photograph by Specialist Austin Berner).

basic skill the Afghans had to learn was to be quiet on the battlefield. The sergeant explains: "One of the most basic soldier skills is when you're in field, you're silent. You know, use hand and arm signals so that no one knows you're there until you want them to know." Since the Afghan soldiers all talked to each other, it was one of the first obstacles the trainers had to address.[7]

Another cultural challenge was that the Afghan recruits all wanted to be infantry instead of any type of combat support personnel. Captain Andrew Schmidt observes, "They had a problem building this army because nobody wants to be a cop or a cook. Everybody wants to be a rifleman." He explains that Afghan men saw the supporting roles as more women's work. "It's hard to build a specialized army because nobody wants to be the finance guy," he notes.[8]

Training Afghans also had to deal with illiteracy among the force, as about 40 percent of the recruits could neither read nor write.[9] Formalized training encountered another barrier. "Since most of them had never been to school, they did not even have experience with the structured environment that education provides," states one report. Afghan recruits had to be socialized to follow daily schedules for training. Given the tribal nature of Afghan society, it was another culture shock to be instructed in multi-ethnic groups.[10]

Early efforts at training the ANA proved slower than projected. Although the Afghan government intended for a force of 70,000 soldiers to be created over the course of five to seven years, less than 2,000 recruits finished basic training in the first nine months of the program. Even three years in, as of March 2005, the ANA numbered only about 43,000, including soldiers still in training. Part of the problem of building up the ANA consisted of a high drop-out rate, where up to 40 percent of recruits failed to complete the initial training or left soon after it finished. Low-pay, poor food, and less than adequate living conditions caused many Afghan soldiers to desert as well.[11]

As a result of the poor initial results, the US created Task Force Phoenix in May 2003 to take over the training mission. Beyond training small units, the task force's mission included building up to company- and battalion-level operations as well as creating schools and logistics for the ANA. With the invasion of Iraq in 2003 diverting Special Forces and active duty units to the new theater of operations, National Guard units took over the training mission in Afghanistan. That summer, the Office of Military Cooperation—Afghanistan started a new training program where 19-man training teams embedded into ANA units upon graduation from basic training.

Because of the cultural differences between Western and Afghan cultures, female service members were not permitted to become trainers. Training policy shifted in 2005, when the embedded training teams were assigned to their ANA counterpart units at the beginning of training rather than after graduation from basic training. The ANA training shifted again in 2007 when Afghan units transitioned from light infantry to motorized infantry, incorporating light tactical vehicles and Humvees. Along with the change in organization, the US began to furnish the ANA with American equipment, including M-16s, because the mismatched donations of military equipment from a number of nations caused difficulties with consistent training and upkeep of equipment for maintenance.[12]

Soldier training schedules evolved over time as well. In 2005, for instance, the basic training bloc for Afghan soldiers was 14 weeks in length, but that shifted in 2007 when it became a 10-week course. At that time, qualified candidates could opt for additional six to eight weeks of advanced training. Major Christopher Miller states that the training consisted of a combination of classroom and practical skills. With a range at the training center, they had the recruits practice rifle marksmanship. The trainers also had the Afghan soldiers practice foot patrols around the base, "which gave us an opportunity to evaluate their skills with moving and patrolling," he notes.[13]

With the pressure of fighting two simultaneous wars in Iraq and Afghanistan, the personnel available to serve as embedded trainers did not always match what was needed. For example, on Master Sergeant José Medina's deployment as an ETT, they had an aviation officer acting as a mentor to an ANA infantry officer. They also had an American logistics officer mentoring an ANA infantry company commander. He observes that instead of basing assignments on military occupation specialty they were assigned by rank. On that deployment, the American trainers did not have enough infantry trainers to meet the needs of the ANA, so they had to be flexible and do the best they could with the resources at hand.[14]

National Guardsman Sergeant Major Stephen Guion explains his understanding of the relationship between the embedded trainers and their Afghan counterparts: "We are here not just to train, but we mentor and advise the leadership of the battalion and company. Our task is to show them the military decision-making process." The trainers had a lot of work to do. Guion adds that the Afghan soldiers "have a very steep learning curve." Tasks that the ETTs completed with their counterparts included weapon qualification, securing the perimeter, and vehicle maintenance. The ETTs also trained the Afghan soldiers how to conduct patrols in villages. They worked and lived closely with the Afghan troops. First Lieutenant Andrew Booth comments on his experience as a trainer: "We are constantly traveling with them, living off the local economy, eating the local food."[15]

Some Afghan soldiers had prior military experience, having fought with the Soviets or with the *Mujahedeen* during the Soviet war in the 1980s. Major Don Bishop worked with a number of Afghan soldiers who had served in the Soviet Army or who had fought against the Soviets. "I actually have a lot of respect for them as soldiers; their warrior ethos," he states.[16] Major John Tabb also trained with an Afghan officer with prior military involvement. "The Afghan company commander I had in the beginning was great. He had fought with the *Mujahedeen* against the Russians. He was a very experienced and fearless leader and he was very tactically proficient," he recounts.[17]

Familiarity with the Soviets in combat also worked against the American-trained embedded trainers. American and Soviet military culture deviated with respect to the non-commissioned officer (NCO) corps. While the Americans emphasized the development and leadership of the NCOs, the Soviet system

Embedded Trainers marine Lieutenant Colonel James F. Werth (left), Lance Corporal Michael J. Subu (wearing glasses), and marine First Sergeant Matthew S. Seamans (far right) meet with Afghan National Army soldiers at an eastern Konar Province, Afghanistan, border checkpoint. January 5, 2008.

focused almost exclusively on leadership from officers alone.[18] The Afghans "view the army more on a Russian mentality," Media notes. In this "Soviet type of mentality, the officers make most of the decisions and they do most of the execution. They don't give much respect to the NCOs." He observes that Afghan NCOs were chosen more on aggressive personalities than on any other standard. In fact, he saw the Afghan NCOs intimidate and physically assault their soldiers. "They use fear and intimidation to get soldiers to do what they want them to do," Medina says, which made a "huge cultural difference between us and the Afghans."[19]

Major Hurel Johnson agrees. Enlisted soldiers were treated "like gofers, not as an integral part of their organization," he states. "We figured it was a carryover from the Russian regime because that's how they treated their enlisted soldiers."[20] It proved to be one of the challenges American trainers had to overcome. Major Doug Ross writes that the "Afghan mentality is that if you are a commander, you stay back in the rear in the office and you send your lieutenants out on these missions." He found it difficult to get his ANA commander to go out on missions with the unit.[21]

Bishop describes a typical day for an embedded trainer. He woke at 5:00 a.m., got dressed, and grabbed breakfast. The soldiers then tended to vehicle upkeep and performing preventive maintenance. After checking the vehicles, the unit attended the day's mission briefing. The trainers generally met up with their Afghan counterparts by 7:30 or 8:00 a.m. They spent the day with the ANA, usually leaving around 6:00 p.m. Bishop noted that his Afghan soldiers specifically asked to learn map reading and how to use GPS. The Americans also taught them basic vehicle maintenance. It was wintertime during the first months of his deployment, so Bishop mentioned that the American trainers would wait to make sure the Afghans had enough wood to heat their compound before they drove back to Camp Phoenix in the evening.[22]

Even with financial assistance from the international community, the government of Afghanistan did not provide enough equipment and support for the Afghan National Army. The ANA was dependent on the US for support. During his 2005–2006 deployment, Master Sergeant Michael Threatt notes the Afghans lacked canteens or pouches to carry food, and the few things they possessed were not in good condition. "A lot of the guys had their stuff taped together or were tied together with string." In addition, their "weapons were not functional and their ammo was corroded." His ANA unit had one troop carrier for the entire 88-soldier company. The three Toyota pickups the Afghans had were civilian

Soldiers with 4th Brigade, 215th Corps, Afghan National Army, practice plotting grid coordinates on a map during an explosive ordnance disposal course aboard Forward Operating Base Delaram II, Afghanistan, on March 15, 2014. The course is designed to instill basic tactics, techniques and procedures for locating, avoiding and disposing of improvised explosive devices (photograph by Corporal Cody Haas).

trucks, so they lacked any crew-serviced weapons. "They had never been trained to maintain any of the equipment they had," he states.[23]

When Major William Woodring deployed in 2005–2006, the ETTs and ANA unit lacked almost everything. He mentions that they had to live in temporary buildings as the main camp had not yet been constructed. Fortunately, they did have hot water, showers, and toilets. Without assistance from contractors, the soldiers had to cook for themselves. They also lacked office supplies, computers, and other basic equipment. They did not have maintenance to keep the generators working, either. Part of his job was just getting the Afghans their weapons, food, firewood, and other basic support. Even when the equipment came in, the Afghans could not necessarily maintain it. Woodring notes, "The first week they got a computer, they destroyed it because they didn't know how to use it."[24] Even in 2009, after years of training, mentorship, and support, according to Corporal Dakota Meyer, "Starbucks runs a tighter ship than the Afghan Army."[25]

Compared to US standards, the Afghans had difficulty with logistics. One problem was illiteracy—the soldiers could not write requisitions. Even if the requisitions had been completed correctly, it was hard to submit them as the physical copies had to get to the capital. In one example, a supply request for an ANA unit had to travel to "the Ministry of Defense in Kabul, which is a two-and-a-half-day drive over land" from where Threatt was located with his Afghan unit. All this assumes "the vehicle makes it and they don't get shot up on the way." Of course, the response had to travel the same route back to their base. "The process was completely ineffective," Threatt asserts.[26] Even when the requisitions were submitted successfully, the turnaround time proved lengthy. Medina complains how it took four to six months for uniforms to arrive. Even then, the ANA soldiers did not have enough body armor for each soldier. Some Afghans had to patrol without proper equipment, such as helmets and vests. Supplies were so limited that the Afghans even shared weapons at times.[27]

Since logistics proved such a challenge, the ANA units did not have enough food and water to go out on patrol for any length of time. "If you can't feed a unit, you can't expect them to go out and operate in the environment for three or four days at a time," states Threatt. His trainers contacted the Combined Joint Special Operations Task Force to secure halal (ritually fit to eat) MREs for the Muslim Afghan soldiers to eat while on missions. The MREs allowed the trainers to go on multi-day missions with their units.[28] Major John Tabb remembers, "the *Kandak* didn't coordinate food and water very well. When I got there, they were relying on the ETTs to provide that stuff of them in the field."[29]

The ETTs sometimes bought equipment for their ANA unit. Threatt discusses how his trainers would have to walk with the ANA squad leader in case the Afghan soldier needed to contact the company commander because the Americans had the radios and the Afghans did not. In order to make the ANA independent, Threatt and his team purchased Motorola ICOM radios for $25 from the local economy for the Afghan soldiers. The Americans also provided the batteries to keep the radios operational.[30]

Living quarters for the ANA units had to be supplemented with American supplies as well. Threatt notes that the Afghan soldiers had tents that lacked heating or air conditioning. His trainers secured funding from one of the American task forces to build a hardened structure for the Afghans. "The bureaucracy of contracting took forever" Threatt complains, "and it was months before they had something to live in." Even after the structures had been built, Threatt and his soldiers had to purchase heaters for them as well as cold weather gear. Threatt explains how his men were able to get US Army field jackets, undergarments, gloves, mittens and socks for the Afghan soldiers. The Americans also provided stoves for the soldiers. Americans arranged for funds so the Afghans could install plumbing for showers, latrines, and hot water.[31]

Without their own helicopters, Afghans could not provide close air support or medical evacuation for their troops.[32] "The ANA had no evacuation support," Medina reports, so American helicopters had to be called for wounded Afghan soldiers. Additional restrictions placed on American medical evacuation caused tension with the Afghans, who did not understand the limited availability of American helicopters.[33] Situations like this undermined the ability for trust to grow between the ANA and Coalition.

When the ETTs deployed into remote areas with their ANA units, they experienced austere conditions. In his location in Oruzgan Province, all supplies had to be brought in by helicopter because it was a three-day drive to Kandahar. Even with air resupply, "there were a couple of times we were completely out of fuel. We were almost out of water." Miller found it nerve wracking when they were down to counting individual bottles of water and closely watching their ammunition supplies dwindle.[34]

Embedded trainers conducted patrols with their ANA units, which resembled many of the presence patrols conducted by American units. Major Rich Lencz states that he would go out on three or four patrols a week with his Afghan counterparts. The ETTs rode in Humvees, while the Afghan soldiers rode in Ford Ranger pickup trucks. Sometimes they walked up mountain trails, while other times they visited local villages. When they were in towns, they visited with the village elders. "After the ANA's patrol leader was done talking to the village elder, he'd have the village elder assist him in passing out the humanitarian assistance" Lencz explains, just as American units did.[35]

Jeremy Galvez had a similar experience when he went on patrol with the ANA. He mentions how the American trainers provided support, on-the-job-training, and additional security on the missions. Just as American troops have done for years, "ANA soldiers are also able to establish a positive relationship with the local populace by distributing candy and toys to local children," he writes. The ANA presence in the villages also gave them the opportunity to discuss local insurgent activity with the village elders.[36]

Major Robert Reed found fighting alongside ANA soldiers challenging. He explains that his most difficult challenge in Afghanistan was controlling the ANA soldiers on the battlefield. "I like to call it herding cats," he says. "They just go." He notes that most of the ANA soldiers had been familiar with and using weapons since they were children. Some of them even started fighting in combat by the age

Chief Warrant Officer Byung Kim, a marine embedded tactical trainer, walks up the mountain with Afghan National Army soldiers during a patrol to Combat Outpost Warheit in Nuristan Province, Afghanistan, on March 2, 2008 (photograph by Staff Sergeant Brandon Aird).

of 12. Despite their familiarity with fighting, they lacked an understanding of tactics. "We'd get hit, and they would just jump out of their Ranger trucks in front of the hills," Reed describes. "That was the tough part—controlling them during the fight," he adds.[37]

Although he did not use the term "herding cats," James Christ observes similar behavior from the Afghan soldiers. "The ANA were running in what appeared to be all directions, doing their notorious unorthodox and independent ANA react to contact." The Afghans fired their weapons indiscriminately toward the enemy positions, lacking fire discipline. In what is almost a contradiction in terms of both disdain and praise, Christ writes, "The typical ANA fighter was often unpredictable, childlike, and usually quite fierce."[38]

Embedded trainers witnessed their ANA counterparts engaging in combat, even as many American troops complained the ANA did not fight.[39] "It is not true to say the Afghan soldier won't fight," Plummer asserts. "They don't shoot well and they weren't trained well, and the US is partly to blame for this, but they will definitely go after the enemy." Despite the challenges and shortcomings the ANA soldiers faced, "they were not afraid of combat. I thought they were very good," Plummer concludes.[40]

Sergeant First Class Gregory Strong's respect for the ANA grew over the course of his deployment. "They got to the point they would fight beside you, and then by the end they were really laying down for us," Strong comments. "They even got to the point of trying to protect us," he adds. He remembers the Afghan soldiers going from a sound sleep to within minutes being ready to fight. "You do a line check once and some are sleeping, and you do another line check and still nothing, and all at once the ANA would posture up. And they were ready to fight," Strong explains.[41] Other service members indicated respect for the ANA and its ability to fight as well.[42]

Even with American mentoring, ANA troops often followed their own way. Medina recounts a time when he and his ANA counterparts discovered an IED. He called for Explosive Ordnance Disposal to come to dismantle it, but the Afghan soldiers were impatient. Instead of waiting, they tried to detonate it themselves. The Americans had to advise them not to use fuel to set the IED on fire or to shoot it with their weapons. Medina describes how the Afghans see fear as a sign of weakness, so they simply do not follow the same safety procedures or have the same safety-mindedness as Americans. He pointed out that the Afghans would not wear seat belts in vehicles either.[43]

Embedded trainers had experiences with the Afghan soldiers invoking *Inshallah*, or the concept of "as God wills." Major John Bates remembers how the Afghan soldiers merely shrugged and said *Inshallah* to getting different sized clothes or boots or losing an item.[44] Christ complains about how the ANA soldiers ran down their fuel supplies by sitting in their Ford Rangers in the winter, running the heat and listening to the radio. When the truck batteries died, the Afghans invoked *Inshallah* instead of acknowledging that their actions had led to this predictable outcome. "The ETT's learned quickly that lack of success in missions with their ANA was often because of *Inshallah*," Christ asserts.[45] Similarly, Medina observes that the Afghans were terrible at planning their fuel needs. It was *Inshallah* if they had what they needed for a mission.[46]

Christ recounts a time when the ANA would not move a semi-truck that had broken down on the highway because it was "disrespectful to God because God had wanted that semi broken down right where it was."[47] Afghans also expressed *Inshallah* with respect to more serious matters. "When people got hurt or killed, it was *Inshallah* to them," Bates states, "and I don't mean that haphazardly. They mean he was a good man and lived a good life but it was just his time. God wanted him back and so now he's back and we don't mourn for him. That's how they were."[48]

American mentors and trainers had firsthand experience of what, according to Western standards, they considered corruption among the Afghan National Army. These perceptions of corruption are confirmed by the Special Inspector General for Afghanistan Reconstruction, which detailed systemic corruption throughout all levels of Afghanistan from the central government down to low-level officials. Though corruption existed in Afghanistan before the Afghan War, the influx of money and goods from the international community, coupled with poor oversight from the US and the international community, exacerbated the corruption from theft to bribery to narcotics.[49]

At the level of the ETTs, trainers observed corruption relating to smaller sums of money or theft. Whenever the Afghans were choosing a vendor for one of their contracts, it led to corruption according to Medina. "It's not a random thing," he explains. The Afghan soldier is "looking for who will give him the best deal, or maybe give him a kickback."[50] Americans also had to safeguard the fuel once it arrived lest the *Kandak* commander try to sell it. Bishop also notes that the fuel would disappear from his ANA unit. Tabb mentions they locked up the fuel to keep it from being sold off by the ANA. The Afghans did not understand that once the fuel was sold, they would not have any more coming and their vehicles would not function. Other items that would be sold by the ANA included parts for their pickup trucks and ammunition.[51] Major Marc Fleurant remembers that "we would see soldiers walking around without boots. We asked them, where are your boots?" It turns out the soldiers were selling their government issued equipment to raise money to give to their families.[52] He does not think that the Afghan culture was going to change quickly. "We are not going to change the way they do business overnight or the way they operate," he muses.[53]

Drug use among the ANA proved to be a problem as well. Lencz estimates that about 70 percent of the soldiers in the ANA unit he embedded with were using hashish, a potent form of cannabis. Some of the Afghan soldiers were on a drug high most of the time, while others restricted use to their free time. "When I found out they weren't going on patrol that day, they go hide somewhere and get high," he observes. Rickard notes that his ANA soldiers "liked to smoke hashish and pass out in the guard towers" when they were on guard duty.[54] Some of the Afghan soldiers grew it on base, until caught, or purchased it at markets.[55]

Despite the frustrations and shortcomings the ETTs observed with the ANA, they generally wanted to believe they had accomplished something during their deployments. In oral history testimony, ETTs indicated that they had made headway. Major William Woodring declares, "Overall, we made good progress. I'm not sure what happened after we left but I know the ANA was better off when I left and when I got there."[56] Lencz believes that during his rotation, the ANA advanced in logistics operations, such as being able to request supplies and project food and water needs.[57] Tabb believes that the ANA made considerable improvement. When he first arrived, the ANA relied almost completely on the US for their logistics. His ETT managed to get them to take responsibility for their logistics operations. In addition, "they also went from being barely able to plan and conduct the company-level operation to being able to conduct a full battalion cordon-and-search with actual orders process and rehearsals," he adds. He also states that the Afghans were more capable in planning and requesting information and equipment from their higher headquarters.[58]

Major Ronald Walck also had a positive experience training his Afghan counterparts. He worked with Afghans from the Central Movement Agency, which drove supply trucks at the airfield. The ETTs had to teach the Afghans how to drive, maneuver, and load and unload the trucks and trailers. When he first arrived, the ANA had no idea what to do and only took action when given specific instructions to do so. Walck explains how the Afghans advances so that "a guy could go out there, drive his truck around an aircraft full of bombs, back it up correctly, its stuff loaded and strapped down." He concludes that the ETTs "professionalized them a little bit."[59]

Others related positive training experiences as well. Galvez wrote to his fellow college students at the University of Nevada, Las Vegas about his time as trainer in Afghanistan. He mentions, "we have seen significant progress in the ANA and their relationship with local villages, resulting in fewer insurgent attacks and more cooperative villagers."[60] Also writing for his fellow Nevada classmates, First Lieutenant Kyle Gunn likewise saw value in his interactions as a trainer with the ANA. He found similarities between Afghan and American soldiers. "Some are highly motivated and truly believe in what they're doing, and some just want a steady paycheck," he explains. He finds that "the Afghans I've been in contact with have been respectful, and a large number support establishing a legitimate government." Gunn believes that the ANA would be capable of independent operations after Coalition forces left the country.[61]

Not all ETTs had positive assessments of their counterparts. Major Christopher Plummer asserts that out of the 800 Afghan soldiers he saw try to qualify on the rifle range, only 80 of them succeeded. "In spite of that, they never really re-fired the failures," he admits. "They went right into the field, deployed and went to combat operations," Plummer says. The training on other combat skills or combat service support proved just as dismal in Plummer's opinion.[62] When he trained Afghan soldiers on the M-16, Meyer notes that some of the Afghans put in the effort to try to master the task but others simply did not care. He did his best to drill the basics and hoped the Afghans remembered them.[63]

While some Afghan units mastered basic soldier skills, they were still unable to operate independent of American forces. "I was sent to the 201st Corps, which was based out of Camp Blackhorse, which is on the outskirts of Kabul," Major Mark O'Neill remembers. "They were probably the best trained Afghans at the time [2006], but that's relative," he continues. He did not believe the Afghans were capable of long-range planning or logistics. Ultimately, O'Neill did not think the Afghans could operate on their own after the Americans left.[64] Lencz's ANA unit also mastered basic tactics and platoon-size maneuvers, but could not do much else. They worked on logistics with their ANA counterparts so by the time the ETT rotation ended in early 2008, the Afghan logistics officer "was capable of planning for how many meals they needed to take with them depending on how many days they were going out and how many men they were taking with them."[65] The Afghans had learned—but not enough to be on their own.

O'Neill felt frustrated that the Afghan soldiers did not appear to show any initiative to get better. "When they don't really show the initiative to help themselves you get frustrated and folks have a tendency to throw their hands up and say, 'if you're not willing to help yourselves than I'm not going to put forth my max effort.'" He felt like hanging out with other Americans and leaving the Afghans to fend for themselves until they improved their attitude.[66] Not only did the ETTs have low morale because the Afghans demonstrated little effort, but they also felt they were neglected in the larger US effort in the Global War on Terror. All the focus of the US military was on the Iraq War surge when O'Neill had been deployed to Afghanistan. "Afghanistan was not in the limelight and the embedded training mission even less so," O'Neill asserts.[67] Major Stephen Boesen agrees. "We really felt like bastard children. If Afghanistan is a secondary effort, ETTs are about four rungs below that in terms of getting support."[68]

Some ETT members deployed both to Iraq and to Afghanistan, so they could compare the experiences of training soldiers from both countries. Iraq had the advantage of "a much higher literacy rate, stronger tradition of professional soldiering and a vastly better infrastructure," according to one observer.[69] Those advantages did not necessarily translate into better outcomes. Staff Sergeant Scott Edwards perceives many similarities between Iraqi and Afghan soldiers. In both cases, he complains that they failed to spend the entire day training, often leaving before the end of the day. Edwards also notes that both armies had difficulty with planning and logistics. For him, he found a big difference between the soldiers: "Afghan soldiers would fight." He trusted the Afghans to stay engaged in a firefight. Iraqis, in his observations, "would run and hide. They wouldn't fight at all."[70]

Major Matt Lillibridge makes the same observation. "The Afghans fight better than the Iraqis, but they have been doing it longer and they are a little bit more tenacious," he states.[71] Conversely, some trainers thought Afghan soldiers were unreliable and undisciplined, worse than Iraqi soldiers.[72] Edwards did not hold out much hope for the training to have lasting effects on either the Iraqis or the Afghans. He believes, "Once we are gone in time for them to take over all the operations by themselves, I think they will just go back to the same way the countries were when we came."[73]

Many of the trainers' complaints about the ANA parallel the criticisms US troops had about the South Vietnamese Army. It, too, was "often ill-equipped, inadequately trained, and poorly led," and when they conducted field operations "they did not always perform well." American soldiers also complained about the South Vietnamese soldiers stealing from them. Korean War troops also griped about the host nation troops. Though "the South Koreans and the GIs did not dislike each other as intensely as the grunts and the South Vietnamese did," historian Kindsvatter asserts, "GIs frequently complained about the lack of fighting spirit in the Republic of Korea Army."[74]

In addition to their work with the ANA, American trainers also mentored the Afghan police forces.[75] At the beginning of Operation Enduring Freedom, the job of training police fell to Germany. The German effort proved slow, underfunded, and short in numbers of trained police forces. In May 2003, the US State Department supplemented the police training mission. At first, the State Department hired contractor DynCorp International to conduct the training. DynCorp created short training courses, ranging from two- to eight-weeks long. Given that the company also trained police in other countries, such as Iraq, the training programs were not designed specifically for Afghanistan. As a result, this effort also did not produce the level of trained forces needed in Afghanistan. In addition, the police lacked vehicles, radios, and weapons. Some policemen were even training with wooden rifles.[76]

and minds" rhetoric. In this instance, the Civil Affairs soldiers rated their efforts as successful as they received the cooperation of the locals.[17]

The CHLC in Herat, in western Afghanistan, focused mainly on infrastructure and economic development. They cited as accomplishments: "canal de-silting projects, underground irrigation systems, school rehabilitation, school furniture project, and a generator project that eventually provided 24-hour power to the regional hospital." Civil Affairs personnel coordinated the repair of numerous irrigation canals, which also provided jobs to the local population.[18]

Over in eastern Afghanistan, in Jalalabad, the capital of Nangahar Province, the CHLC focused on building medical capacity and providing supplies to the locals. The Civil Affairs team provided blankets, medical books and medical supplies to the Nangarhar Islamic University Medical Hospital as well as giving toys, food, clothing, and school supplies to the local orphanages. The soldiers believed their activities "significantly enhanced the image of U.S. forces among the political leaders of the Jalalabad region."[19] Despite these humanitarian and construction projects the CHLCs, by design, carried a "light footprint," and funding proved slow, so the work that the Civil Affairs teams could accomplish proved fairly small-scale.[20]

Civil Affairs teams often worked in remote locations and areas that were still hostile, areas where nongovernmental organizations would not go for safety reasons. International aid agencies did not approve of the work of the Civil Affairs teams because they believed the military "blurred the lines separating private and military programs, placing civilians at risk from Afghans angry with American soldiers." Part of the confusion stemmed from lax uniform standards at the beginning of the war. Special Operations Forces, including the Civil Affairs teams, often wore civilian clothing or Afghan clothing to blend in with the population. They sometimes grew beards as well. As a result of the complaints of civilian agencies, military officials tightened uniform standards.[21]

Some soldiers also criticized the behavior of NGOs. "Here's my problem with these nongovernmental organizations," explains Major Christopher Plummer. "They weren't out in the provinces where they needed to be." Instead, he asserts, they operated in Kabul, the capital, or stayed on one of the main FOBs for safety. He complains that the NGOs only wanted to operate in areas without enemy activity. Given the massive needs of the Afghans, particularly for electricity, running water, and other basic infrastructure, Plummer believed the NGOs did not do enough. As a result of the non-appearance of the international aid organizations, "the US military had to shoulder 90 percent of the burden," Plummer asserts. He points out that service personnel are not trained in development, infrastructure, and nation building. Plummer does admit, however, that the NGOs feared injury or death, which was why they were reluctant to push into less secure areas.[22] These thoughts reveal a key challenge for reconstruction efforts in Afghanistan: the international community intended the projects to help win over the loyalty of the population, but until the population cooperated with the Coalition, they could not act to secure the area from insurgent activity.

Given a limited number of Civil Affairs units in the active and reserve forces, conventional units participated in civil affairs activities, such as the distribution of supplies. In one example, soldiers from the 101st Airborne handed out pencils, school supplies, toys, food, and blankets in an Afghan village outside Kandahar.[23] Sergeant First Class James Buck provided similar aid in Gardiz. He describes, "it's a culture shock when you go into these villages because these people are so poor." Buck observes that the villagers are a bit apprehensive at first, but once they realize the soldiers are handing out supplies, "then they go crazy. They take stuff, hide it behind a bush, and come back for more."[24] Captain Katie Morris recalls that the Afghan children went wild for her pens, especially colored pens. "Every time I went out, all my pens would be stolen out of my pocket," she remembers. She asked family and friends to keep sending more to her so that she would always have enough to hand out.[25]

Likewise, conventional units contributed to small infrastructure projects, such as building a school. Major Daniel Wilson, a logistics officer, comments, "My soldiers sit inside all day. Their morale tends to drop. Getting about doing a project like this reminds them what they are here for." The activity boosted the morale of Second Lieutenant Jason Johnson, who acknowledges that "it definitely gives us a sense of purpose" rather than simply managing paperwork from a desk. Afghans enthusiastically supported many of these early infrastructure projects. "It's amazing how happy the villages are and how happy the kids are," observes Specialist

Technical Sergeants Michelle Stokes and Brandon Livingston, counter-improvised explosive device team out of Forward Operating Base Shank, hand out school supplies and toys to children in the village of Polerad in Logar Province, Afghanistan, on October 3, 2009 (photograph by Specialist Melissa Stewart).

Kenneth Norris. In an exhibition of *Pashtunwali,* the local Afghans hosted the logistics soldiers to lunch. The Afghans served rice, okra and stew as well as naan, the local flatbread.[26]

Despite the best intentions and efforts of service members, it was difficult to discern whether the efforts were convincing the Afghans to support the central Afghan government rather than the Taliban. One military officer explains, "We wanted hard quantitative metrics that would tell us that X project is producing the desired outcomes, but we had a hard time defining those metrics." For example, "we had no idea how to measure if [a] hospital's existence was reducing support for the Taliban."[27] The military never did find usable or consistent measures of effectiveness.[28]

While infrastructure projects proved problematic, military units also provided medical care to the Afghans. The purpose of these Medical Civic Assistance Programs, or MEDCAPs, was both to provide medical assistance and a military presence. Many of the medical issues the service members treated had to do with poor sanitation. "We treat skin problems, bad teeth and lots of digestive problems from bad food," explains one soldier. Some of the dietary problems stem from giving children raw cow's milk. They also treat everyone for worms. The Afghans lack Western sensibilities concerning sanitation and hygiene. "It's very hard to make people understand that they have to separate sewage, bathing and cooking, and they must boil their water," he adds.[29]

Leo Jenkins remembers going on one MEDCAP in the summer of 2005. As soon as the line started forming, "every man, woman, and child from the entire village stood ready to receive treatment for some type of ailment." The people often did not know their age, guessing an age range when asked. Jenkins observes that most of the villagers had never had medical or dental treatment before. "I spent the first couple of hours cleaning out minor wounds, many of which have been festering for some time," he recalls. In the average American's experience, a minor wound would be treated with a quick cleansing, Neosporin, and a bandage. "It seemed like that level of treatment must have been like performing surgery in this village," he muses, indicating the backwardness of Afghanistan compared to the US. Once the Afghans realized that the medics handed out Tylenol and Pedialyte, he noticed that they got back in line to "score as much free shit as they could get their hands on" he criticized, as if Americans do not do the same thing at times.[30]

Also important to the livelihoods of many Afghans was the health of their farm animals, so American troops provided veterinary care as well. For example, after treating many of the local villagers for worms in Zabol Province, a veterinarian turned her attention to the animals. "We're going to keep the animals alive. Going to increase productivity and build their numbers so they can afford to feed their families," explains the vet. Of note to the Afghans, the veterinarian was a female soldier. Optimistically, she enthused, "women here don't work with large animals. Seeing me work with cattle is opening up their view to the world quite a bit."[31] Contemplating different cultural values, Colonel Walter Herd muses disdainfully, "you heal a warlord's child and he likes you; you strengthen his herd

Air Force Major Tim Gacioch, Bagram Provincial Reconstruction Team (PRT), treats a young Afghan boy for a fungal infection during a medical civil affairs program on April 6, 2007. Medics with the Bagram PRT treated ailments ranging from anxiety to ringworm during the daylong event (photograph by Staff Sergeant Thomas Doscher).

of goats and he LOVES you," suggesting animals rate more highly than his own children.[32]

Stemming from the experiences of the CHLCs, the US government created the first Provincial Reconstruction Teams in Afghanistan. The first one opened in Gardiz, in eastern Afghanistan, in November 2002.[33] At first, the PRT was vaguely defined as a "unique Inter-agency team that will manage reconstruction and stabilization at the regional level." It stood as a civil-military operations effort in what was called a "semi-permissive environment," which meant that friendly forces controlled the area, but there continued to be a threat from hostile forces operating there.[34] Over time, the PRT concept became more defined. One PRT commander explains it as "a team that conducts non-kinetic [i.e., non-combat] effects in conjunction with other teams in a particular battle space, at the tactical level, to support counterinsurgency operations." The PRT is meant to assist in securing an area while it "strengthens the reach, the influence, the capacity, the legitimacy of the [Afghan] government." Additionally, the PRT is supposed to facilitate "reconstruction and development by building roads, bridges, schools, creating jobs, economic activity."[35]

As the PRT concept evolved, the Army listed these activities of the PRT in 2011: "to improve stability in a given area by helping build the host nation's capacity; reinforcing the host nation's legitimacy and effectiveness; and bolstering that the host nation can provide security to its citizens and deliver essential

US Army Specialist Kathy Tanson of the 40th Infantry Division Agribusiness Development Team, California National Guard, greets a young boy as he passes through the Veterinary Civil Action Program held in Barbur Village, Chowkay District, Konar Province, Afghanistan, on May 2, 2010 (photograph by Sergeant Corey Idelburg).

government services. The PRT assists provincial-level governments to meet the expectations of their citizens."[36] No matter how broadly or narrowly defined, the teams working on PRTs had great expectations placed on their shoulders to engage with the local population, win their support for the central Afghan government, and provide some level of economic development.

Given the number of responsibilities placed on PRTs, it is notable that most of the teams consisted of fewer than 100 members. The PRTs often had 80–100 personnel, mostly military, with limited staffing from other government agencies, such as the State Department, the United States Agency for International Development (USAID), and the Department of Agriculture. At first, Army lieutenant colonels led the teams, followed later by similarly ranked officers from the other military services. The PRTs consisted of a "combat service support section that handles logistics, a force protection platoon, a civil affairs team, a civil military operations center, and special staff that provides technical expertise" in other areas, such as engineering, agriculture, and more.[37]

The Gardiz PRT had a rocky start, but began to show progress with positive interactions with the population. "At first our teams might have had rocks thrown at them, but now we're starting to get cooperation" such as the locals telling the team where to find a weapons cache, relates Colonel Phil Maughan. Though the area was still considered a non-permissive environment in 2002, with a serious threat from insurgents, "people are starting to be more open than in the past," Maughan states. Colonel Roger King, a spokesman for the US military forces, explains "you cannot have a stable environment without cooperation from the local populace." In order to win over the population, the PRT had to remain non-threatening and provide positive outcomes.

While some of the local Afghans remained skeptical of the American presence in Gardiz, the majority appeared "excited at the prospect of more aid and jobs." The locals soon became accustomed to seeing the camouflage uniforms of American military personnel.[38] The PRTs quickly became the "centerpiece of the counterinsurgency efforts," which placed the population at the center of US military efforts. Over the next months and years, the US expanded the PRTs. By July 2005, there were 22 PRTs in Afghanistan, with the US running 13 of them and NATO leading 9.[39]

While most of the military personnel staffing PRTs came from the Army, the Army's forces were stretched thin with simultaneous operations in Iraq and Afghanistan. In 2004, Secretary of Defense Donald Rumsfeld directed the Navy and Air Force to relieve the pressure on the Army and Marine Corps. One way of accomplishing this goal was having Navy and Air Force support PRTs.[40] Army Captain Katie Morris deployed to a PRT in Ghazni, which was on Polish FOB at the time. She considered her teammates a "ragtag group" consisting of 85 people, including National Guard infantrymen, Navy corpsmen, a Navy commander, three active-duty Army physicians, a logistics officer, and a civil affairs reservist group from California, among others.[41]

At first, there was no real training for PRT personnel. Often, officers came as individual augmentees with little idea or understanding about the role of PRTs or their duties and responsibilities inside the organization.[42] By 2005, personnel underwent some preparation before deploying to PRTs. Navy Commander John Wade, selected to be a PRT commander, underwent three and a half months of pre-deployment training under the direction of First Army at Fort Bragg, North Carolina. One part of the training focused on individual soldiering skills, while the other concentrated on stability, reconstruction, and peacekeeping operations.[43]

Navy Commander Mike Varney had similar experiences when he trained as a PRT commander. It included unit-level tasks and combat skills. Given that the Navy does not train its personnel with personal weapons the same way as the Army or Marine Corps, the naval personnel trained to use 9 mm and M-16 weapons.[44] Morris, who also trained at Fort Bragg, recalls cultural training as well. She remembers that her training had the benefit of discussions with current PRT personnel, who came stateside to help train the newcomers. She also learned from civil affairs soldiers and a representative from the USAID.[45]

With team members from different services, cultural differences between the branches became apparent. Major Ronald Walck muses that the single most important lesson he learned professionally from his PRT experience was "that officers from different branches of the military are raised differently and think differently." He notes that although the Marine Corps had different terminology, "their mindset is a lot like that of the Army," making it easier to interact with soldiers than with service members from the Air Force or the Navy.[46] Navy Commander Wade describes a moment, training with his mostly Army team, when the cultural differences became noticeable. Out of habit, he responded to an Army colonel with a navy "aye-aye," creating an awkward moment. When Wade turned his attention back to the platoon, he noticed that their body language had changed. "They wouldn't look at me in the eye, and I could tell they were concerned or had something on their minds," he recalls.

After a few minutes, a platoon sergeant spoke up, "Excuse me, sir.... We're really honored that you came out to meet with us here today." He continued to explain that the soldier were proud to be on his team and appreciate the significance of the mission. He adds, "as you're leading our soldiers, can you do it with a little less 'aye-aye' and a little more 'hooah?'" "Hooah" is a commonly used term of affirmation in the Army. Wade reflects, "What it takes to lead a sailor is different than a soldier, and what it was going to take for me to lead this organization was going to be much different than what I had been trained to do in my previous 17 years."[47]

Varney likewise noted differences in Navy and Army culture, and favored his service, the Navy. The majority of his PRT personnel—around 80 percent—came from the Army. He thought the soldiers "all focused on finding the enemy and killing them." He believed it was his intervention and that of the other Navy commanders that placed the proper focus on the mission. "We used to say, 'a little less kill 'em, a little more hooah, and we'll get it all.'"[48] Similarly, Army personnel typically did not think highly of many Navy and Air Force PRT commanders.[49] It appears traditional interservice rivalry persisted through this conflict as it had in earlier eras.

Each PRT proved unique, though there were common activities such as meeting with Afghans, interacting with the local community, overseeing various projects, and promoting the government. The PRT personnel often attended meetings, called *shuras*, with local elders. Wade recalls attending *shuras* on the provincial and district levels as they could not reach the 200 villages in their extensive area of operations.[50] Numerous service members have commented on how much small talk is involved in *shuras*. Lieutenant Sean Parnell observes, "Small talk here is an art form. It can go on for hours before anything of substance is brought up."[51] Lieutenant Colonel Michael Forsyth concurs, noting "it takes hours to get to the heart of the matter because of all the flowery talk."[52]

Army Lieutenant Colonel Robin Fontes, PRT commander in Tarin Kowt, describes some of her experiences with the local community. The area, like many parts of Afghanistan, lacked modern infrastructure. All the roads in the area were rough dirt roads with one-story mud buildings. Locals hand-pumped water,

Colonel Stephen Quinn, 189th Infantry Brigade commander, eats lunch with village elders after a *shura* at the Shinkai District Center, Zabul Province, Afghanistan, on February 17, 2011. Quinn is in Zabol Province to observe Provincial Reconstruction Team Zabul in action (photograph by Staff Sergeant Brian Ferguson).

and sewage removal consisted of drainage ditches. The only two-story buildings sat in the center of the town. One of them belonged to the governor, though it also lacked electricity and running water. Fontes remarks that there were about 30,000 residents in Tarin Kowt, though she rarely saw the women and children. "It was very, very rare to see a woman on the streets, and never without a burqa," Fontes recalls. Children came out when the PRT personnel walked around, especially if they had something to hand out, but not when they drove through town. "You might drive down the street," she explains, "and they would go back inside their yard and close the door," suggesting the locals were still wary about the presence of the PRT.[53]

Morris describes how the PRT personnel would leave in the morning to conduct a survey, talk to the local Afghans, or check up on the progress of one of their projects. "Then stuff happens on Afghan time," she observes. It was always an open question as to whether the Afghans would come or not. As long as the situation remained non-hostile, she could stay, have lunch, and accomplish some tasks. As with other military operations, the team returned to base, wrote up their reports, and conducted a battle update brief and after action review. Morris notes that some of their missions could last for a couple of weeks if the team worked farther out from the PRT.[54] The PRTs also dealt with natural disasters and disease outbreaks in their areas of operation. Some PRTs, such as the one in Mehtar Lam in Laghman Province in the east, accomplished less because of ambushes and IEDs in the area, which severely curtailed their activities.[55]

Air Force Captain Jon Polston, lead engineer attached to Laghman Provincial Reconstruction Team, inspects a bridge in Mehtar Lam, Laghman Province, on September 7, 2011. The civil engineer team from the PRT traveled to the Jugi Bridge in Mehtar Lam to assess the structural integrity following its completion, ensuring it would withstand the Afghan weather for years to come (photograph by Staff Sergeant Ryan Crane).

As a female service member, Morris commented on how she interacted with the conservative Afghan culture. "I think the reaction to a female soldier is always funny," she says. The Afghan women showed interest in speaking with her, but "talking to them was different too because they have a burqa on. I don't think they understood how to take us at first," she muses. Morris recalls one encounter with a 72-year-old warlord named Bashee, a major landowner in the province who had six wives already. Morris remembers he asked her to be wife number seven. "I said no," she notes.[56] Fontes did not find any issue with the Afghans as a female PRT commander. She explains, "If you wear the uniform and you don't do anything to mark yourself as female—you know, like, as long as you don't wear a scarf or something or makeup—then they don't have to respond to you that way."[57] Similarly, Kimberly Evans remarks, "I'm a uniformed member of the military and [they] just sort of treat me as generals."[58]

Relations with the PRTs and local Afghans became strained because of the quick rotation of personnel. While Army units typically had year-long deployments, the other services and government agency personnel often stayed for shorter periods. New people often rotated through the PRTs, and even with a year-long rotation, many projects took longer to finish. Fontes explains how this affected the relationship by stating, "Afghans understand because they know that we're going to rotate, and they get really sick of it, too. But you always hear them say, 'Well, you'll be gone. The guy two times ago promised me this, and he left and didn't do anything. You'll do the same thing.'"[59]

Like the earlier Civil Affairs units, PRTs coordinated and funded a variety of projects, which often differed from area to area. For example, the Ghazni PRT assisted with the reconstruction of a women's ward, installed generators, and dug a well. The PRT prioritized hospitals, water sources, and refurbishing schools, all using local labor and materials to boost the economy.[60] In Lashkar Gah, the PRT started sports teams to build rapport with the locals. They provided equipment for soccer, volleyball, and cricket.[61]

At the Panjshir PRT, "one of our projects was trying to get a paved, travelable road all through the province. It's a pretty mountainous area, especially in the northern part," explains Major Nicholas Dickson. Part of the challenge was getting funds and coordination to keep the road going beyond the boundary of their area of responsibility. "That level of coordination was almost unattainable," he complains, "just because it was so frustrating dealing with the ISAF command structure."[62] The PRTs also had to deal with local corruption in the bidding and building process.[63]

Given the limitations on resources as a result of simultaneous wars in Iraq and Afghanistan, development projects in Afghanistan were "twice as hard, cost twice as much, and took twice as long as one planned."[64] As an example, Michael Waltz explains:

> You would build a school, and it would have no teachers. Find the teachers, and they would have no materials. Get the teachers, books, supplies, and facility in place, and the students would be too intimidated by the Taliban sympathizers to come. Convince local elders and families to send the students, and the next week the Taliban would burn the whole thing down, intimidate and sometimes beat the teachers, and threaten the villagers so that you had to start all over.[65]

Despite their best intentions, occasionally projects created new, unanticipated tensions in an area. In one example, the PRT in Konar created a cash-for-work program to clear an aqueduct of trash and to clean up hypodermic needles from the nearby riverbank in the village of Yargul. The project inadvertently caused conflict with another area village, whose elder believed he should have been put in charge of the project. Eventually, the PRT created a new project to mollify the second village. As soon as the funds for the projects ran out, however, the villagers abandoned the work.[66] Major Brian Elliot explains that the underlying purpose of the project was not really the clean grate but "what we wanted was to make sure that the people that lived next to the wall weren't going to throw a grenade over." He muses that one could consider the project a failure on the grounds that the trash problem remained unresolved. On the other hand, "we created some goodwill with the Yargul villagers that lived next door to us," so "that, in my mind, is probably good enough."[67]

The PRTs worked to ensure the success of the national government through governance in the provinces and districts. When Evans commanded the PRT in Herat, one of her goals was to "extend the provincial government's reach" by going out into outlying areas, conducting surveys, and starting projects. Evans observes that the bureaucrats in Herat did not know how to govern. "For the first time in life I missed bureaucrats," she admits. "We ended up spending a lot of time mentoring them."[68] The PRTs encouraged the villages to work through the districts.

Districts, in turn, submitted requests to the provincial governor. The PRT worked with the governor about how to prioritize, apply resources, and manage risk.[69] Varney mentions that he focused on connecting tribal elders with local government officials. He thought the elders were the best way to deal with the local population and to determine community needs. The PRT could then have the elders make requests through the district government. He notes that PRTs had to be seen as working with the provincial or district government officials instead of as a separate or independent organization. Varney adds, "there was always a term over there that everything should have an Afghan face on it."[70]

Team members from PRTs often believed they had made positive contributions during their deployments. Acknowledging that it was a long-term process, Lieutenant Colonel Anthony Hunter believes, "I think you will win them over." He thinks the PRTs allow the Afghans to take charge and rebuild. It was an experience he would do again "in a heartbeat," Hunter asserts. Others felt the same way, though it should be noted that they served prior to the Taliban resurgence.[71] "I think we did as a whole accomplish a lot of really good things," Dickson remarks. In addition to the various projects, he touts the establishment of a professional engineering association that could advise the local government. "As a whole I think what I'm most proud of was moving that PRT closer to the point of when it could legitimately be closed down and we can pull out of that province," he states.[72]

Despite the efforts of PRT personnel, numerous government reports and scholarly analyses found fault with PRTs due to incoherent strategy, lack of interagency coordination, funding problems, and other issues.[73] Over time, the responsibilities of PRTs began to be handed over to ministries in the Afghan government, development agencies, nongovernmental organizations, and even the private sector. All PRTs were phased out by the end of 2014.[74]

Alongside the PRTs, Civil Affairs teams continued to work out of FOBs. Both the PRTs and Civil Affairs drew on a pool of funds designated the Commander's Emergency Response Program (CERP) to fund projects. These ventures ranged from small-scale building projects, such as constructing office space in a district center, to paving roads to connect distant villages to district and provincial centers.[75] The amount of CERP funds available in Afghanistan grew significantly over time, and with greater resources came greater restrictions on the use of those funds.[76]

Another way that US troops worked with—or perhaps it is better conceived as working against—Afghans was with poppy eradication. The cultivation of poppy for opium fed a drug trade that financed the insurgency, increased government corruption, interfered with construction efforts, and undermined security.[77] The British government initially took responsibility for counternarcotics operations, but the US became involved with a strategy to combat narcotics in 2005. Unfortunately, neither the British nor the American efforts had lasting effects. The Special Inspector General for Afghanistan Reconstruction concludes that "no counterdrug program undertaken by the United States, its coalition partners, or the Afghan government resulted in lasting reductions in poppy cultivation or opium production—and, without a stable security environment, there was little possibility of success."[78]

Afghanistan provides a substantial portion of the world's opium, and the amount grown increased during the Afghan War.[79] Major Matthew Brown quips, "when someone says Afghanistan doesn't have the capacity to do something, I usually respond with, 'well, it got the capacity to provide the entire world's worth of opium.'" He notes that the Afghans grow and harvest the crop by hand, and they can bring in three crops each year. "The stuff grows like a weed out there. It's drought resistant if they don't irrigate. The seeds can be stored without cold storage or anything," Brown observes.[80] Despite the international community's efforts, poppy continues to be a staple of the Afghan economy.

For a brief time, American service members participated in counterdrug programs with their ANA counterparts. Major John Bates recalls that they used bush hogs and mowers in the poppy fields, but they would often get stuck in the canals. The ANA then used bulldozers to fill in the canals, so the tractors could cross into the fields. They could not leave the canals filled with dirt, however, because they were used by the Afghan farmers to irrigate their food crops. Bates explains, "So one-third of your force is getting you into the jerib [field], and one-third of your force is fixing what you just broke." He also notes that the eradication was done by lottery, but everyone believed Afghan officials were taking bribes from farmers to leave their fields alone. There were also rumors spreading "telling people to flood your field so the tractors can't get to them."[81]

Major Doug Ross observed similar difficulties with counternarcotics

US Marines with Fox Company, 2nd Battalion, 5th Marine Regiment, Regimental Combat Team 6, patrol through a poppy field on their way to Patrol Base Mohmon in the Lui Tal District, Helmand Province, Afghanistan, on April 17, 2012 (photograph by Lance Corporal Ismael E. Ortega).

operations in Musa Qala, in Helmand province. "We started seeing that very little of the fields were being cut. It was just one or two swaths of some of the fields. A lot of fields were not being touched," he remembers. Ross believed the Afghan National Police were corrupt, accepting payments to leave fields untouched. He understood that even for those fields they mowed, the provincial governor ordered than no more than half the field be plowed because he "didn't want to devastate every farmer." Ultimately, Ross thought the people got the wrong message from the whole enterprise.[82]

Sergeant First Class Gregory Strong provided security for poppy eradication. "Once we had the security lines set up," he explains, "then DynCorp would go inside and eradicate the poppy." Strong remembered that they engaged in firefights with insurgents on a daily basis, and ANA soldiers and ANP lost their lives. From his perspective, the Afghans farmed poppy because the Taliban threatened them into doing so. "The farmers, of course, would do what the Taliban told them because they would threaten to kill the farmers' families if they didn't grow the poppy," he observes, highlighting a key challenge to any counternarcotics program.[83]

By 2010, both US officials and the international community shifted their emphasis to improving governance in Afghanistan in order to transfer responsibilities to the national government. By improving governance, officials intended to increase efficiency and provide goods and services to the population, thereby improving the people's support for the national government. State Department and USAID personnel took the lead responsibility on many aspects of the governance mission, while US military forces worked with the provincial- and district-level Afghan government officials.[84]

Forsyth had observed Afghans on three deployments, and on his deployment in 2009–2010 he worried about their capability for governing themselves. He admits that his confidence started to fade almost as soon as he started his tour. "In my dealings with the Afghan government officials I began to encounter disturbing signs of weakness on their part that they did not care to resolve," he notes. In particular, he criticizes the centralized nature of the Afghan government. He perceives that too much centralization made it impossible for local officials to make decisions independently. They always consulted national government officials in Kabul. Since local officials were hesitant to act, Forsyth asserts that "the constant struggle on our part to develop competence, facilitate decision-making, and demand transparency wore down my confidence over time." When he reflected on some of his encounters, Forsyth's frustration became clear. In his journal, Forsyth writes, "It is all supposed to have an Afghan lead, they are still so incapable that we will have to do a lot of handholding." He despairs that after eight years of mentoring, Afghans still appeared unable to run the bureaucracy without direct assistance.[85]

Infrastructure and small-scale construction projects continued through the end of Operation Enduring Freedom, even as the force started to draw down. As one Civil Affairs soldier comments, their job was "solving problems as they come." Even as FOBs were being shut down in 2012, Civil Affairs teams continued to work small infrastructure and other projects in the areas where they operated. For instance, outside Kandahar, in Zhari, Civil Affairs teams built up the district center right up until the closing of the FOB in early 2013.[86]

From the start of Operation Enduring Freedom, Civil Affairs and combat units provided humanitarian aid and supported small-scale reconstruction efforts in Afghanistan. Those efforts led to the creation of PRTs, which continued the work. The service members who worked with Afghans prided themselves on their accomplishments but also became increasingly frustrated with the overall lack of progress in Afghanistan. As the insurgency mounted, it became ever more difficult to promote reconstruction. The growing violence prompted President Barack Obama to order a surge in troops in Afghanistan to quell the increasingly successful Taliban insurgency.

Local Afghan contractors work together to maintain a steady flow of cement on June 30, 2012, in Ghariban, Zharay District. Workers came from surrounding villages and partnered with a team from the 445th Civil Affairs Battalion to rebuild the compound (photograph by Specialist Tyler Meister).

•• 8 ••

Surge and Draw-Down

Despite the efforts of American troops with working with the Afghan security forces, the Taliban increased their presence and influence across areas of Afghanistan, principally in the eastern and southern provinces where Pashtun influence proved strongest. Troops experienced increasing levels of violence, particularly with improvised explosive devices. The military attempted new programs to protect local populations, such as Village Stability Operations, and military offensives to wrest back control of provinces from the Taliban. President Barack Obama focused America's attention on the "necessary" war in Afghanistan, ordering a surge in troops to reverse the gains the Taliban had made. The surge proved temporary. American troops spent the last two years of Operation Enduring Freedom [2012–2014] turning over responsibilities and forward operating bases to the Afghan government and security forces. At the end of Operation Enduring Freedom, troops did not have confidence that the Afghans would be able to handle security on their own. With unabated activity from the Taliban insurgency, Coalition military forces continued its operations past 2014.

Violence across Afghanistan increased year by year. One observer, visiting four times between the spring of 2003 and the spring of 2010, found that expanding violence required ever more robust security measures, including "bigger and more heavily armed convoys with more armor and more restrictions on travel."[1] Waltz experienced shock at how much security had declined in Afghanistan from his 2006 tour to his 2009 deployment.[2] Sergeant First Class Heath Clark describes the conditions in Helmand in 2009. He stated that a two and a half hour drive took 18 hours because of horrible road conditions. "The roads were all bombed out," he explains, "When I say bombed out I'm talking about 20, 30 foot wide craters, cars on fire, trucks on fire, split in half, bridges were down to one lane. It was something like out of a movie."[3] Indeed, the US Army sent a Stryker battalion to Kandahar Province, in part, to counter the increased IED threat there. M1 Abrams tanks were also deployed in Helmand for the same purpose. With increased violence came increased measures for force protection. Waltz observes that many commanders mandated their troops go outside the wire in MRAPs instead of Humvees or other vehicles, which restricted the areas where the troops could travel. After incidents where patrols and combat outposts were nearly overrun, the numbers of servicemen required to go out on patrols or to protect combat outposts also increased, limiting the flexibility and maneuver-ability of the troops.[4]

Insurgents continued to deploy ever more complex and effective IEDs. When the US brought in Stryker armored vehicles to survive roadside bombs, the Tali-ban simply built larger weapons to punch through the vehicles.[5] The Taliban tar-geted Highway 1, or the Ring Road, that connected many of the country's major cities. "On a single day in August 2008," a journalist reports, "insurgents burned 60 trucks that were hauling supplies on the highway for NATO and cut the road with massive IED explosions."[6] So many IEDs were set in the Zari Panjwai District of Kandahar Province that it became known as "the IED capital of the world."[7] The troops dubbed another road in the Arghandab River Valley "Devil's Alley" because of the number of IED explosions there.[8]

In addition to roadside bombs, the insurgents planted explosives along routes the troops walked on dismounted patrols. Many of these bombs were con-structed from homemade explosives and housed in common plastic jugs. With pressure-sensitive triggers, insurgents could place them anywhere an unsus-pecting combatant might walk. Insurgents even managed to plant bombs in the branches of trees in orchards. As a result, "blown-off limbs quickly became the

US Marine Sergeant Anthony Zabala of 1st Combat Engineering Battalion of 2nd Marine Expeditionary Brigade runs to safety as an Improvised Explosive Device (IED) explodes in Garmsir District of Helmand Province on July 13, 2009. A foot patrol was advancing painstakingly with metal detectors and bare hands to defuse bombs planted on a rough track when an explosion shot a cloud of dust and rocks into the sky in southern Afghani-stan's Helmand Province at dusk, killing Sergeant Michael W. Heede Junior and Staff Ser-geant David S. Spicer (Manpreet Romana/AFP via Getty Images).

signature injury for America's surge troops in the south" of Afghanistan.[9] Troops adapted to the mine threat. As one service member, Kingsley, explains, in order to avoid the dangers of pressure-plate triggers, the troops moved out in single file. "Theoretically, as long as you walk where the guy in front of you walked, and nothing blows up, you'll be safe," Kingsley states.[10] Major Brendan McEvoy relates how his unit added rollers to the front and back of their vehicles as well as toting concertina wire to try to snag the pressure plates. "We just *Mad Maxed* the crap out of them," he describes, invoking a pop culture reference. He relates that the activity "was a lot of fun, and it was good because the soldiers kind of got a chance to take it on themselves to be innovative."[11]

In order to undermine the increasing Taliban influence, Special Forces in Afghanistan instituted a new program called Village Stability Operations (VSO) to target Pashtun areas across southern Afghanistan. It launched in March 2009 and ran until 2013. The program started as an effort to protect locals from the Taliban by building up local security forces, working with village elders, and improving governance.[12] As Lieutenant Colonel D. Scott Mann explains, Special Forces soldiers "lived in the villages, wore Afghan garb, and immersed themselves in the community." While living with the villagers, they met with the elders as well as recruited and trained men to defend the area from insurgents.[13] Colonel Don Bolduc praised the VSO effort when he said, "we're going to win by securing the populace and preventing the insurgents' negative influence." Special Forces soldiers also distributed humanitarian aid and trained local police.[14]

In Major Edward Woodall's 2010 deployment to Afghanistan, he participated in the VSO program in Kandahar Province. His team went in the Zari Panjwai District, which had last seen a Coalition presence with the Canadians a few years prior to his deployment. Woodall described setting up the program "in the middle of nowhere." It was one of three VSOs they set up in the district. As a sign of how dangerous the area had become, he secured a convoy of Jingle trucks for the mission, but they hit IEDs on the way there, causing Afghan casualties. After the Zari Panjwai District, he helped establish three more VSOs, two of which were on the Afghan/Pakistan border, also an area with a strong insurgent presence.[15] Special Forces officer Michael Waltz describes a successful VSO in Khakrz, in Kandahar Province. The Taliban had taken over the village and used it to launch attacks against Kandahar City. Waltz explains that after the Americans established the VSO there, the villagers resisted the Taliban, defended themselves, and reopened the local bazaar for business again.[16]

In conjunction with the VSO program, Afghan President Hamid Karzai established the Afghan Local Police (ALP) in July 2010. The ALP lacked the arresting authority of the Afghan National Police, but their presence in villages increased security in places where no other Afghan security forces were present. The program expanded beyond the ability of Special Forces soldiers to train, so conventional units deployed to support the expansion of the VSO/ALP mission. In 2012, the program included 80 districts with more than 17,000 local police. At the time, there was great excitement about the future of the program.[17]

The initial success of the ALP program tuned into "enormous top-down

Areerob's husband, First Lieutenant Matthew Jarzen, commanded a Forward Retrograde Element, which is "a team comprised of both soldiers and civilian contractors responsible for assisting units with everything from closing Forward Operating Bases (FOBs), retrograde of materials and supplies, customs searches and managing container accountability." He notes, "it's not the sexy job." It required him to fly to different FOBs to determine how to shut it down or how to transfer it to the Afghan National Army. Jarzen mentions that each FOB he helped close or transfer had unique elements so that there was "no cookie-cutter, one-size-fits-all solution."[62]

American troops needed to close permanently over 300 bases. Major General Darrell K. Williams explains, "as you looked around those base camps, you were essentially in a small city. In some cases, we literally had to turn it into the desert as it was when we first found it." Even on the large FOBs that were being kept operational, such as Bagram and Kandahar Air Field, parts of the encampments were downsized or handed over to the Afghans. The busiest phase of the draw-down happened between September 2013 and January 2014.[63]

Service members on FOBs dutifully packed up to return to the US. Troops tore down wood huts and filled containers with personal items to ship back home. As the Americans readied to leave, the Afghans moved onto the base. Since the

Staff Sergeant Daniel Hall, along with other 19th Movement Control Team aerial porters, muscles a "tricon" shipping container into a 774th Expeditionary Airlift Squadron C-130 Hercules cargo plane at Forward Operating Base Salerno, Khowst Province, Afghanistan, September 22, 2013. The 19th MCT, a small squadron of Air Force surface movement controllers and aerial porters, have the herculean task of overseeing the vast majority of retrograde operations at FOB Salerno (photograph by Master Sergeant Ben Bloker).

Soldiers from the 608th Engineer Construction Management Team organized for contractors to remove 16 structures using a Hydraulic Excavator to load wood and metal from barracks huts to be hauled off to the solid waste management complex in support of retrograde missions at Bagram Airfield, Afghanistan, on December 7, 2014 (photograph by 4th Sustainment Brigade).

Afghan government could not maintain the FOBs at the same level that the Coalition had done, "Western troops have scaled back the bases to make them more defensible, and removed water treatment machines, generators and other amenities that are too expensive to run."[64] Working on a FOB in Zhari District near Kandahar that was in the process of shutting down, a civil affairs soldier, Sergeant Neil Arrieta, describes it as going from a "small city" to "like a ghost town."[65] Even in Kandahar, one of the larger bases that the US retained during the draw-down, the once bustling boardwalk became a "ghost town" as well.[66]

Turning over FOBs to the Afghan National Army did not guarantee continued success. Marine Corps logistics officer Christine Hannigan asserts that what they left for the Afghan security forces was "ridiculous." She explains: "They were not trained well. They were not at all equipped to deal with the Taliban. It was openly discussed on base that they were not prepared to take care of Camp Leatherneck. We just let them fail knowing it would be a complete disaster."[67] The shift from Coalition to ANA operations accelerated in 2013–2014. For comparison, the vast majority of operations—95 percent—were led by the US or NATO in 2011. In 2014, the Afghans purportedly led 95 percent of operations without US or NATO assistance.[68] Coalition forces focused mostly on training. Decreased troop levels also meant that the Taliban attacked Afghan security forces more frequently, which led to a rise in Afghan deaths.[69]

Reduced Coalition forces allowed the Taliban to move openly in a number of areas. In Nangarhar Province, for example, the Taliban disrupted elections by simple intimidation. In parts of southern and eastern Afghanistan, reported the *New York Times,* "the Taliban did not have to pick up their rifles to disrupt the vote" because "residents were too frightened or too disenchanted with the national government in general to turn out to vote." While some areas in the northern provinces and around Kabul remained secure for elections, heavily Pashtun areas were not. The Taliban sent night letters "threatening to kill or cut the fingers off voters and warnings of potential attacks on voting centers."[70]

Taliban fighters initiated their spring offensive in 2014 largely against the ANA. As reported at the time, "Afghan forces will be in an unrelenting fight just to hold ground," as Coalition forces had handed over most operations already. The Taliban and ANA appeared evenly matched in some cases, "inflicting nearly equal casualties on each other."[71] As the offensives continued into summer, the Taliban successfully regained territory near the capital, Kabul, and other areas outside their traditional strongholds. Fighters made inroads near district centers and around closed Coalition bases, "as the Taliban felt more emboldened to launch attacks without fear of reprisal."[72]

In autumn 2014, the US and Afghanistan signed a bilateral long-term security agreement that established that 9,800 American and an additional 2,000 NATO troops would remain in Afghanistan to train Afghan security forces after the end of Operation Enduring Freedom in December. American Special Operations Forces would continue counterterrorism operations against insurgent leadership. The Taliban's successful spring and summer offensives suggested that the Afghan forces alone were unable to meet the country's security needs. Afghan forces suffered high casualty rates and persistent logistics problems. The US and NATO divided the country into training zones with the US in the east and south, Italy in the west, and Germany in the north.[73]

Signs of the draw-down were everywhere. The last troops on a closing base had to contend with MREs, much like the early days of the war, as cooks and kitchens packed up. In another signal of abandonment, the post-exchange closed, garbage pickup ended, and the Internet provider removed its equipment.[74] Items that could not be taken home were sold to the Afghans or destroyed. Brigadier General John G. Ferrari announced, "we don't want to leave Afghanistan like the Soviets did, with equipment strewn across the battlefield."[75] In addition, as troops withdrew from Afghanistan, they were, in some cases, replaced by contractors, obscuring the level of continued US commitment to Afghanistan. At the end of 2014, US troops numbered 9,800, while contractors numbered around 23,500. Colonel Ken Dyer explains, "you can't separate the military logisticians anymore from defense contractors. We are very much integrated."[76]

As US and NATO military forces left, the security situation in Afghanistan deteriorated. In several areas of the country, the Taliban made headway against Afghan security forces. The Taliban had also attacked in larger numbers than they had during their spring offensive. Afghan security forces sustained heavy casualties in fighting in Helmand, losing around 1300 soldiers between June and November 2014. A factor that contributed to high casualties was the absence of close air support from US forces. Without the assistance of American or NATO air assets, reports suggest that "the police and military stay tethered to their checkpoints," which allows insurgents freedom of movement.

The Taliban regained territory they had lost during the surge, such as the area around Marjah in Helmand. Further, the fighting continued into November, later in the year than was usual. In response to these developments, US military officials requested a more aggressive role for US troops in 2015. President Obama agreed to the request, authorizing combat support for Afghan security forces for another year with a new anticipated total withdrawal date for 2016. He severely restricted the use of air power, however, permitting it only if Afghan forces faced obliteration.[77]

On December 8, 2014, US and NATO troops officially closed Operation Enduring Freedom, lowering the flags at their headquarters. With a reduced presence of Coalition troops, the Taliban committed to fight "until all foreign troops have left Afghanistan."[78] The new NATO mission, Resolute Support, started on December 31, alongside the US military counterterrorism component named Operation Freedom's Sentinel. According to NATO, the mission for Resolute Support comprised: "supporting planning, programming and budgeting; assuring transparency, accountability and oversight; supporting the adherence to the principles of rule of law and good governance; supporting the establishment and sustainment of such processes as force generation, recruiting, training, managing and development of personnel." Training support was pledged through 2020 and financial support through 2024.[79] From a deployment high point of about 142,000 US and Coalition troops in 2009, around 12,500 to 13,500 NATO forces remained for Resolute Support in 2015. In addition, US forces numbering about 5500 remained in Kabul.[80]

The beginning of Resolute Support Mission/Operation Freedom's Sentinel did not signify the end of combat in Afghanistan. Given that the violence in Afghanistan did not abate, the number of international troops in Afghanistan hovered around 17,000 with the bulk coming from the US. While the main headquarters centered in Kabul, other bases were established in Mazar-e-Sharif, Herat, Kandahar, and Langhman. As the Taliban continued to gain ground, US military forces engaged in a larger mission than had been anticipated. The Taliban made offensive gains, capturing the city of Kunduz in 2015, prompting an American offensive to retake the city. Helmand Province also fell to the Taliban.

Military officials authorized combat missions against Taliban forces and limited air support resumed. Special Operations Forces conducted raids against insurgent targets. A new al-Qaeda affiliate, al-Qaeda in the Indian Subcontinent (AQIS), popped up in eastern Konar and Nuristan provinces in 2015. The US military forces typically used drones to attack insurgents in these provinces.[81] One Special Forces soldier fought in such an intense firefight that he probably set a record for firing rounds from a Carl Gustaf recoilless anti-tank rifle.[82]

The ISAF color guard salutes during the playing of the national anthem during the ISAF Joint Command and XVIII Airborne Corps colors casing ceremony on December 8, 2014, at North Kabul Afghanistan International Airport, Afghanistan (photograph by Staff Sergeant Perry Aston).

Further complicating the situation, another terrorist organization, a branch of the Islamic State, joined the conflict in Afghanistan in 2014. This group comprised "splinter Taliban groups from Afghanistan and Pakistan that came together under the black flag of the Islamic State because they were disillusioned by the way the war was going" under the current Taliban leadership. The Islamic State fighters proved more extreme in their methods than the Taliban.[83] US troops continued to deploy and to fight in Afghanistan, though the public thought the war ended.

As the security situation in Afghanistan failed to improve, President Obama reversed his decision to withdraw all American troops, keeping a force of around 8,400 through the end of his second term in 2016. At first, Obama had restricted the use of air power to support Afghan security forces only if they were in immediate danger of being overrun. The Taliban gains prompted Obama to change course. The president authorized more permissive rules of engagement for the counterterrorism mission, allowing Special Operations Forces soldiers to expand their role in fighting the insurgents. Obama also directed the SOF forces to fight the Islamic State affiliate in Afghanistan, giving the troops additional resources to do so, including drone strikes. Publicly the president still claimed that American military forces were restricted to training and advising Afghan security forces rather than committing to continued combat operations. Even with more robust American support for Afghan Army offensives, the Taliban continued to expand the territory they controlled.[84]

Security conditions continued to deteriorate under the Donald Trump administration to the point that, in 2018, the Afghan government held only about half of the country's districts. Afghan security forces continued to sustain heavy casualties. Trump authorized a small, temporary surge in troops, and Special Operations Forces received further permission to escalate combat against insurgent forces. American assistance allowed Afghan government forces to retain hold on major cities. Unfortunately, the Taliban continued to hold considerable rural territory. In a strange twist of events, American drone strikes sometimes supported Taliban forces engaged in firefights against Islamic State fighters. Meanwhile, the Trump administration resumed negotiations with the Taliban that had started under the Obama administration to reach a peace settlement and to finally withdraw American troops from Afghanistan.[85]

While the surge forces in Afghanistan temporarily established security in Taliban-influenced provinces in Helmand and Kandahar, the withdrawal of substantial Coalition forces allowed the Taliban's resurgence. Though Operation Enduring Freedom officially came to a close in December 2014, combat in Afghanistan did not. The Taliban steadily regained territory it had lost, new terrorist affiliates began activities in the country, and Afghan security forces suffered heavy losses as the fighting continued unabated. Assumptions that international forces would leave Afghanistan by 2015, then 2016, proved optimistic. With continued Taliban gains, the mission kept extending year-by-year so that American troops remained in Afghanistan into 2021. Looking back on 20 years of war, were the sacrifices of so many Americans, Coalition partners, and Afghans worth it?

•• 9 ••

Meaning and Memory

In February 2020, after almost 18 months of negotiations, the United States and the Taliban reached a tentative peace deal. As part of the arrangement, the remaining US forces would leave within 14 months. In exchange, the Taliban "pledges to engage in talks with the Afghan government and commits not to allow terrorist groups to use Afghan soil to plot attacks against the United States or its allies." The pact also assumed lower levels of violence and a prisoner swap.[1] Two days after signing the peace deal, the Taliban resumed offensive operations against Afghan security forces, which did not increase confidence in the longevity of the accord.[2]

The first deadlines of the deal—starting talks between the Afghan National Government and the Taliban by March 10, 2020—passed without progress. Violence increased year-over-year in March, causing high numbers of Afghan security force casualties. "The numbers show Taliban doing nothing for peace and everything to continue their campaign of terror against Afghans," the Afghan National Security Council's spokesman, Javid Faisal, wrote on Twitter.[3] Since then, peace talks between the United States, the Government of Afghanistan, and the Taliban stalled.

In April 2021, the Biden administration announced the full withdrawal of US forces from Afghanistan by September 11, 2021. The administration then moved the deadline earlier to August 31, 2021, regardless of conditions on the ground or the success of a peace settlement. With the war approaching 20 years in duration, Biden explained his rationale for leaving: "I will not send another generation of Americans to war in Afghanistan with no reasonable expectation of achieving a different outcome."[4] A US intelligence assessment in June 2021 estimated that the Taliban could defeat the Government of Afghanistan as soon as six months after the US military withdrawal was completed. The majority of US troops had already departed by early July 2021.[5] Meanwhile, the Taliban, which had quietly been taking over districts throughout the country, stepped up its efforts at seizing control of Afghanistan. District after district fell to the Taliban. The rapid disintegration of the Afghan security forces took the Biden administration by surprise, prompting a massive air lift campaign in August to evacuate remaining US troops, State Department personnel, US citizens, and Afghan allies. The Taliban quickly reclaimed control of Afghanistan, reestablishing a fundamentalist Islamic regime. On August 30, the final US flight took off from Kabul International Airport. The war was over.

Even before the collapse of the Afghan government, veterans who had deployed to Afghanistan harbored mixed feelings towards the conflict. For those who deployed early in the Afghan War, their recollections tended toward a call to service as a result of the September 11, 2001, terrorist attacks, pride in their service, and optimism for Afghanistan's future. For those who deployed later in the war, they also felt pride in their service but felt conflicted or outright cynical about the war. Mostly, the troops focused on shared sacrifices with the men and women with whom they have served, and for combatants, they particularly emphasized a brotherhood of combat.

In the immediate aftermath of the September 11, 2001, terrorist attacks on the United States, Captain Cameron Sellers, an Arizona National Guardsman, volunteered to deploy to Afghanistan. He equated his service in Afghanistan to that of the World War II generation responding to the surprise Japanese attack on Pearl Harbor. He writes, "Now our generation will fight terrorism so that our kids will not have to live through another World Trade Center."[6]

September 11 inspired Leo Jenkins to join the Army, but in his memoir Jenkins dedicates the book to "his brothers" in arms "so those outside of our fraternity may better understand our unique and valuable personalities." He ends the dedication with William Shakespeare's famous "band of brothers" quotation from *Henry V,* which includes the lines "We few, we happy few, we band of brothers/ For he to-day that sheds his blood with me/ Shall be my brother."[7] Comradeship, or primary-group cohesion, between combatants is a common element in warfare. Historian Gerald Linderman points out that in earlier wars, "observer-commentators reserved for it [comradeship] elevated, sometimes fulsome, descriptions,"[8] much like Jenkins and others continued for the Afghan War.

"Brotherhood" served as a more common theme than the patriotic motivation to bring justice to the perpetrators of September 11. Lieutenant Nathaniel Fick, who served in 2001–2002, emphasizes the shared sacrifices of service. He writes with pride, "I took sixty-five men to war and brought sixty-five home." He adds "I hope life improves for the people of Afghanistan and Iraq, but that's not why we did it." Instead of fighting for some larger cause, "we fought for each other."[9]

Lieutenant Sean Parnell echoes those sentiments in his memoir about his 2006 deployment. He intends for it "to tell the world of [his platoon's] amazing accomplishments and to secure their place in American military history." Though the memoir delves into detail of the deployment and firefight in Bermel, the larger war in Afghanistan does not feature prominently. For Parnell, the men he served with in Outlaw Platoon became his family and it is a story of brotherhood.[10]

Sergeant Clinton Romesha, who survived the attempted Taliban overrun of Combat Outpost Keating, also embraces the band of brothers theme: "We were soldiers who loved one another with a fierceness and a purity that has no analog in the civilian world."[11]

Optimism for an ultimate victory in Afghanistan came in the early years of the Afghan War, before the Taliban insurgency gained a clear momentum. Deployed in 2004–2005, Captain Robert Anders believes that his unit was "successfully winning the war *without* killing people" through counterinsurgency operations in Paktika Province. He acknowledges that the mission to "eliminate the sanctuary for terrorists" had not been accomplished completely during his year-long deployment, but Anders believes his unit had made progress to that end. He recommends a sustained large deployment of forces to finish the war and noted that the US military and their families had "answered the call valiantly" to serve.[12]

Deployed in 2006, Colonel Dominic Cariello asserts that "Afghanistan is a success story that's just not getting a lot of press."[13] Command Sergeant Major Jeff Janke, who also served in 2006, states it was a "noble mission" in Afghanistan, and "I do believe we will finish this one out and I think it'll be successful."[14]

Even during the years when the insurgency was not yet at full-strength, some service members harbored mixed feelings about their deployments. Specialist Johnny Rico deployed in 2004, and his firebase was demolished soon after his unit returned to the US. "I couldn't help but think back about Afghanistan and harbor a slight regret," Rico muses. "What was the point in shedding blood, sweat, sperm, and tears to secure a place and make it safer if you were just going to blow it all up?" he wonders. Moreover, the nation's attention had turned to Iraq by this time.[15] Serving in 2006–2007, Captain Benjamin Tupper believes, "The truth for me was that the war in Afghanistan is a conundrum of positive, humanistic goals bloodied by the violence used to combat those who resist them."[16]

Major Rusty Bradley acknowledges that his feelings about the war in Afghanistan have changed over time. He fought in Kandahar in 2006. At the time, he felt pride in what he believed was "the most strategically significant battle in Afghanistan that you never heard of, and its effects [had] a direct impact in the War on Terror." Bradley describes how he has been asked frequently if he believes the war in Afghanistan was worth it. He explains that before 2008, his ready answer was "yes," and after 2008 it switched to "no." He changed his mind because of what he saw as politically motivated alterations to the rules of engagement, unchecked corruption in Afghanistan, and the withdrawal of troops against military advice. From the vantage point of 2014, Bradley admits, "I am not sure how I feel about Afghanistan anymore. Honestly, I am not sure I ever will know how I feel about the place."[17]

Other service members also felt their deployments to Afghanistan made for mixed memories. "Looking back now it was the best, and most definitely the worst time of my life," declares Chad Mauger.[18] These mixed emotions track with what veterans of other US wars in the twentieth century have experienced: "Veterans typically denounced combat's horrors and hardships, yet they could not deny that their wartime experience had somehow been exciting, adventuresome, a source of pride, or an emotional high point," explains historian Kindsvatter.[19]

Some service members believed there was purpose in the war in Afghanistan. Colonel Michael Creedon, who deployed to Afghanistan twice as a Civil Affairs officer, believes it was worth clearing the conditions in Afghanistan that contributed to September 11 in order to prevent a similar incident from happening again, though he also acknowledges that the US did not succeed in its mission to connect the population with the centralized government in Kabul.[20]

Grant McGarry, an Army Ranger who served in the Pech Valley in 2010, not only wrote his story to honor the men with whom he served but to chastise Americans who did not sacrifice for the war. "What it boils down to is that most people in today's society just do not have the courage or the intestinal fortitude to sacrifice their freedom so that others can enjoy the fruits of their blood, sweat, and tears," he writes.[21] Similarly, Marine Corps Corporal Dakota Meyer defends the war in Afghanistan: "I'm not going to sit here and let you say my guys died for nothing."[22]

Marine Corporal Jeff Sibley, who had fought in Sangin, admits, "once the Marines left, though, the Taliban came back. I don't think about it. I don't want our losses to be in vain."[23] At the end of Operation Enduring Freedom, in 2014, Lt. Colonel Michael Waltz still believed it was in the nation's interest to stabilize Afghanistan and prevent it from becoming another haven for terrorists.[24]

More cynicism about the conduct and ultimate outcome of the war became evident as the insurgency in Afghanistan grew stronger. Michael Golembesky wrote about Marine Special Forces in the Bala Murghab Valley in 2009. Once again, the main theme of his book was to honor the men with whom he served in Afghanistan. About the meaning of the war, he states, "We went in eager for victory. We chose to fight, we won our battles. In the end, none of it seemed to matter." He muses that "Afghanistan has no winners and losers, just those who survive and those who die." He, too, focuses on the brotherhood of combat.[25]

A survey in one marine platoon which served in Sangin in 2011 demonstrated that few of them held optimistic views about the "endgame" in Afghanistan. One in five thought the Afghans would ultimately side with the national government against the Taliban; 25 percent believed the Afghan National Army could be trained to defeat the Taliban; and the majority, 55 percent, judged that "when we leave, Afghanistan will remain a mess."[26] Sergeant Neil Arrieta, a Civil Affairs soldier serving in 2012, asserts that the "Taliban are never going to win militarily" but "their ability to disrupt is permanent." He does not think the US will outlast the Taliban.[27]

Army infantryman Jay O'Brien, who served in Kandahar Province in 2013, connected his service to the attacks on September 11, 2001, but ultimately decided the war had no larger meaning. On September 11, he had been 25 years old. O'Brien perceived the terrorist attack as his opportunity to live up to the "Greatest Generation" of World War II. "I felt that my generation needed to step up, like my grandfather's did in 1941," he recalls. He felt proud joining the Army, "but I'm not proud of my deployment or what I did in Afghanistan. It wasn't of worth to my country and it didn't mean anything in the big scheme of things."[28]

Army combat medic David Bently, who served in Konar Province in 2009–2010, despaired at the mismanagement of the war. Though he is proud of his service, it appeared to him that "we just repeated the first six months of a war 18 years in a row." Bently further worried that the conflict would never end; "many who served in the Iraq and Afghanistan campaigns will have children retracing their parents' steps in combat."[29] In truth, the military *has* publicized father-and-son duos who have deployed together as feel-good stories of family patriotic service, and sons *have* followed in their fathers' deployment footsteps.[30] Public affairs personnel have put a positive spin on what could otherwise be perceived as a rather negative development.

Marine Miles Lagoze, who deployed in the Sangin-Kajaki area in 2011, believes the entire nation should be held accountable for the conflict in Afghanistan. He explains that he does not want people to perceive service members as victims or that responsibility rests on the shoulders of the politicians who sent the troops to Afghanistan. "I think the soldiers are responsible, the politicians are responsible, but also the American people are complicit. Our tax money funded the war," he asserts. Everyone bears some blame because, collectively; "We didn't really give a shit. We didn't notice it. We didn't pay attention."[31]

By 2020, victory appeared a distant possibility. Former marine Thomas Gibbons-Neff muses on the dismantling of Kandahar Air Field and the hundreds of other outposts that have been demolished since the end of Operation Enduring Freedom in 2014. "Now, mostly, the sandbagged and Hesco-barriered earthworks serve as decrepit monuments to failed strategies and halcyon days of victory that never came. They are the American version of the rusted Soviet tanks that litter much of the countryside," he writes.[32] In the end, the service member response to their war ran the gamut from optimistically supportive to outright negative.[33]

The mixed feelings and pessimism about Afghanistan's future stand in stark contrast to official pronouncements about the war from the White House and the Pentagon, which always cast the conflict in the best possible light. The story of the official misinformation campaign about the war in Afghanistan is told in the *Washington Post* "Afghanistan Papers." Unit commanders, naturally, wanted to show they had made progress of some kind on the ground during their year abroad. As Lieutenant General Michael Flynn observes, "Then they all said, when they left, they accomplished that mission. Every single commander. Not one commander is going to leave Afghanistan … and say, 'You know what, we didn't accomplish our mission.'"[34] Medal of Honor recipient Dakota Meyer makes a similar observation when he notes that his command publicly stated they "had made progress in eastern Afghanistan, but I didn't see it."[35]

When the Biden administration announced the full withdrawal of US troops from Afghanistan, veterans of the war conveyed mixed feelings, though they tended toward the negative. Spokespeople for the military assured the press that the troops who died in Afghanistan did not die in vain, despite the lack of a clear-cut victory.[36] Marine Corps Master Sergeant Tony Villa does not want to think America's time in Afghanistan had been wasted. "I'd like to think that there were good things that came out of it," he muses, "But who knows?"[37] Air Force Technical Sergeant William Monahan laments, "the notion of a sudden withdrawal without the closure of strategic victory diminishes the sacrifices of all those individuals" who lost their lives in Afghanistan.[38]

Although marine Peter Lucier believed for a long time that the US needed to withdraw the actual decision to do so left him feeling empty. "I thought I'd be happy," he reports, but "it doesn't feel like a win."[39] Amber Chase, a thrice-deployed mortuary affairs soldier, reacted bitterly, stating, "It makes every life we lost over there pointless."[40] Navy Corpsman Tyler Burdick echoes a similar sentiment, "A lot of guys got hurt and a lot of guys got killed, and it was all for nothing—and that's hard."[41]

The meaning of the war has changed for many service members, particularly for those who served during the opening years of the conflict. As the war became mired in an increasingly aggressive Taliban insurgency and as the national security forces appeared unable to combat it, more Americans have come to believe the war in Afghanistan was a mistake. Depending on the question, pollsters have found different answers from the public regarding their support for the war in Afghanistan. Phrased as a "mistake" or "not a mistake," Gallup polling demonstrates that most Americans supported the war effort throughout the conflict. At the very beginning, in November 2001, a mere 9 percent believed the war was a mistake. The number of Americans with a negative view of the war reached 43 percent in August 2010, where it remained stable for almost a decade with only a temporary shift in 2014. Except for a brief time in 2014 when 49 percent of respondents indicated the war was a mistake, the majority, 52 percent, consistently supported the war.

The data indicate partisan differences, with Democrats twice as likely as Republicans to report the war was a mistake.[42] "Regardless of the wisdom of the initial intervention," states a University of Maryland Critical Issues October 2019 poll, "a plurality of respondents (44 percent) also felt that the United States has an obligation toward the Afghan government and segments of Afghan society affected by the war."[43] Phrased as cost versus benefit to the US, a May 2019 Pew Research Center poll found that 58 percent of veterans and 59 percent of the public did not believe the war in Afghanistan was worth fighting. A partisan divide exists among veterans as well. Asked whether the war in Afghanistan was worth fighting, 46 percent of Republican veterans agreed but only 26 percent of Democratic veterans agreed.[44] These polls assume, of course, that Americans are aware of US operations overseas. A July 2018 Rasmussen poll found that only 58 percent of likely US voters knew that the country was still fighting in Afghanistan.[45]

After the Biden administration's announcement of the US withdrawal from Afghanistan, the headlines in the news media tended toward pessimism and declarations of defeat. The *Washington Post* reports, "some analysts worry that the U.S. exit could precipitate the collapse of the struggling Afghan army and a worsening of the country's civil war as various warlords fight for power."[46] Columnist and opinion writer Max Boot warned of a Taliban takeover.[47] *Washington Post* Afghanistan/Pakistan bureau chief Pamela Constable worries about the negative effects of the US withdrawal on the Afghan people.[48]

They were right to worry. In the summer of 2021, the Taliban launched a series of attacks against provincial capitals, "testing for defensive weak points and assessing the government's capacity to provide air support as US and NATO forces withdraw."[49] By June, the Taliban had approached several provincial capitals, including the country's second largest city, Kandahar. They had reportedly purchased heavy weapons for continued offensive operations. One Taliban commander claimed that they will retake the capital, Kabul, "as conquerors" and re-establish the harsh Islamic rule that prevailed before the US-led invasion of 2001.[50] To the surprise of most analysts, the Taliban followed through remarkably quickly, capturing Kabul in August as US and NATO forces withdrew, taking civilian support staff, their citizens, and Afghan allies with them.

On the issue of the withdrawal of troops from Afghanistan, majorities of Americans were supportive, though political affiliation affects the results. Polling registered voters in July 2021, 59 percent supported President Biden's withdrawal of troops, while 25 percent opposed it. By political affiliation, 76 percent of Democrats approved, while 42 percent of Republicans did so. Independents supported the withdrawal at 59 percent.[51] An April 2021 *Economist*/YouGov poll found a similar 58 percent support from registered voters, also showing majority approval from Democrats and Independents.[52] Americans were divided on whether the withdrawal was a victory (18 percent) or defeat (22 percent), with most unsure, as if the Taliban had not yet taken over country.[53] As the Taliban made dramatic gains in August 2021, polls shifted to asking people about how the withdrawal was handled, and majorities indicated it went poorly.

Though there is currently no interpretation that the troops in Afghanistan were "stabbed in the back" by civilian leaders, some service members do criticize leadership at various levels.[54] What comes through is a frustration that the United States never established clear criteria for success in Afghanistan, and worse, "the goalposts kept moving."[55] As Craig Whitlock points out, the first objective clearly stated the mission was to destroy al-Qaeda and make certain Afghanistan could not be a base for terrorist attacks again. The George W. Bush administration broadened the mission to modernize Afghanistan through medicine, education, and national security, among other measures. Here, too, the administration "offered no benchmarks for achieving [the goals] and gave no indication of how long U.S. troops would have to remain" to accomplish them.[56] The pattern continued for the Barack Obama and Donald Trump administrations. Analysts criticized the Biden administration for leaving without reference to conditions on the ground.[57]

Memories and legacies of the Afghan War will also be influenced by images in popular culture, as has happened to World War I, World War II, the Korean War, and the Vietnam War. It is not only the history of the war that is important, but what images viewers see about service members and the war—are those images supportive of the effort or critical? Are service members portrayed as heroes, victims, or anti-heroes? How are the causes and outcomes of the war framed? How all of these are seen in major studio film productions, for example, shape public memory of war.

Given that Operation Enduring Freedom lasted 13 years, and combat extended through Operation Freedom's Sentinel until 2021, major Hollywood film studios have made very few feature-length films about the war, suggesting that the topic is not considered a sure-fire money maker. Hollywood studios made the same calculation about the Vietnam War, with the major films about that war coming years after the end of the conflict. The three top Hollywood films about the Afghan War have focused on discreet events conducted by elite units that have mostly lent themselves to depictions of heroism. Since at least the 1980s, American culture has placed military service personnel on a pedestal, so it is entirely expected that depictions of the armed forces in major Hollywood studio productions would highlight heroism.[58] The focus on elite units—Navy SEALs and Special Operations Forces—emphasizes how military personnel are set apart from the regular citizenry as opposed to being members on par with it. And these elite units are even set apart and regarded more highly than regular conventional units.

The first major Hollywood studio production, *Zero Dark Thirty* (2012), portrays a fictionalized account based on real events of the intelligence gathering and resulting 2011 SEAL Team 6 raid on a compound in Abbottabad, Pakistan, that killed al-Qaeda leader Osama bin Laden.[59] The film depicts Maya (Jessica Chastain) as a lone-wolf CIA analyst who spends a decade tracking down the courier who leads her to bin Laden. Her persistence pays off with the raid that eliminated him. The men of SEAL Team 6, led by Justin (Chris Pratt), are shown laughing, joking, and playing around before the raid, all to make the characters likeable and sympathetic. On the mission, they are level-headed, professional, and competent as they breach the walls of the compound, quickly dispatch the adults of the house, including bin Laden, and collect intelligence from the office. The entire military operation is handled with professionalism, and they react to unfolding events with cool heads. The men of SEAL Team 6 are heroes, and the raid is a resounding success. Though the scenes depicting torture and the apparent support for the idea that torture-gleaned intelligence proved controversial, most critics and audiences reacted positively to the film.[60]

Also focusing on an elite unit, the movie *Lone Survivor* (2013), based on the memoir of the same name, tells the story of a reconnaissance patrol from SEAL Team 10, which was overrun by Taliban forces.[61] Only one member survived, Marcus Luttrell, played by Mark Wahlberg. Additional members of the military died when their Chinook helicopter was hit by an RPG and crashed into a mountainside, killing all on board. Though the film explains the immediate mission of locating a high-value target Taliban commander, it does not delve into the larger context of the Afghan War. Instead, it focuses on intense combat action scenes when the men fight for survival. The movie portrays the Taliban as pure evil as it shows them beheading a man. It also highlights *lokhay warkawal,* the local honor code that obligates the villagers to provide Luttrell's protection from the Taliban.[62] Though the film changes some of the details of the real-life account, it is largely accurate. The actual Marcus Luttrell wrote his book and supported the film in order to "immortalize" his teammates. "That's all I ever really wanted," Luttrell admits.[63] Critics and audiences have largely given the film positive reviews, confirming the popularity of the heroism portrayed in the movie.[64]

The film *12 Strong* (2018) tells the story of the first Special Forces Operational Detachment–Alpha (ODA) on the ground in Afghanistan in October 2001 at the beginning of the war.[65] It is based on the book *Horse Soldiers* by Doug Stanton. Unusually, the movie includes an actor who is a veteran of the actual events depicted on the screen, Rob Riggle. He plays Lieutenant Colonel Max Bowers in the film, who happened to be the actual commanding officer of then-marine Captain Rob Riggle.[66] Given the large number of World War II veterans in the population, it was fairly common for military veterans to play roles in war films during the 1950s and 1960s. With the very small percentage of veterans among today's population, it is rare for the same to happen presently.

Though based on true events, *12 Strong* manages to recreate a trope in American war cinema where a small group of American soldiers are outnumbered by an enemy force but through their scrappy ingenuity manage to overcome the odds.[67] This is a particularly difficult trick to accomplish given that the US stood as the lone superpower of the world at the time of the events. The 12 men of the ODA team were outnumbered but had the devastating firepower of American bombers at their disposal. Indeed, the greatest inaccuracy of the movie is depicting less air support than had been the actual case. The director chose to invent a scene where the Americans, on horseback, miraculously ride a gauntlet through smoking Taliban armor and vehicles to take out a Taliban truck-mounted rocket launcher. The Taliban are shown as evil, with the Taliban commander callously murdering a woman for educating girls, which was against the regime's laws. The movie creates a scene where the Northern Alliance commander, General Dostum, kills the Taliban leader in revenge for taking the lives of his family. The operation is a success, and the Americans are heroes, returning to their loving families by Christmas. Of the major Hollywood films, it is the one that provides the most context for understanding the war. Critics were not particularly impressed with the simplistic storytelling, though audiences gave it slightly better reviews. Though the film has significant star power with Chris Hemsworth, Michael Shannon, and Michael Peña, it trails *Zero Dark Thirty* and *Lone Survivor* in popularity.[68]

Perhaps the tag line for Netflix's *War Machine* (2017) captures best the mixed feelings of service members on Afghanistan: "We're gonna liberate the sh*t out of you."[69] *War Machine* is a part tongue-in-cheek recreation of the events that led to the removal of General Stanley McChrystal in Afghanistan based on the *Rolling Stone* article written by Michael Hastings.[70] Though it was not produced by a major Hollywood studio, it had the backing of a major media company. It is based on real-life events and does not highlight an elite unit. Rather, its focus is on the commanding general of Afghanistan and his staff. It gives a fairly negative portrayal of soldiers. In this case, the soldiers act unprofessionally, drink heavily, and openly criticize the Obama administration. It shows a disconnect between the commanding general and his commander-in-chief. It also showcases the strategic conflict between counterinsurgency—protecting the population from the Taliban—and counterterrorism—going after the remnants of al-Qaeda. A German politician, played by Tilda Swinton, intimates that the Coalition has overstayed its welcome in Afghanistan and questions the suitability of a surge in troops that McChrystal is advocating. If the Afghans simply want the foreigners to leave, the German politician states, the Coalition will never win the war, no matter if McChrystal gets his surge in troops. Looking back from 2021, the comment appears prescient. Neither critics nor audiences cared much for the fictionalized satire of this film, suggesting that audiences do prefer to view service members as heroes rather than flawed and frustrated by a difficult and perhaps unwinnable war.[71]

Some of the films about the Afghan War have come from small, independent film studios, which lack the audience reach of major Hollywood studio movies or major media outlets like Netflix. One of these, *The Kill Team* (2019), had a limited release.[72] Though it garnered critical support, audiences did not care for the far less than heroic depictions of US Army soldiers murdering Afghan civilians.[73] The fictionalized account is based on the real events of five soldiers who murdered civilian Afghan men in the Maywand District in Kandahar Province and planted evidence to make the deaths look justified. This story focused on regular soldiers rather than on an elite unit. Director Dan Krauss changed the soldiers' names in the film, but otherwise stuck to the facts of the case.

The story is told through the perspective of Specialist Andrew Briggmann, the fictionalized character based on real-life Private Adam Winfield. Briggmann is manipulated by Staff Sergeant Deeks (real-life Staff Sergeant Calvin Gibbs), the mastermind of the murders, into finally participating in one of them.[74] Deeks' character is understated and even a bit humanized by showing him talking to his son on his laptop computer. This depiction stands in stark contrast to an otherwise similar character, Sergeant Barnes, from the Vietnam War film *Platoon* (1986), who also condones the murder of Vietnamese civilians. Barnes is a larger-than-life character, packed with muscles, scars, and an intimidating attitude. Deeks, on the other hand, appears as a regular soldier. He manipulates much more discreetly and suavely to isolate Briggmann from the rest of the team, and then to threaten him quietly, until he joins them.

The depiction of the soldiers in *The Kill Team* is generally accurate, capturing banter and the youth of actual service members. (The major Hollywood studio films tended to have actors who were older than the service members they portrayed.) Though the murders are depicted accurately, the movie lacks overall context. It never explains why the US is in Afghanistan or even what the soldiers are doing in Kandahar. At best, the audience is given to understand that soldiers are going after "bad guys" who set roadside bombs. Perhaps the director assumes audiences understand the overall context of the war and the specific events in southern Afghanistan in 2009–2010. This will not likely always be the case.

Perhaps the film with the most verisimilitude is another small studio release, *The Outpost* (2020), based on the book of the same name by Jake Tapper about the events at COP Keating. It provides context for the part of the war in Nuristan, depicts soldiers frankly, and shows both the battle and its psychological aftermath on the men. Given the length of Tapper's book, the film had to streamline the narrative to fit into a two-hour length. As a result, the film condenses some of the events. For example, it includes the roll-over death of Lieutenant Benjamin Keating (Orlando Bloom), though he served in a different unit three years before the attack at the heart of the film. Director Rod Lurie, a West Point graduate, pays attention to details, creating a setting that looks and sounds authentic. Veterans of COP Keating were on set, contributing to the accuracy of the film, including Specialist Daniel Rodriguez, who plays himself in the movie.[75]

Like *12 Strong* and *Lone Survivor*, *The Outpost* battle at COP Keating shows the 53-strong American force outnumbered by 300–400 Taliban fighters, swarming down the sides of the mountains that ring the outpost. The combatants at Keating fought for a considerable time on their own before air support arrived to rain rockets, bombs, and strafing fire on the enemy forces. Lurie focuses the narrative on the actions of the two real-life Medal of Honor recipients Staff Sergeant Clint Romesha (Scott Eastwood) and Staff Sergeant Ty Carter (Caleb Landry Jones). The film also includes scenes about the aftermath of the battle, including the emotional struggles that prompt Carter to speak to an Army psychologist (Celina Sinden). Veterans and families of the soldiers who died at COP Keating appreciated the honesty of the film and believed that it honored the fallen.[76] Film critics praised the film along the lines of the *Washington Post's* Ann Hornaday, who concluded the movie honored "service and sacrifice without lapsing into empty triumphalism."[77] Indeed, the men respond to save themselves and each other under extreme duress. Yet, the heroism is not jingoistic. Like many of the veterans who wrote memoirs, this film emphasizes the "band of brothers" connection between the combatants.

There are also a number of documentary films on the Afghan War, some of which have positive portrayals of the war and others which focus on negative themes. The documentary *Restrepo* (2010), about fighting at an outpost in the Korengal Valley, gives a sympathetic portrayal of the soldiers deployed there.[78] Once again focusing on regular soldiers rather than an elite unit, the men are nevertheless heroes for facing a faceless enemy—the Taliban are never shown—and viewers are told repeatedly that the Korengal Valley was the most dangerous place in Afghanistan at the time of filming in 2007–2008. Though the danger to the troops is clearly demonstrated, the documentary lacks context. Why are the men fighting? What is the mission?

All viewers are told is that constructing Observation Post Restrepo changed the operational situation in the valley, though it is not explained exactly how. Instead, viewers are meant to connect emotionally with the soldiers and be concerned with their plight. Even though the documentary ends with the announcement that 50 soldiers died in the valley and that the US abandoned it in 2010, a viewer is not necessarily left with an interpretation of defeat. Instead, viewers focus on the sacrifices the troops made in the war. They are framed as heroes simply for being there, taking fire, and enduring the deployment. Both critics and audiences had extremely positive reactions to the documentary that exceeded those of *Zero Dark Thirty*.[79] Reality rather than Hollywood proved the most attractive here.

Most documentaries did not gain the number of viewers that watched *Restrepo*, so the following images of the military could not have had as much an impact on audiences. *Legion of Brothers* had a limited release in 2017, and it focused on the first ODA teams to fight in Afghanistan, much like *12 Strong*.[80] The very few critics who reviewed the documentary gushed about its authenticity and heroism, though they all mentioned how disjointed the storytelling had been. Audiences, however, did not care for it as much.[81] Indeed, the film lacks an overall narrative, shifting between the activities of the veterans in the present day and recollections of the war. It also combines the stories of multiple ODA teams without much explanation of the different areas where they operated. If a viewer did not already understand the overall history of the war in Afghanistan, the documentary would be difficult to follow. Had this been a major Hollywood studio film, critics probably would have eviscerated the director for poor storytelling.

Another documentary in very limited release is *Combat Obscura*, which shows a slice of life during a marine deployment in 2010–2011. It is a compilation of video taken by Marine Corps videographers, not officially released by the Marine Corps or Department of Defense. In addition to the sequences depicting the men taking fire and goofing off in their quarters, the documentary includes scenes that reveals marines intimidating children and killing an unarmed shopkeeper. Given that the armed forces never display images of service members killed in combat, the documentary daringly includes the death of a marine, Justin Levy. When asked why he made the film, Miles Lagoze explains, "we want to give people the experience of the war, the uncertainty of it, and the paradoxes." Furthermore, he wanted to reflect on the experiences of the men and the absurdity of the war. He adds, "There wasn't even a definition of what the outcome was going to be, what winning would even look like, or anything, really. And just the waste of life."

Lagoze intentionally did not want audiences to have a sense of closure about the war. In his decision to include the death of Levy, he notes that while there were plenty of images of dead Iraqis or Afghans, US service members were off limits. "We didn't want to value one life over the other," he explains.[82] The 14 critics documented on Rotten Tomatoes all liked the documentary, interpreting it through the victimhood lens—the men were changed by their negative experiences in Afghanistan, rather than them being inherently bad people. The critics also appreciated the authenticity and honesty of the footage.[83] Hardly any audience members reacted to the film, so it is difficult to discern what the overall reaction to it is.

The Discovery Channel's television mini-series *Taking Fire* also has little in way of an audience. It is based on the videos taken by soldiers at COP Michigan in the Pech Valley, during one of the deadlier phases of the insurgency there. The soldiers took fire every day. It captures exactly the daily lives of soldiers, the banter, the danger of taking enemy fire, the loss of men from roadside bombs, and more. It is authentic and not particularly dramatized. The few people who rated it liked the series, though they are a self-selected group.[84] It clearly resonated with the few audience members who are still actively watching stories about the Afghan War. Though US troops continued to be deployed in Afghanistan through July 2021, not many Americans were paying attention. The war fades into the background except for when major announcements are made—such as the total troop withdrawal. Otherwise, Americans go about their daily lives, oblivious to the war in Afghanistan.

No single narrative of the war has taken hold of popular culture, but given the final withdrawal of troops, this might become a period of reflection. Will the memorialization of the Afghan War ultimately "simplify and glorify" the conflict or will it lead to disillusionment?[85] What is clear, thus far, is that Americans consider the service members who deployed, fought, died, or survived the Afghan War mainly as heroes.

Conclusion

As he stepped down as commander of US forces in Afghanistan in July 2021, Army General Austin "Scott" Miller said, "our job now is just not to forget." He wanted the nation to remember the Afghan War, particularly for those families who lost someone during the conflict.[1] The US war in Afghanistan has rarely been at the forefront of Americans' attention, earning the moniker "the forgotten war" soon after the US invaded Iraq in 2003. Yet this "forgotten war" became America's longest war to date. Though imperfect in execution and uneven in results, American service members proved earnest in their efforts, if ultimately limited in their capacity, to secure Afghanistan from al-Qaeda terrorists and a resurgent Taliban and to create a version of liberal democracy for the Afghan people.

Many US troops sincerely believed they were preventing Afghanistan from becoming a haven for terrorists and in so doing, defending the United States. Years into Resolute Support Mission/Operation Freedom's Sentinel, US troops continued to assist the Afghan security forces in the hopes that it would not appear that the US had lost the war and to avoid comparisons to America's failed war in Vietnam.[2] With the Taliban continuing to fight in mid–2021 despite a signed peace deal, it did not appear that the United States was on its way to claim success in Afghanistan. Even though the experiences of US troops in Afghanistan varied over time and location—fighting in the mountains of the Korengal Valley differed from dodging IEDs in Helmand—several conclusions can be drawn about the overall American experience there.

In Afghanistan, Iraq, and the other areas where the US has been waging a "Global War on Terror," the conflicts have been costly both in terms of treasure and lives. According to one estimate, the combined costs of the US wars on terror approaches $6.4 trillion. The war in Afghanistan constitutes an expenditure of $2.261 trillion.[3] More importantly, tens of thousands have died. As of July 2021, there had been 2452 American military fatalities in Afghanistan.[4] Coalition allies have suffered military deaths as well. One study examines the fatalities of US and Coalition troops by determining the percentage of deaths at the time of the highest troop deployment to Afghanistan. According to this calculation, American fatalities constitute 2.3 percent of peak deployment numbers.

Though Coalition allies Canada and the United Kingdom deployed numerically fewer personnel (with peak deployment numbers of 2,905 and 9,500

202

respectively, in February 2011), they suffered higher per capita fatalities: 5.4 percent for Canada and 4.7 percent for the UK, demonstrating that key Coalition partners sacrificed for the war effort alongside the US.[5]

Though the Pentagon does not keep track of the contractors who are employed by the US who die, analysts estimate that over 3,800 have been killed in Afghanistan through April 2021, exceeding US military deaths. Excluding contractor fatalities distorts the true human losses of the war as an accurate assessment should include them and show deaths twice as high as reported. Afghans suffered the most. Scholars figure over 47,000 Afghan civilians have died, though given the rural environment in the country this number may not be terribly accurate. Somewhere between 66,000 and 69,000 Afghan soldiers and police have been killed, far exceeding Coalition deaths.[6] Since violence continues in Afghanistan, these numbers will surely climb. Though the war is over for the United States in mid–2021, it is certainly not over for the Afghans who have suffered 40 years of almost continuous conflict so far.

Was the Afghan War another Vietnam? Though there are similarities with America's war in Vietnam, the conflict in Afghanistan proved quite different in several meaningful ways. With frequent troop rotations, the war in Afghanistan lived up to the adage ascribed to Vietnam that the US fought a one-year war over and over again. Both wars involved counterinsurgency operations and an enemy that proved both capable and elusive. The helplessness troops faced with improvised explosive devices in Afghanistan echoed similar responses from troops in Vietnam to booby-traps. Service members themselves made conscious references to the Vietnam War, as when a soldier shouted "Charlie in the wire" when Taliban breached the perimeter of COP Keating, or when helicopters dropped off troops in a dried rice paddy in Afghanistan. Trainers for the Afghan National Army and police forces grumbled about the corruption and lack of performance from their mentees, much like Americans complained about the South Vietnamese army.

Both in Vietnam and in Afghanistan, Americans brought their consumerism overseas, creating vast bases that sported American food, shopping, and services. Unlike the Vietnam War where public support faltered, a majority of Americans fairly consistently supported the war in Afghanistan. Though the war in Afghanistan lasted far longer than the one in Vietnam, Afghanistan did not remain in the news headlines or feature prominently in American life as the war in Vietnam did. Where the draft generated controversy during the Vietnam War, the war in Afghanistan was fought by an All-Volunteer Force. Simply put, the war in Afghanistan remained in the background of American life for most of the 20 years the US fought there. It never became a flash point like the Vietnam War.

It is also important to note that the war in Afghanistan is not the Iraq War, either, though both happened simultaneously. Troops who served in both theaters remarked on their differences in terms of people, the environment, and the fighting, and they cautioned others not to conflate the two wars. There are, of course, similarities as they were both fought by the same all-volunteer force using the same methods and technology. The US toppled both governments, attempted to establish elected democracies in both countries, and faced insurgencies in both areas. Both theaters saw female personnel engage in combat out of necessity. Though both Iraq and Afghanistan are Muslim countries, they have different ethnicities, languages, terrain, cultures, and politics. Iraq is more Western, educated and urban than Afghanistan. The Iraq War also had the priority in terms of troop numbers, air power, and other equipment, with Afghanistan a secondary economy-of-force theater.

Though often taken aback by what Westerners perceived as social and cultural backwardness, most American troops attempted to respect the very different Afghan culture they encountered in their deployments. Troops tried to interact with the local population, drink tea with village elders, eat Afghan food, and respect the cultural boundaries of interacting with women. One of the most welcome cultural elements troops came across was *Pashtunwali*, most often observed as hospitality. When invited inside an Afghan's home, it also included protection, though troops never fully trusted that aspect of *Pashtunwali*.

Even with an openness to cultural differences, frustrations remained. The Afghan habit of talking extensively before getting down to business during meetings often exasperated Americans, who wanted to dive right into work. Americans also complained about the Afghan culture of corruption, which they observed both at the individual level and systemically in the army, police, and government. A Muslim religious concept, *Inshallah,* or "as God wills" caused irritation as well, as troops believed it led to inaction and inattentiveness in training, on missions, and in daily operations. Since Western societies rarely stop for religious observations anymore, some troops became frustrated when activities ceased on Muslim holy days.

Even though the troops tried to respect cultural boundaries when interacting with Afghan women, such as having female troops conduct searches and ask questions of Afghan women, Americans acculturated to Western concepts of equality condemned the way Afghan men separated and subordinated Afghan women. On the other hand, Afghan men also needed to accommodate Coalition women in uniform, something far outside of their cultural norms. Another aspect of Afghan culture which appeared strange to Americans was the physical affection common between men, such as hand-holding. Even after 20 years of interactions, many of these cultural differences could not be overcome.

Many of the troops' frustrations with Afghans stemmed from the Americans sincerely wanting to improve conditions for the Afghan government and security forces. When mentoring Afghan government officials, the Afghan National Army, or the Afghan police forces, American troops, naturally, measured success by Western standards, which Afghans consistently failed to achieve. More realistic metrics of success, based on what the Afghans were capable of accomplishing, might have reduced frustration on both sides.

For the troops deployed to Afghanistan, living spaces ranged from large, safe forward operations bases that resembled the ones stateside to austere and remote combat outposts. Whether living on a large FOB or remote COP, troops universally complained of the *Groundhog Day*–like repetitive daily routines. Even in the more remote outposts, troops relied on technology to maintain communications within Afghanistan and through satellites to drone operators in the US. They also used technology to watch movies and television shows and play video games in their downtime, just like home. Modern communications technology often kept the troops in frequent contact with friends and family back home, which on one hand created unprecedented connection with the home front, and on the other hand could create difficulties for troops dealing with family matters while on a deployment. Modern communications proved to be a double-edged sword.

Service member experiences in Afghanistan reinforce the divide between military and civilian and between support personnel and frontline combatant. As Army Ranger Colby Bradley writes, "prepare yourself to see some shit and do some shit that nobody back home will understand."[7] As much as troops were surrounded by the familiar on base, they were exposed to the dangers of the theater, such as rocket attacks on bases and roadside bombs outside the gates.

Combatants felt just as much separated them from the "Fobbits" on base as they were from civilians back home. They chafed at military courtesies observed on bases, as well as strict uniform standards.

Combatants felt a world of difference between the large, generally safe bases and the exposed remote locations constantly vulnerable to enemy attack. On patrol, they were frequently exposed to ambushes, IEDs, and firefights. As time passed for the veterans of the Afghanistan war, the sharpness of the divide between combatant and Fobbit faded a bit and evolved into a broader understanding of shared sacrifice. "Infantrymen don't have a monopoly on heart," Lieutenant Sean Parnell admits, and so-called Fobbits "can inspire and elevate just as equally as those of us who rolled out beyond the wire."[8] Perhaps they, too, could be included in the "band of brothers."

Combat in Afghanistan varied over time and location. After the initial attacks on al-Qaeda and the Taliban caused the terrorists to retreat into Pakistan and the government to fall, patrols proved fairly quiet. While Special Operations Forces hunted down the remnants of the terrorist and Taliban leadership, conventional forces conducted patrols and handed out humanitarian aid. Operations focused mainly on the eastern provinces on the border with Pakistan and at one point pushed into Nuristan, a particularly isolationist and hostile province. There, remote outposts were vulnerable to attack. Meanwhile, the Taliban regrouped and rearmed, launching a counteroffensive in 2006. From this point forward, US and Coalition troops and Afghan security forces had to contend with more frequent ambushes, suicide bombers, improvised explosive devices, and eventually insider attacks of Afghan security forces on Coalition personnel and fellow Afghans. The Taliban reoccupied the southern provinces of Helmand and Kandahar, necessitating major combat operations there to briefly retake the territory. Special Forces continued to conduct night raids to kill or capture insurgent and terrorist leadership.

Through blogs, memoirs, and oral histories, combatants attempted to explain the experiences of battle using analogies for sights, sounds, smells, physical sensations, and mental frames of mind. Given the troops' familiarity with modern technology, many of their descriptions invoked machinery and other technologies—fireworks, Christmas lights, wood-chippers, jackhammers, and the like—to make their experiences understandable. Troops even invoked machinery to describe the heat in Afghanistan—from ovens to hair dryers blowing dust in their faces. Troops pulled comparisons from nature, too—thunderstorms for combat and hornets and dragonflies to describe darting and hovering aircraft and helicopters. They pulled analogies from everyday life to make their experiences understandable to themselves and to the people back home.

Although troops chafed at what they perceived as overly restrictive rules of engagement that placed their lives and the lives of their fellow service members at risk during combat, with a few tragic exceptions, they generally avoided deliberately harming Afghan civilians. The Taliban often made it difficult to avoid civilian casualties, as the insurgents had no problems hiding among the population and using civilians for protective cover.

Given the prominence of entertainment in American culture, troops made many references to popular culture, particularly Hollywood films, in describing their experiences in Afghanistan. Many likened the people, languages, terrain, or combat to the original *Star Wars* film. Another reference was *Mad Max* to describe the environment and adaptations the troops made to their vehicles to deal with the terrain and roadside bombs. Terrain features reminded some soldiers of the Harry Potter films or *Lord of the Rings.* Indeed, the very nickname of troops who served their deployments in Forward Operating Bases, "Fobbits," comes from the Hobbits of *Lord of the Rings.* Troops also invoked images from the Stone Age, Biblical era, and old western movies. Many summoned the image of alien worlds to describe the dust that reminded troops of the moon to terrain that appeared Mars-like. Even the insects seemed other-worldly.

The US and Coalition forces held the advantage in advanced technology, such as the use of night vision devices. Modern technology allowed a relatively small number of combat troops to rain down destruction from the air on insurgent forces. Only in a very few instances—Wanat and COP Keating—did the insurgents come close to overrunning an American position. As a result of overwhelming American firepower, the Taliban turned toward more asymmetric tactics, such as improvised explosive devices and terrorizing the population to undermine the efforts of the Afghan government and Coalition forces. The use of IEDs created a feedback loop where the US would devise countermeasures, the insurgents created bigger bombs, the US brought in more robust vehicles, and the insurgents found new ways to use the bombs effectively. The IEDs certainly lowered morale for the troops who encountered them on a daily basis, particularly down in the southern provinces of Kandahar and Helmand. Whether a roadside bomb or an ambush, many troops believed the enemy held the initiative in combat rather than the Coalition.

Though typically a Special Operations Forces role, training the host nation's security forces fell to conventional forces, including the National Guard, in Afghanistan. Part of the reason for the shift to conventional forces had to do with the strain on US forces fighting insurgencies in Iraq and Afghanistan at the same time. Often the troops designated as Embedded Training Teams did not match skills precisely with the Afghans they had to train. When mentors went into combat with their Afghan trainees, they sometimes likened it to herding cats. Nevertheless, most instructors believed they had accomplished some progress with the Afghan soldiers—and later police—that they trained. One of the biggest obstacles that they faced at this, and other levels of government, were behaviors that the Americans deemed corrupt according to Western standards. Afghans horded equipment or sold it for money for their families. Higher level officials demanded bribes or kickbacks. As these actions were partly cultural, they proved difficult to manage as they were not going to be eliminated. Many Americans experienced increasing frustration with the culture of corruption, and some gave up on the Afghans.

Though an overly used and trite phrase, it is nevertheless somewhat appropriate to state that Americans attempted to "win the hearts and minds" of the Afghans. At the start of the war, troops handed out humanitarian aid. They provided medical and veterinary care as well as sponsored infrastructure development, such as the building of roads, schools, clinics, and wells, even if the results proved uneven. In so doing, the US devoted considerable financial resources in their attempts to improve the lives of the Afghans. According to the Special Inspector General for Afghanistan Reconstruction, the US has invested about $36 billion on reconstruction, education, and infrastructure projects. Unfortunately, some of those funds were wasted due to corruption or simply misaligned goals. Some clinics or schools remained unused, for example, because the Afghans did not have the personnel to run them.[9] Improving the lives of women in Afghanistan proved one success, with the United States Agency for International Development indicating that the lifespan for Afghan women rose from 47 to 60 years in the 20 years of US involvement. Girls attend school, and women participate in the economy in ways not allowed under Taliban rule.[10] Analysts fear that these gains will disappear since the Taliban regained power in Afghanistan.

When looking back at nearly 20 years of war in Afghanistan, with the Taliban forces back in control, the future of a secure, democratic Afghanistan looks dim. Service members who deployed early in the conflict wrote blogs, memoirs, and other documents with an optimistic interpretation of the ultimate success of the US war. They felt their time in Afghanistan served a purpose toward the goal of securing the US from another terrorist attack. As the war dragged on into a second decade, the troops exhibited more mixed feelings concerning the war, focusing most on the "band of brothers" comradeship they felt. By the time the Biden administration announced the final withdrawal of American troops, service members shared frustration at the apparent failure to secure Afghanistan while also not wanting the fallen service members to have died for nothing.

Though many of the troops recounted difficulties, frustrations, and sometimes outright failures during their deployments, their experiences of working with the Afghans, interacting with the Afghan population, and fighting a difficult insurgency, the vast majority of the troops who deployed did so honorably and are proud of their service, even if the ultimate outcome was a failure. As one marine sums up at the end of Operation Enduring Freedom: "I'd like to say the world

has watched, or at least our nation has, as this era of American/NATO intervention in Afghanistan has flowed, ebbed, flowed, and ebbed again." He knows, however, that a minority has paid attention to the war, and very few are aware of the
nation "being 'at war,'" he observes. Though he acknowledges that Afghanistan
may become a failed state, it "would be due to so many more factors than how
ably U.S. and allied troops performed their given missions."[11]

Glossary

ALP   Afghan Local Police

ANA   Afghan National Army

ANP   Afghan National Police

AQIS   al-Qaeda in the Indian Subcontinent, an al-Qaeda affiliate

AVF   All-Volunteer Force

CASEVAC   Casualty Evacuation

CHU   Containerized Housing Unit used in the Iraq War

CAB   Combat Action Badge

CAR   Combat Action Ribbon

CAS   Close Air Support

CERP   Commander's Emergency Response Program

CIB   Combat Infantry Badge

CHLC   Coalition Humanitarian Liaison Cells

CJCMOTF   Combined Joint Civil Military Operations Task Force

COIN   Counterinsurgency

CONEX   Container Express

CONOP   Concept of Operations

COP   Combat Outpost

DFAC   Dining Facility

Down Range   Troops deployed overseas

DShK   Soviet-era machine gun

DUSTWUN   Duty Status Whereabouts Unknown

EOD   Explosive Ordnance Detachment

ETT   Embedded Training Teams

FET   Female Engagement Team

FOB   Forward Operating Base

Fobbit   Nickname for personnel who spend their deployments on Forward Operating Bases

GMT   Greenwich Mean Time

GO   General Order

Green-on-Blue   An Afghan attack on US or Coalition personnel

Green-on-Green   An Afghan attack on Afghan security force personnel

HESCO   Cloth interiors with wire mesh on the outside that are filled with dirt

HMMWV   High Mobility Multipurpose Wheeled Vehicle or Humvee

ICOM   Two-way radio

IED   Improvised Explosive Device

Inshallah   Islamic saying meaning, "If God wills"

IR   Infrared laser

ISAF   International Security Assistance Force

JDAM   Joint Direct Attack Munition

JOC   Joint Operations Center

JRTC   Joint Readiness Training Center, Fort Polk, LA

JTAC   Joint Tactical Air Controller

209

K2   Karshi-Khanabad Air Base

KAF   Kandahar Air Field

Kandak   Battalion in the Afghan National Army

LGB   Laser-Guided Bombs

LZ   Landing Zone

M240   Belt-fed machine gun

M4   Standard-issue carbine for most US military personnel

M-ATV   Mine-Resistant All-Terrain Vehicle

Ma deuce   Nickname for the M2 .50 caliber machine gun

Mark-19   Automatic grenade launcher

MEDCAP   Medical Civic Assistance Program

Medevac   Medical Evacuation

MRAP   Mine-Resistant Ambush Protected vehicle

MRE   Meal Ready to Eat

Mujahedeen   Mostly Arabic combatants who fought the Soviets in Afghanistan

MWR   Morale, Welfare, and Recreation

NATO   North American Treaty Organization

NCO   Non-Commissioned Officer

NGO   Non-Governmental Organization

NOD   Night Optical/Observation Device

NVG   Night Vision Goggles

ODA   Operational Detachment Alpha (Special Forces unit)

OEF   Operation Enduring Freedom

OIF   Operation Iraqi Freedom

OP   Observation Post

Pashtunwali   Pashtun code of honor, status, and hospitality

PJ   Pararescue Jumper

PID   Positive Identification

PMCS   Preventative Maintenance Checks and Services

POG   People Other Than Grunts, pronounce "pogue"

PRT   Provincial Reconstruction Team

PX   Post Exchange

REMF   Rear Echelon Motherfucker, a Vietnam-era slang term for troops in the rear

ROE   Rules of Engagement

RPG   Rocket Propelled Grenade

SEAL   Sea, Air, and Land

Shura   local council

SITREP   Situation Report

SOF   Special Operations Forces

Squirter   Nickname for enemy combatants running from the battlefield

TIC   Troops in Contact with enemy fighters

TOC   Tactical Operations Center

UAV   Unmanned Aerial Vehicles

USAID   United States Agency for International Development

VBIED   Vehicle-Borne Improvised Explosive Device

VSO   Village Stability Operations

Wadi   Dried riverbed

Chapter Notes

Introduction

1. Johnny Rico, *Blood Makes the Grass Grow Green: A Year in the Desert with Team America* (New York: Presidio, 2007), 201–202.

2. Kevin Clifford, quoted in Meredith Fischer, "Watchful Waiting at Base," *Richmond Times Dispatch*, July 19, 2004.

3. "Afghanistan: The Forgotten War," S4, E28, *NOW on PBS*, https://www.thirteen.org/programs/now-on-pbs/now-on-pbs-afghanistan-the-forgotten-war/, aired on July 17, 2008. There is also a documentary by Bill Genile, *Dateline Afghanistan: Reporting the Forgotten War*, released February 10, 2009, on DVD.

4. Gil Barndollar, "Afghanistan—The Forgotten War Turns 17," *The Hill*, October 7, 2018, https://thehill.com/opinion/international/410204-afghanistan-the-forgotten-war-turns-17.

5. Dominic Tierney, "Forgetting Afghanistan: Americans Are Debating Whether to Fight ISIS, Without Acknowledging That They're Already at War," June 24, 2015, *The Atlantic*. The war in Afghanistan did not play a major role in the 2016 presidential campaign in the U.S. Hasib Danish Alikozai, "Afghanistan: The Forgotten War of the U.S. Presidential Campaign," *Voice of America*, September 2, 2016, https://www.voanews.com/east-asia-pacific/afghanistan-forgotten-war-us-presidential-campaign.

6. Links to all of the articles in the "Afghanistan Papers" can be found here: https://www.washingtonpost.com/graphics/2019/investigations/afghanistan-papers/afghanistan-war-confidential-documents/.

7. Meredith H. Lair, *Armed with Abundance: Consumerism & Soldiering in the Vietnam War.* (Chapel Hill: University of North Carolina Press, 2018), 26. Lair argues that because of the prevalence of combat narratives in the Vietnam War, "combat and deprivation continue to dominate the war stories we like to tell" (21).

8. Jake Tapper, *The Outpost: An Untold Story of American Valor* (New York: Little, Brown and Co., 2012), 620. The reference to the one-year war fought ten times comes from Neil Sheehan, *A Bright Shining Lie: John Paul Vann and America in Vietnam* (New York: Random House, 1988). During his 2007 deployment, Special Forces officer Michael Waltz thought, "it seemed as though we had fought six one-year wars over and over," Michael G. Waltz, *Warrior Diplomat: A Green Beret's Battles from Washington to Afghanistan* (Lincoln, NE: Potomac Books, 2014), 199; Brian Glyn Williams, a professor of Islamic history, described the Afghan War as 18 one-year wars since troops deployed every 12 months. Kevin Maurer, "Witness to a War," *Washington Post Magazine*, September 9, 2019, accessed September 18, 2019, https://washingtonpost.com/news/magazine/wp/2019/09/09/feature/the-afghanistan-war-is-likely-ending-one-longtime-correspondent-asks-was-it-worth-it/; Wesley Morgan, *The Hardest Place: The American Military Adrift in Afghanistan's Pech Valley* (New York: Random House, 2021), 393.

9. Lisa M. Mundey, "The Combatants' Experiences," in *Understanding the U.S. Wars in Iraq and Afghanistan.* Beth Bailey and Richards H. Immerman, eds. (New York: New York University Press, 2015), 187; Lair, 15–16.

10. Seth G. Jones, *In the Graveyard of Empires: America's War in Afghanistan* (New York: W. W. Norton & Company, 2010), 3–85. The most comprehensive volume on the entirety of the war thus far is Carter Malkasian, *The American War in Afghanistan: A History* (New York: Oxford University Press, 2021).

11. Anthony Tucker-Jones, *The Afghan War: Operation Enduring Freedom, 2001–2014* (Barnsley, South Yorkshire: Pen & Sword, 2014), 27, 29–30; See also Doug Stanton, *12 Strong: The Declassified True Story of the Horse Soldiers* (New York: Scribner, 2017). Jones, *Graveyard*, 90–91; Michael G. Walling, *Enduring Freedom, Enduring Voices: U.S. Operations in Afghanistan* (New York: Osprey, 2015), 27.

12. Richard W. Stewart, ed., *American Military History Volume II: The United States Army in a Global Era, 1917–2003* (Washington, DC: United States Army Center of Military History, 2005), 465; Tucker-Jones, 39. See also Richard W. Stewart, *Operation Enduring Freedom: The United States Army in Afghanistan, October 2001-March*

2002 (Washington, DC: U.S. Army Center of Military History, 2004) and Donald P. Wright, *A Different Kind of War: The United States Army in Operation Enduring Freedom (OEF), October 2001-September 2005* (Fort Leavenworth, KS: Combat Studies Institute, 2010); Jones, *Graveyard*, 91.

13. Stephen Tomat quoted in Steve Call, *Danger Close: Tactical Air Controllers in Afghanistan and Iraq* (College Station: Texas A&M University Press, 2007), 18.

14. Tucker-Jones, 39–40; Stewart, *American Military History*, 465–466; Walling 28–36. For a description of the development of the tactics, techniques, and procedures developed for close air support in OEF, please see Call, *Danger Close.*

15. John Hendren and Richard T. Cooper, "Fragile Alliances in a Hostile Land," in Clint Willis, ed., *Boots on the Ground: Stories of American Soldiers from Iraq and Afghanistan* (New York: Thunder Mountain, 2004), 70–73; Tucker-Jones, 40–41; Jones, *Graveyard*, 94. See also Eric Blehm, *The Only Thing Worth Dying For: How Eleven Green Berets Fought for a New Afghanistan* (New York: Harper Perennial, 2010).

16. Jones, *Graveyard*, 94; Tucker-Jones, 51; Stewart, *American Military History*, 469; Stewart, *Operation Enduring Freedom*, 30–44; Walling, 52–65. See also Sean Naylor, *Not a Good Day to Die: The Untold Story of Operation Anaconda* (New York: Berkley Caliber Books, 2005); Lester W. Grau and Dodge Billingsley, *Operation Anaconda: America's First Battle in Afghanistan* (Lawrence: University Press of Kansas, 2011).

17. Stewart, *American Military History*, 469; Donatella Lorch, "The Green Berets Up Close," in Willis, 25–31; Jonathan Steele, *Ghosts of Afghanistan: Hard Truths and Foreign Myths* (Berkeley, CA: Counterpoint, 2011), 283; Walling, 68, 84; Thomas Barfield, *Afghanistan: A Cultural and Political History* (Princeton: Princeton University Press, 2010), 313; "Population, Total—Bosnia and Herzegovina," *World Bank*, accessed July 3, 2020, https://data.worldbank.org/indicator/SP.POP.TOTL?end=1996&locations=BA&name_desc=false&start=1991. Afghanistan is about 13 times bigger than Bosnia and Herzegovina. "Country Size Comparison," *My Life Elsewhere*, accessed July 3, 2020, https://www.mylifeelsewhere.com/country-size-comparison/afghanistan/bosnia-and-herzegovina; Jones, *Graveyard*, 117, 127. Carter Malkasian argues that Rumsfeld was essentially correct: the longer the U.S. stayed in Afghanistan, the more Americans were seen as an occupier. The association of the U.S. with the government in Kabul undermined the democratically elected government. See Malkasian, *The American War*, 454–459.

18. Vishal Chandra, *The Unfinished War in Afghanistan, 2001-2014* (New Delhi: Pentagon, 2015), 16; Seth G. Jones, *Counterinsurgency in Afghanistan* (Santa Monica, CA: RAND, 2008), 38; Walling, 95; Brian F. Neumann and Colin J.

Williams, *The U.S. Army in Afghanistan: Operation Enduring Freedom, May 2005-January 2009* (Washington, DC: U.S. Army Center of Military History, 2020), 14–15.

19. Jones, *Graveyard*, 109; Tim Bird and Alex Marshall, *Afghanistan: How the West Lost Its Way* (New Haven: Yale University Press, 2011), 4. Colin Jackson describes the U.S. strategy in Afghanistan evolving in five phases, which he refers to as "triumph and tutelage," counterinsurgency, the surge, transition, and "a long goodbye." Colin Jackson, "U.S. Strategy in Afghanistan: A Tragedy in Five Acts," in *Our Latest Longest War: Losing Hearts and Minds in Afghanistan* Reprint Edition, ed. by Aaron O'Connell, (Chicago: University of Chicago Press, 2018), 71–108; Neumann and Williams, 19.

20. Barfield, 314–318; North Atlantic Treaty Organization, International Security Assistance Force History, accessed May 24, 2019, https://www.nato.int/cps/en/natohq/topics_69366.htm. Hereafter NATO, ISAF History; Carlotta Gall, *The Wrong Enemy: America in Afghanistan, 2001–2014* (New York: Houghton Mifflin Harcourt, 2014), 131; Bird and Marshall, 156; Walling, 114; Neumann and Williams, 27–28; Carlotta Gall, "U.S. Hands Over Southern Afghanistan Command to NATO," *New York Times*, August 1, 2006.

21. Gall, *The Wrong Enemy*, 131; Neumann and Williams, 14; Barfield, 319.

22. Antonio Giustozzi, *Koran, Kalashnikov, and Laptop: The Neo-Taliban Insurgency in Afghanistan* (New York: Columbia University Press, 2008), 102–103, 108–113; Gall, "U.S. Hands Over Southern Afghanistan Command to NATO"; Jones, *Graveyard*, 163.

23. Jones, *Graveyard*, 142; Jones, *Counterinsurgency*, 9–10.

24. Tapper, 354.

25. Gall, *Wrong Enemy*, 129–130; Neumann and Williams, 37–38; Barfield, 319; See also Jones, *Graveyard*, 209–212; Jack Fairweather, *The Good War: Why We Couldn't Win the War or the Peace in Afghanistan* (New York: Basic, 2014), 248–262.

26. Barfield, 319; Chandra, 105, 109, 113; McCaffrey quoted in Chandra, 113; Gall, *Wrong Enemy*, 191; Neumann and Williams, 77; Williams, 222–223.

27. Gall, *Wrong Enemy*, 194; Neumann and Williams, 28–29, 61, 73; John McGrath, *Wanat: Combat Action in Afghanistan, 2008* (Fort Leavenworth, KS: Combat Studies Institute, 2010), 182; Williams, 234; See also Clinton Romesha, *Red Platoon: A True Story of American Valor* (New York, Dutton, 2016). Air support and field artillery played a similar role in stopping an enemy assault on an American position in Gowardesh in June 2006. See John C. Mountcastle, "Firefight Above Gowardesh," in *Vanguard of Valor: Small Unit Actions in Afghanistan*, ed. by Donald P. Wright (Fort Leavenworth, KS: Combat Studies Institute, 2012).

28. Neumann and Williams, 77; Gall, *Wrong Enemy*, 219; Jason W. Davidson, "The Costs of

War to the United States Allies Since 9/11," Watson Institute, Brown University, Mary 12, 2021, accessed May 13, 2021, https://watson.brown.edu/costsofwar/files/cow/imce/papers/2021/Davidson_AlliesCostsofWar_Final.pdf; Amin Saikal, *Modern Afghanistan: A History of Struggle and Survival* (New York: I.B. Tauris, 2012), 260–261; Williams, 236–237.

29. Steele, 34; Williams, 237.

30. Steele, 35; Gall, *Wrong Enemy*, 230–231; Williams, 238.

31. Chandra, 172; Ahmed Azam, "2 Coalition Soldiers Killed by Attackers in Afghan Uniforms," *New York Times*, February 13, 2014.

32. Gall, *Wrong Enemy*, 272–273; Williams, 239, 251; Chandra, 115.

33. Malkasian, *The American War*, 384–385; 412–413.

34. Mark Mazzetti and Eric Schmitt, "In a Shift, Obama Extends U.S. Role in Afghan Combat," *New York Times*, November 22, 2014; NATO, ISAF History; Fazelminalah Qazizai, "The Taliban Are Getting Stronger in Afghanistan as U.S. and NATO Forces Exit," *NPR Morning Edition*, June 8, 2021; Cleve R. Wooston, Jr., Dan Lamothe, and John Wagner, "Biden Forcefully Defends Afghan Pullout Despite Taliban Gains," *Washington Post*, July 9, 2021, https://www.washingtonpost.com/politics/biden-afghanistan-taliban/2021/07/08/3fe9ef50-dfd3–11eb-ae31–6b7c5c34f0d6_story.html; Lara Seligman, "Sources: U.S. Troop Withdrawal from Afghanistan Complete 'For All Intents and Purposes,'" *Politico*, July 7, 2021, https://www.politico.com/news/2021/07/07/us-troop-withdrawal-afghanistan-498671; Alex Horton, Dan Lamothe, and Susannah George, "U.S. Escalates Airstrikes on Taliban, Officials Say, as Afghan Military Loses Ground," *Washington Post*, July 23, 2021, https://www.washingtonpost.com/world/2021/07/23/us-afghanistan-airstrikes/.

Chapter 1

1. Parnell, 272.

2. William A. Taylor, *Military Service and American Democracy: From World War II to the Iraq and Afghanistan Wars* (Lawrence: University Press of Kansas, 2016), 156–157; Miranda Summers Lowe, "The Gradual Shift to an Operational Reserve: Reserve Component Mobilizations in the 1990s," *Military Review* (May-June 2019), https://www.armyupress.army.mil/Journals/Military-Review/English-Edition-Archives/May-June-2019/Summers-Lowe-Reserve-1990s/; George M. Reynolds and Amanda Shendruk, "Demographics of the U.S. Military," Council on Foreign Relations, accessed October 15, 2019, https://www.cfr.org/article/demographics-us-military; Department of Defense, "Selected Manpower Statistics FY 2001," Selected Manpower Statistics, Historical Reports FY 1994–2009, p. 20, accessed September 20, 2019, https://www.dmdc.osd.mil/appj/

dwp/dwp_reports.jsp; Department of Defense, "Selective Reserve by Rank/Grade," September 30, 2001, accessed February 24, 2020, https://www.dmdc.osd.mil/appj/dwp/dwp_reports.jsp; Kelly Ann Holder, "They Are Half the Size of the Living Vietnam Veteran Population," Census Bureau, April 11, 2018, accessed June 18, 2019, Census.gov/programs-surveys/acs/; Quick Facts: United States, U.S. Census Bureau, accessed June 18, 2020, https://www.census.gov/quickfacts/fact/table/U.S./PST045219; Jennie W. Wegner, Caolionn O'Connell, and Linda Cottrell, "Examination of Recent Deployment Experience Across the Services and Components," (Santa Monica, CA: RAND Corporation, 2018), 3, https://www.rand.org/pubs/research_reports/RR1928.html.

3. Wegner, O'Connell, and Cottrell, 1, 6. Nearly all the oral history interviews that the author has read from the Operational Leadership Experiences through the U.S. Army Combat Studies Institute indicate multiple deployments to one or both theaters of operation; Mundey, in Bailey and Immerman, 177; Dan Lamothe and Alex Horton, "For Afghanistan Veterans, Old Feelings of Frustration and Loss Surface as the U.S. Prepares to End Its Longest War," *Washington Post*, April 14, 2021, https://www.washingtonpost.com/national-security/afghanistan-withdrawal-veterans-biden/2021/04/14/92ce7798–9c96–11eb-8a83–3bc1fa69c2e8_story.html; U.S. Military Casualties—Korean War Casualty Summary, Defense Casualty Analysis System, accessed August 26, 2020, https://dcas.dmdc.osd.mil/dcas/pages/report_korea_sum.xhtml; U.S. Military Casualties—Vietnam War Casualty Summary, Defense Casualty Analysis System, accessed August 26, 2020, https://dcas.dmdc.osd.mil/dcas/pages/report_vietnam_sum.xhtml; U.S. Military Casualties—Persian Gulf War, Defense Casualty Analysis System, accessed August 26, 2020, https://dcas.dmdc.osd.mil/dcas/pages/report_gulf_sum.xhtml; Chart by Jin Wu and Karen Yourish, in "U.S. to Withdrawal 7,000 Troops from Afghanistan, Officials Say," by Thomas Gibbons-Neff and Mujib Mashal, *New York Times*, December 20, 2018, accessed June 18, 2020, https://www.nytimes.com/2018/12/20/us/politics/afghanistan-troop-withdrawal.html;

4. Taylor, 169–178.

5. Steven Wallace, Interview by Jenna Fike, Operational Leadership Experiences Project, Combat Studies Institute, Ft. Leavenworth, Kansas, October 6, 2010, http://cgsc.cdmhost.com/cdm/singleitem/collection/p4013coll13/id/2055/rec/1.

6. Rich Lencz, Interview by Brad Helton, Operational Leadership Experiences Project, Combat Studies Institute, Ft. Leavenworth, Kansas, September 5, 2008, http://cgsc.contentdm.oclc.org/cdm/singleitem/collection/p4013coll13/id/1240/rec/1; For individual soldier tasks, see Headquarters, Department of the Army, *Warrior Skills Level 1: Soldier's Manual of Common Tasks*,

Soldier Training Publication No. 21–1-SMCT (Washington, D.C.: Department of the Army, May 2011). "See Yourself Culturally" includes identifying values, beliefs, and norms of culture; identifying influences that shape culture; and identifying the effect of bias on interpersonal interactions, among other elements. See 3–222 to 3–223.

7. Wallace interview.

8. "Actions Needed to Further Improve the Consistency of Combat Skills Training Provided to Army and Marine Corps Support Forces," GAO-10-465, Government Accountability Office, April 2010, accessed August 26, 2020, https://www.gao.gov/assets/310/303355.html.

9. Hurel Johnson, Interview by Laurence Lessard, Operational Leadership Experiences Project, Combat Studies Institute, Ft. Leavenworth, Kansas, September 17, 2007, http://cgsc.contentdm.oclc.org/cdm/singleitem/collection/p4013coll13/id/777/rec/1; Sean Parnell and John R. Bruning, *Outlaw Platoon: Heroes, Renegades, Infidels, and the Brotherhood of War in Afghanistan* reprint edition (New York: William Morrow, 2013), 123; Dietra Korando, Interview by John McCool, Operational Leadership Experiences Project, Combat Studies Institute, Ft. Leavenworth, Kansas, October 5, 2005, http://cgsc.cdmhost.com/cdm/ref/collection/p4013coll13/id/39; William Woodring, Interview by Laurence Lessard, Operational Leadership Experiences Project, Combat Studies Institute, Ft. Leavenworth, Kansas, December 12, 2006, http://cgsc.contentdm.oclc.org/cdm/singleitem/collection/p4013coll13/id/648/rec/1.

10. Stuart Farris, Interview by Laurence Lessard, Part II, Operational Leadership Experiences Project, Combat Studies Institute, Ft. Leavenworth, Kansas, December 6, 2007, http://cgsc.contentdm.oclc.org/cdm/singleitem/collection/p4013coll13/id/1020/rec/2; John Bates, Interview by Brad Helton, Part II, Operational Leadership Experiences Project, Combat Studies Institute, Ft. Leavenworth, Kansas, June 24, 2008, http://cgsc.cdmhost.com/cdm/singleitem/collection/p4013coll13/id/1095/rec/2; Stephen Boesen, Interview by Shawn O'Brien, Operational Leadership Experiences Project, Combat Studies Institute, Ft. Leavenworth, Kansas, July 7, 2008, http://cgsc.contentdm.oclc.org/cdm/singleitem/collection/p4013coll13/id/1360/rec/1.

11. Boesen interview.

12. Neil Arietta, Interview by Lisa M. Mundey, August 18, 2019, Personal transcript.

13. Bates interview.

14. Christian Anderson, Interview by Angie Slattery, Operational Leadership Experiences Project, Combat Studies Institute, Ft. Leavenworth, Kansas, November 10, 2010, http://cgsc.cdmhost.com/cdm/singleitem/collection/p4013coll13/id/2125/rec/1; Slusher interview; See also Diego Davila, Interview by Shawn O'Brien, Operational Leadership Experiences Project, Combat Studies Institute, Ft. Leavenworth, Kansas, June 10, 2008. http://cgsc.cdmhost.com/cdm/singleitem/collection/p4013coll13/id/1484/rec/1.

15. Anderson interview.

16. Dominic Cariello, Interview by John McCool, Operational Leadership Experiences Project, Combat Studies Institute, Ft. Leavenworth, Kansas, February 16, 2007, http://cgsc.contentdm.oclc.org/cdm/singleitem/collection/p4013coll13/id/720/rec/1.

17. Ross Davis, Interview by William Adler, Operational Leadership Experiences Project, Combat Studies Institute, Ft. Leavenworth, Kansas, December 19, 2007, http://cgsc.contentdm.oclc.org/cdm/singleitem/collection/p4013coll13/id/900/rec/1; See also Jeff Janke, Interview by Laurence Lessard, Operational Leadership Experiences Project, Combat Studies Institute, Ft. Leavenworth, Kansas, February 16, 2007, http://cgsc.cdmhost.com/cdm/singleitem/collection/p4013coll13/id/734/rec/1 and Ronald Walck, Interview by Shawn O'Brien, Operational Leadership Experiences Project, Combat Studies Institute, Ft. Leavenworth, Kansas, May 21, 2008, http://cgsc.contentdm.oclc.org/cdm/singleitem/collection/p4013coll13/id/1270/rec/1.

18. Woodring interview.

19. Boesen interview.

20. Anderson interview.

21. Davila interview.

22. John Schroeder, Interview by John McCool, Operational Leadership Experiences Project, Combat Studies Institute, Ft. Leavenworth, Kansas, February 16, 2007, http://cgsc.cdmhost.com/cdm/singleitem/collection/p4013coll13/id/733/rec/1.

23. Boesen interview.

24. John Hollar, Interview by Angie Slattery, Operational Leadership Experiences Project, Combat Studies Institute, Ft. Leavenworth, Kansas, May 25, 2011, http://cgsc.contentdm.oclc.org/cdm/singleitem/collection/p4013coll13/id/2359/rec/1.

25. Cariello interview; Kevin Busy, Interview by Allen Skinner, Operational Leadership Experiences Project, Combat Studies Institute, Ft. Leavenworth, Kansas, May 18, 2012, http://cgsc.cdmhost.com/cdm/singleitem/collection/p4013coll13/id/2683/rec/1; John Tabb, Interview by Marty Deckard, Part I, Operational Leadership Experiences Project, Combat Studies Institute, Ft. Leavenworth, Kansas, May 27, 2008, http://cgsc.contentdm.oclc.org/cdm/singleitem/collection/p4013coll13/id/1108/rec/1.

26. José Medina, Interviewed by Leo Hirrel, Quartermaster School, December 12, 2011.

27. Art Martori, "Guard Gets Set for Afghanistan: Virtual Battlefield Tests Arizona Troops," *East Valley Tribune* (Mesa, AZ), January 13, 2007.

28. Robert Reed, Interview by Angie Slattery, Operational Leadership Experiences Project, Combat Studies Institute, Ft. Leavenworth, Kansas, May 18, 2011, http://cgsc.contentdm.

oclc.org/cdm/singleitem/collection/p4013coll13/id/2341/rec/1.

29. Tabb Interview, Part I.

30. Marvin Linson, Interview by Angie Slattery, Operational Leadership Experiences Project, Combat Studies Institute, Ft. Leavenworth, Kansas, April 20, 2011, http://cgsc.contentdm.oclc.org/cdm/singleitem/collection/p4013coll13/id/2319/rec/1; See Also Edward Woodall, Interview with Joey Strudnicka, Operational Leadership Experiences Project, Combat Studies Institute, Ft. Leavenworth, Kansas, December 3, 2013, http://cgsc.contentdm.oclc.org/cdm/singleitem/collection/p4013coll13/id/3159/rec/2; Gabriel Diana, Interview by Lisa Beckenbaugh, Operational Leadership Experiences Project, Combat Studies Institute, Ft. Leavenworth, Kansas, May 14, 2013, http://cgsc.contentdm.oclc.org/cdm/singleitem/collection/p4013coll13/id/3072/rec/1; Michael Gray, Interview by Joey Strudnicka, Part II, Operational Leadership Experiences Project, Combat Studies Institute, Ft. Leavenworth, October 15, 2014, http://cgsc.contentdm.oclc.org/cdm/singleitem/collection/p4013coll13/id/3247/rec/4; Brendan McEvoy, Interview by Joey Strudnicka, Operational Leadership Experiences Project, Combat Studies Institute, Ft. Leavenworth, Kansas, November 13, 2013, http://cgsc.contentdm.oclc.org/cdm/singleitem/collection/p4013coll13/id/3124/rec/7; Andrew Boissonneau, Interview by Joey Strudnicka, Operational Leadership Experiences Project, Combat Studies Institute, Ft. Leavenworth, Kansas, September 17, 2014, http://cgsc.cdmhost.com/cdm/singleitem/collection/p4013coll13/id/3242/rec/1.

31. Michael J. Forsyth, *A Year in Command in Afghanistan: Journal of a United States Army Battalion Commander, 2009–2010* (Jefferson, NC: McFarland, 2017), 60–61, 72; Medina Interview.

32. Busy Interview; Forsyth, 82.

33. Robert S. Anders, *Winning Paktika: Counterinsurgency in Afghanistan* (Bloomington, IN: AuthorHouse, 2013), 6–7.

34. Timothy McGuire, in Christopher Koontz, Ed., *Enduring Voices: Oral Histories of the U.S. Army Experience in Afghanistan, 2003–2005* (Washington, DC: Center of Military History, United States Army, 2008), 406.

35. Paul Darling, *Taliban Safari: One Day in the Surkhagan Valley.* (Lawrence: University Press of Kansas, 2019), 2.

36. Forsyth, 90; See also Parnell, 5; Christy Erwin, Interview by Lisa Beckenbaugh, Operational Leadership Experiences Project, Combat Studies Institute, Ft. Leavenworth, Kansas, October 21, 2013. http://cgsc.contentdm.oclc.org/cdm/singleitem/collection/p4013coll13/id/3126/rec/2; and Marian Eide and Michael Gibler, *After Combat: True War Stories from Iraq and Afghanistan* (Lincoln: University of Nebraska Press, 2018), 80.

37. Adrian Lewis, *The American Culture of War: The History of U.S. Military Force from World War II to Operation Iraqi Freedom* (New York: Routledge, 2007), 389; Lair, 148; Kindsvatter, 139. In his Vietnam War memoir, Philip Caputo comments on the "alien landscape." Philip Caputo, *A Rumor of War* (New York: Picador, 1996), 68.

38. Parnell, 272.

39. Rico, 146.

40. Michael Golembesky and John R. Bruning, *Level Zero Heroes: The Story of U.S. Marine Special Operations in Bala Murghab, Afghanistan* (New York: St. Martin's, 2014), 31.

41. Walter Morris Herd, *Unconventional Warrior: Memoir of a Special Operations Commander in Afghanistan* (Jefferson, NC: McFarland, 2013), 137; Forsyth, 126.

42. Golembesky, 45.

43. Alvin Tilley, Interview by Angie Slattery, Operational Leadership Experiences Project, Combat Studies Institute, Ft. Leavenworth, Kansas, June 29, 2011, http://cgsc.contentdm.oclc.org/cdm/singleitem/collection/p4013coll13/id/2373/rec/1.

44. Rico, 146; See also Farris interview Part II, Meredith Fischer, "VA Soldiers Learn Drill of Life in Afghanistan," Richmond Times Dispatch, July 25, 2004; Leo Jenkins, "First Deployment, Winter 2004," in Marty Skovlund, Jr., Violence of Action: The Untold Stories of the 75th Ranger Regiment in the War on Terror (Colorado Springs: Blackside Concepts, 2014), 143.

45. Mike Elmore quoted in Walling, 30.

46. Farris interview Part II; See also Robin Fontes in Koontz, 460; McGuire, in Koontz, 407; and Eugene Augustin in Koontz, 435.

47. Fontes, in Koontz, 460; Andrew Simkewicz, in Andrew Carroll, ed., *Operation Homecoming: Iraq, Afghanistan, and the Home Front, in the Words of U.S. Troops and Their Families* (New York: Random House, 2006), 67; Rico, 76.

48. Forsyth, 79; Golembesky, 45; Tilley interview.

49. Golembesky, 45.

50. Anonymous service member quoted in Eide and Gibler, 65; See also Wallace interview; Golembesky, 37.

51. Anders, 49.

52. Mike Toomer quoted in *Doonesbury.com's the Sandbox: Dispatches from Troops in Iraq and Afghanistan*, ed. by David Stanford (Kansas City: Andrews McMeel, 2007), 275.

53. Toomer in Standford, 276–277.

54. Rico, 75, 80.

55. Nathaniel Fick, *One Bullet Away: The Making of a Marine Officer* (Boston: Houghton Mifflin, 2005), 122.

56. Anthony Hunter, in Koontz, 487; See also Amber Smith, *Danger Close: My Epic Journey as a Combat Helicopter Pilot in Iraq and Afghanistan* (New York: Atria, 2016), 216; Meredith Fischer, "VA Soldiers Learn Drill of Life in Afghanistan," Richmond Times Dispatch, July 25, 2004. The

"Wild West" was a common theme to describe Afghanistan for deployed troops.

57. Anders, 17.

58. The "old West" and "wild West" have complicated cultural interpretations. See Patricia Nelson Limerick, *The Legacy of Conquest* (New York: Norton, 1987); James R. Grossman, ed., *The Frontier in American Culture* (Berkeley: University of California Press, 1994); and Karen R. Jones and John Wills, *The American West: Competing Visions* (Edinburgh: Edinburgh University Press, 2009, ProQuest Ebook Central, accessed May 18, 2020.

59. Matt Smenos, in Standford, 217.

60. Kingsley, "Lost in the Sauce," in Skovlund, 372.

61. Anders, 169–170.

62. Rusty Bradley and Kevin Maurer, *Lions of Kandahar: The Story of a Fight Against All Odds* (New York: Bantam, 2015), 109.

63. Lou Albans, Interview by Laurence Lessard, Operational Leadership Experience Project, Combat Studies Institute, Ft. Leavenworth, Kansas, January 21, 2009, http://cgsc.contentdm.oclc.org/cdm/singleitem/collection/p4013coll13/id/1726/rec/6.

64. Evan Wright, "Not Much War, but Plenty of Hell," in Clint Willis, ed. *Boots on the Ground: Stories of American Soldiers from Iraq and Afghanistan.* (New York: Thunder Mountain, 2004), 129; Darling, 22–23. See also D. Scott Mann, *Game Changers: Going Local to Defeat Violent Extremists Special Forces & Law Enforcement Edition* (Leesburg, VA: Tribal Analysis Center, 2015), 26.

65. Doug Stanton, *Horse Soldiers: The Extraordinary Story of a Band of U.S. Soldiers Who Rode to Victory in Afghanistan* (New York: Scribner, 2010), 101.

66. Woodall interview; Michael Gray, Interview by Joey Strudnicka, Part II, Operational Leadership Experiences Project, Combat Studies Institute, Ft. Leavenworth, October 15, 2014, http://cgsc.contentdm.oclc.org/cdm/singleitem/collection/p4013coll13/id/3247/rec/4.

67. Boissonneau interview. Service members complained about the unpleasant smells in Iraq, too. See Mundey, in Bailey and Immerman, 179.

68. Forsyth, 79.

69. Eric Cox, "The Cave: Wounded," in Skovlund, 396.

70. Hunter, in Koontz, 487.

71. Brian Glyn Williams, *Afghanistan Declassified: A Guide to America's Longest War.* (Philadelphia: University of Pennsylvania Press, 2012), 51; Fick, 122. Leo Jenkins also describes the terrain as looking exactly like the area in Arizona where he grew up. Jenkins, 68.

72. Rico, 75.

73. Romesha, 78; Kristine Schellhaas, *15 Years of War: How the Longest War in U.S. History Affected a Military Family in Love, Loss, and the Cost of Service* (Life Publishing, 2016), 225.

74. Thomas W. Young, *The Speed of Heat: An Airlift Wing at War in Iraq and Afghanistan* (Jefferson, NC: McFarland, 2008), 38.

75. Erik Jorgensen, Interview by Douglas Cubbison, 10th Mountain Division, Fort Drum, New York, January 22, 2007, http://cgsc.contentdm.oclc.org/cdm/singleitem/collection/p4013coll13/id/1005/rec/1.

76. Parnell, 19; Stephanie L. Carl, "Combined Task Force Bronco Keeps Vehicles Ready to Roll," U.S. Department of Defense Information, December 30, 2004.

77. Bradley, *Lions of Kandahar,* 97.

78. Wallace interview.

79. Craig Mullaney, *The Unforgiving Minute: A Soldier's Education* (New York: Penguin, 2009), 226.

80. Waltz, 66, 111.

81. Linderman, 241; Troops in all 20th century U.S. wars found beauty at moments. Peter S. Kindsvatter, *American Soldiers: Ground Combat in the World Wars, Korea, and Vietnam* (Lawrence: University Press of Kansas, 2003), 65.

82. "Mountains," Peter R. Blood, ed. *Afghanistan: A Country Study.* Washington: GPO for the Library of Congress, 2001. Accessed January 28, 2018, http://countrystudies.us/afghanistan/32.htm.

83. Steve Truax quoted in Young, 38.

84. Mike Langley quoted in Young, 45.

85. Bradley, *Lions of Kandahar,* 104.

86. Parnell 148–149; Dementors appeared in *Harry Potter and the Prisoner of Azkaban* (2004).

87. Reed interview.

88. Clint Douglass, in Carroll, 74; Internet Movie Database, accessed January 28, 2018, http://www.imdb.com/title/tt0126158/?ref_=nv_sr_1.

89. "The Bala Hissar Gate," British Library Online Gallery, accessed February 8, 2018, http://www.bl.uk/onlinegallery/onlineex/apac/photocoll/t/019pho0000430s3u00001000.html.

90. Andrew Stock, "On the Shoulders of Dead Men," in Christine Dumaine Leche, ed., *Outside the Wire: American Soldiers' Voices from Afghanistan.* (Charlottesville, VA: University Press of Virginia, 2013), 119.

91. Mullaney, 226.

92. Jason Thompson quoted in Harry Spiller, *Veterans of Iraq and Afghanistan: Personal Accounts of 22 Americans Who Served.* (Jefferson, NC: McFarland, 2014), 95.

93. Rico, 75–76.

94. Anders, 385.

95. Anders, 48.

96. Parnell 20; See also Tupper, 11.

97. Quoted in J.S. Newton, "NC Troops Weather Seasonal Winds in Afghanistan," *Fayetteville Observer,* reprinted in Associated Press, May 22, 2002. See also Paul Haven, "Beige Haze Over Kandahar Plays Havoc with Soldiers and Machines," *Associated Press,* March 7, 2002.

98. Curtis Garrett quoted in Young, 33.

99. Haven, "Beige Haze Over Kandahar."

100. Anonymous service member quoted in Eide and Gibler, 80.

101. Bradley, *Lions of Kandahar*, 176.

102. Anders, 7.

103. Terry Sellers, in Koontz, 381; The same description appears in Golembesky, 37–38; Smith, 229; James F. Christ, *ETT... Embrace the Suck! Embedded Tactical Trainers with the Afghan National Army* (Independently Published 2017), 163–164.

104. Mullaney, 226.

105. Edward Smith quoted in Haven, "Beige Haze Over Kandahar."

106. Thomas Doherty, Interview by Lisa M. Mundey, December 28, 2018, Personal transcript.

107. Rico, 147; José Githens, "Run Little Girl Run... It's Not Safe Here," in Leche, 50.

108. Chris Wells, Interview by Pete Boisson, Operational Leadership Experiences Project, Combat Studies Institute, Ft. Leavenworth, Kansas, July 25, 2005, http://cgsc.contentdm.oclc.org/cdm/singleitem/collection/p4013coll13/id/317/rec/1; See also Busy interview; Michael J. Doidge, "Flipping the Switch: Weapons Platoon Movement to Contact in Zhari District," in *Vanguard of Valor: Small Unit Actions in Afghanistan*, ed. by Donald P. Wright (Fort Leavenworth, KS: Combat Studies Institute Press, 2012), 67.

109. Rico, 145.

110. Bradley, *Lions of Kandahar*, 109.

111. Charlie Duggan, Jr., quoted in Walling, 180.

112. José Githens, "Run Little Girl Run... It's Not Safe Here," in Leche, 50.

113. Bradley, *Lions of Kandahar*, 134.

114. Tupper, 9.

115. Lauren Fish and Paul Scharre, "The Soldier's Heavy Load," *Center for New American Security*, September 26, 2018, accessed July 3, 2020, https://www.cnas.org/publications/reports/the-soldiers-heavy-load-1; Tupper, 10; Darling conveys the same message. Darling, 3.

116. Bradley, *Lions of Kandahar*, 106.

117. Christopher Plummer, Interview by James Evenson, Operational Leadership Experiences Project, Combat Studies Institute, Ft. Leavenworth, Kansas, June 6, 2006, http://cgsc.contentdm.oclc.org/cdm/singleitem/collection/p4013coll13/id/206/rec/1.

118. Christy Erwin, Interview by Lisa Beckenbaugh, Operational Leadership Experiences Project, Combat Studies Institute, Ft. Leavenworth, Kansas, October 21, 2013, http://cgsc.contentdm.oclc.org/cdm/singleitem/collection/p4013coll13/id/3126/rec/2.

119. Tapper 323; Anders 388–390.

120. Tupper 169; See also Lencz interview.

121. Anders, 443.

122. Kindsvatter, 41–42.

123. Anders, 412, 431.

124. Stock, in Leche, 118.

125. Logan A. Lewis, "The Cave," in Skovlund, 391–392.

126. Smith, 180.

127. Anders 434, 442, 448–449, 463.

128. Busy interview.

129. Rico, 219.

130. Tapper, 59; Michael Creedon, Interview by Lisa M. Mundey, June 3, 2020, Personal Transcript.

131. Rico, 145.

132. Romesha, 78.

133. Tapper, 60; Romesha, 78; Michael S. Mundey, personal communication, July 20, 2020. William Donnelly, personal communication, August 25, 2020. Camel spiders are in the class Arachnida, order Solifugae, family Galeodes. "Camel Spiders," *National Geographic*, accessed July 3, 2020, https://www.nationalgeographic.com/animals/invertebrates/c/camel-spider/.

134. Stanton, 178; Rico, 9; Paul Haven, "Look in Those Boots, Soldier! Troops Not the Only Thing Occupying Southern Afghan Base," *Associated Press*, March 8, 2002; Helen Thorpe, *Soldier Girls: The Battles of Three Women at Home and at War* (New York: Scribner, 2014), 134; Kindsvatter, 43. Lice particularly vexed World War I doughboys. World War II troops dealt with mosquitoes, ticks, flies, fleas, gnats, mites, leeches, sweatbees, spiders, scorpions, land crabs, chiggers, biting and stinging ants. Troops in Vietnam complained of mosquitoes and leeches. Kindsvatter, 43–44.

135. Thompson quoted in Spiller, 95.

136. Rico, 134.

137. Forsyth, 89.

138. Parnell, 36.

139. Bradley, *Lions of Kandahar*, 12.

140. Evan Wright in Willis, 121.

141. Romesha, 82–83.

Chapter 2

1. Meredith H. Lair, *Armed with Abundance: Consumerism & Soldiering in the Vietnam War* (Chapel Hill: University of North Carolina Press, 2018), 5.

2. Lair, 28. The epilogue, "From Vietnam to Iraq," illustrates the parallels of consumer culture in the Iraq War, much of which is also relevant for the Afghan War. See Lair, 222–237. For conditions in Iraq, see Mundey in Bailey and Immerman, 179–180.

3. Herd, 88. Zulu time is mentioned frequently in memoirs, interviews, and newspaper articles; Greenwich Mean Time, accessed March 13, 2020, https://greenwichmeantime.com/timezone/asia/afghanistan/; Evan Wright, "Not Much War, but Plenty of Hell," in Willis, 123–124.

4. Stanton, 65, 349.

5. Neumann and Williams, 21.

6. Scott Kaufman, quoted in Walling, 48–49.

7. Seena Simon, "100 Percent Totally Self-Sufficient; Tanker Airlift Control Element Members Help Coordinate Airfield Operations in Afghanistan," *Air Force Times*, January 28, 2002.

8. Ray quoted in Walling, 72.

9. Sean D. Naylor, "Life Savers: New Armor Stemmed Casualties in Bagram, but Surgical Team Still Had Its Hands Full," *Army Times*, April 22, 2002.

10. Barry Bearak, "A Nation Challenged: The Battle," *New York Times*, March 12, 2002.

11. Mary Beth Sheridan, "Afghan Base Evolve with 'Open-Ended' Commitment by U.S.," *Washington Post*, June 1, 2002. The Post-Exchange system had been established in 1895 and became the military's standard shopping venue by the Vietnam War. See Lair, 148–149; Michael Tarm, "U.S. Base Becoming Center of Trade, Relative Prosperity," *Daily Review*, January 15, 2003.

12. Mark Kennedy, "War Room Is Key to Afghan Operations," *San Diego Union-Tribune*, February 18, 2003.

13. Sean Naylor, "It's Not Over: Soldiers of the 101st Airborne Division Face Constant Risk Every Day in Kandahar," *Army Times*, February 4, 2002.

14. Matthew Cox, "AC Will Help Soldiers Beat Unrelenting Desert Heat," *Army Times*, May 27, 2002; Sean Naylor, "Kandahar Proving to Be Harsh Host," *Army Times*, February 4, 2002; Kimberley Hefling, "Pssst! Swap Scarf for Knife? U.S. Troops Barter and Beg for Scarce Items on Afghan Base," *Associated Press*, February 6, 2002; Kimberly Hefling, Cold Showers, Meal Packets, and Oh-So-Public Latrines: U.S. Forces Tough It Out in Afghanistan," *Associated Press*, January 29, 2002.

15. Evan Wright in Willis, 134.

16. Evan Wright in Willis, 134; Walling, 50.

17. Romesha, 81.

18. Schellhaas, 256.

19. Jay Kirell, "Here's What Happens When Your Local Porta Potty Cleaner Just Up and Leaves," *Task & Purpose*, accessed June 18, 2019, https://taskandpurpose.com/u/jay_kirell. Bob Vila hosted *This Old House*, *Bob Vila's Home Again*, *Bob Vila*, and *Restore America with Bob Vila*. "About Bob Vila," accessed July 27, 2020, https://www.bobvila.com/pages/about-bob.

20. Evan Wright in Willis, 124. Dysentery proved a common ailment for troops in the wars the U.S. fought in the 20th century. Kindsvatter, 44–45; Meredith Fischer, "Medics Take Post in Ghazni," *Richmond Times Dispatch*, July 26, 2004; See also Augustine in Koontz, 434; Sean Naylor, "Kandahar Proving to Be Harsh Host," *Army Times*, February 4, 2002.

21. Kindsvatter, 95–97. Troops secured alcohol in World War I, World War II, and Korea, while beer was issued to troops in Vietnam. See also Lair, 172 for alcohol rations in Vietnam; Schellhaas, 237; See also Michael S. Mormino in Spiller, 80; Junger, 151; "A Day in the Life of a CJC-MOTF Soldier," PowerPoint slides, OEF D-152 CD, Civil Affairs & Psychological Operations, "Operation Enduring Freedom: Historical Collection," 126th Military History Detachment, 2003,

U.S. Army Heritage and Education Center, Carlisle Barracks, PA; Thorpe, *Soldier Girls*, 146, 159. See also "In Afghan Killings Case, Questions Over Alcohol," *CBS News*, March 16, 2012, https://www.cbsnews.com/news/in-afghan-killings-case-questions-over-alcohol/.

22. Herd, 71.

23. Declan Walsh, "Fighting Tooth and Nail in Afghanistan: Burger King and Manicures Raise Morale for U.S. Troops," *Guardian*, September 27, 2004; See also Drew Brown, "Ban on Sex for Soldiers in Afghanistan Is Lifted… Sort Of," *Stars and Stripes*, May 14, 2008, https://www.stripes.com/news/ban-on-sex-for-soldiers-in-afghanistan-is-lifted-sort-of-1.78800; "U.S. Soldiers in Afghanistan Using Craigslist to Have Sex with Each Other on Base," *Daily Mail*, July 30, 2013, https://www.dailymail.co.uk/news/article-2381367/U-S-soldiers-Afghanistan-using-Craigslist-hook-base.html.

24. Thorpe, *Soldier Girls*, 150–151, 220. Thorpe reports one account of a female soldier who went to Germany to obtain an abortion; Evan Wright in Willis, 124; Steven Beardsley, "U.S. Soldier Gave Birth While Deployed to Afghanistan," *Stars and Stripes*, October 25, 2012, https://www.stripes.com/news/us-soldier-gave-birth-while-deployed-in-afghanistan-1.194562. Oral history interviews and memoirs did not include any references to unwanted sexual activities. For discussion of sexual assault, please see U.S. Commission on Civil Rights, "Sexual Assault in the Military," September 2013, https://www.usccr.gov/pubs/docs/09242013_Statutory_Enforcement_Report_Sexual_Assault_in_the_Military.pdf; "Department of Defense Annual Report on Sexual Assault in the Military: Fiscal Year 2016," accessed August 27, 2020, https://sapr.mil/public/docs/reports/FY16_Annual/FY16_SAPRO_Annual_Report.pdf; and the documentary by Kirby Dick, *Invisible War* (Independent Lens, 2013); Brown, "Ban on Sex"; See also "Penalties Imposed for Soldiers Who Get Pregnant," *NPR Morning Edition* transcript, December 23, 2009, https://www.npr.org/templates/story/story.php?storyId=121798362.

25. Thorpe, *Soldier Girls*, 146, 153, 222.

26. "Report Blames Lapses on Stryker Commander—532-Page Report Finds Colonel Ignored Doctrine, Proper Procedure in Leading Undisciplined BCT," *Military Times*, March 27, 2013, https://www.militarytimes.com/2013/03/27/report-blames-lapses-on-stryker-commander-532-page-report-finds-colonel-ignored-doctrine-proper-procedure-in-leading-undisciplined-bct/.

27. "In Afghans Killings Case," *CBS News*; Michael Martinez, "Opiates Killed 8 Americans in Afghanistan, Army Records Show," *CNN*, April 23, 2012, accessed June 5, 2020, https://www.cnn.com/2012/04/21/us/afghanistan-soldier-drug-overdoses/index.html. C.P. O'Brien, M. Oster, and E. Morden, eds., *Substance Use Disorders in the U.S. Armed Forces*, Washington, DC: National

Academies Press, February 21, 2013, accessed June 5, 2020, https://www.ncbi.nlm.nih.gov/books/NBK207276/.

28. Thorpe, *Soldier Girls*, 186, 198–199.

29. Sean D. Naylor, "Soldiers in Afghanistan Value Safety Over Fashion," *Army Times*, February 18, 2002.

30. Matthew Cox, "AC Will Help Soldiers Beat Unrelenting Desert Heat," *Army Times*, May 27, 2002; Charles J. Hanley, "A Army Base, Movies, Email Means 'It's Getting Better All the Time,'" *Associated Press*, March 22, 2002. The military screened movies for troops starting in World War II. Kindsvatter, 95; The U.S. military provided similar recreational activities for service members deployed to Vietnam, with the addition of alcohol. Lair, 116, 134; Amy Waldman, "A Nation Challenged," *New York Times*, March 31, 2002.

31. Matthew Cox, "AC Will Help Soldiers Beat Unrelenting Desert Heat," *Army Times*, May 27, 2002.

32. James Brooke, "Vigilance and Memory: Kandahar; Pentagon Tells Troops in Afghanistan: Shape Up and Dress Right," *New York Times*, September 12, 2002; See also Doherty Interview. Vietnam-era bases also decreed state-side grooming standards. See Lair, 38.

33. Chris Brummitt, "Troops Live It Up a Little in Afghan Desert Base," *Associated Press*, October 27, 2002; Evan Wright in Willis, 120.

34. Graham Thomson, "A Town Like Ponoka: Kandahar Air Field an Enclave of Western Ways," *Edmonton Journal*, February 16, 2007; "Base Improvements: A New Look for Kandahar," Department of Defense, October 20, 2003.

35. Rajiv Chandrasekaran, *Little America: War Within the War for Afghanistan* (New York: Alfred A. Knopf, 2012), 156–158.

36. Chandrasekaran, 157–158.

37. Declan Walsh, "Fighting Tooth and Nail in Afghanistan: Burger King and Manicures Raise Morale for U.S. Troops," *Guardian*, September 27, 2004.

38. Carlotta Gall, "At Afghan Bazaar, Military Offers Dollars for Stolen Data," *New York Times*, April 15, 2006.

39. Meredith Fischer, "'Welcome,' Company C/ Virginia National Guard Troops Become Part of Task Force Thunder," *Richmond Times Dispatch*, July 15, 2004.

40. Meredith Fischer, "The 'Good Base" Has a Lousy View," *Richmond Times Dispatch*, July 16, 2004; Meredith Fischer, "Watchful Waiting at Base," *Richmond Times Dispatch*, July 19, 2004; Walsh, "Fighting Tooth and Nail in Afghanistan"; "AAFES Rolls Out Tastes of Home for Deployed Troops," U.S. Department of Defense Information, November 8, 2004; Thorpe, *Soldier Girls*, 162; Smith, 177.

41. Marvin Linson, Interview by Angie Slattery, Operational Leadership Experiences Project, Combat Studies Institute, Ft. Leavenworth, Kansas, April 20, 2011, http://cgsc.contentdm.oclc.org/cdm/singleitem/collection/p4013coll13/id/2319/rec/1.

42. Meredith Fischer, "Soldiers Condemn Attack on Voter Registration Site," *Richmond Times Dispatch*, July 29, 2004.

43. Creedon interview.

44. Meredith Fischer, "Welcome to Camp Tiger; Lots of Rock to Go Around," *Richmond Times Dispatch*, July 23, 2004; Meredith Fischer, "Meeting Children of War," *Richmond Times Dispatch*, July 26, 2004.

45. Stanton, 65.

46. Bradley, *Lions of Kandahar*, 21.

47. Lair, 85; Anders, 158, 457.

48. Kyle Kivioja, Interview by Sean Kaubisch, Operational Leadership Experiences Project, Combat Studies Institute, Ft. Leavenworth, Kansas, April 10, 2015, http://cgsc.contentdm.oclc.org/cdm/singleitem/collection/p4013coll13/id/3269/rec/1.

49. Dakota Meyer and Bing West, *Into the Fire: A Firsthand Account of the Most Extraordinary Battle in the Afghan War* (New York: Random House, 2012), 9. Combat Outposts are not found in military doctrine, which explains the flexible use of the term. See also Timothy Hsia, "A Quick Review of Combat Outposts," *Small Wars Journal*, November 27, 2008, https://smallwarsjournal.com/blog/journal/docs-temp/138-hsia.pdf.

50. Romesha, 52.

51. Romesha, 53.

52. Christopher Niemeyer, in Spiller, 82.

53. Chad Rickard, *Mayhem 337: Memoir of a Combat Advisor in Afghanistan* (BookBaby, 2019), xiv, 90.

54. Romesha, 8, 60, 81, 119; COP Keating was named after First Lieutenant Ben Keating, continuing a naming trend from the Vietnam War to name military installations after the fallen. The naming convention became problematic in Afghanistan when outposts were abandoned or shut down after being named for a fallen service member. See Lair, 194; Tapper, 330

55. Casey Crowley quoted in Walling, 175.

56. Dave Lamborn quoted in Walling, 174.

57. Anders, 11, 47–48, 457.

58. Rico, 75–76.

59. Tapper, 296.

60. Rico, 255.

61. Romesha, 65; Tapper, 366.

62. Rickard, 38.

63. McGrath, *Wanat*, 102–103.

64. Eric Long, Interviewed by Leo Hirrel, January 24, 2012, Quartermaster School.

65. Eric Lanham, Interview by Laurence Lessard, Operational Leadership Experiences Project, Combat Studies Institute, Ft. Leavenworth, Kansas, February 22, 2007, http://cgsc.contentdm.oclc.org/cdm/singleitem/collection/p4013coll13/id/1003/rec/1.

66. Michael Slusher, Interview by Laurence Lessard, Operational Leadership Experiences

Project, Combat Studies Institute, Ft. Leavenworth, Kansas, February 16, 2007, http://cgsc.cdmhost.com/cdm/singleitem/collection/p4013coll13/id/504/rec/1.

67. Rico, 258; See also Mormino in Spiller, 78.
68. Romesha, 90.
69. Kindsvatter, 51–54; Rico, 269.
70. Parnell, 251–252.
71. Rickard, 152.
72. John Schroeder, Interview by John McCool, Operational Leadership Experiences Project, Combat Studies Institute, Ft. Leavenworth, Kansas, February 16, 2007, http://cgsc.cdmhost.com/cdm/singleitem/collection/p4013coll13/id/733/rec/1.
73. Waltz, 308.
74. Millhouse quoted in Walling, 82.
75. Resentment from combatants toward non-combat troops is common in America's wars. See Kindsvatter, 246–251.
76. Lair, 8, 26–27; Kindsvatter, 248.
77. Tupper, 110. For Iraq, see Mundey in Bailey and Immerman, 180. One military blogger described service members on FOBs as "Fobalonians." "Thanksgiving in the Land of Sandcastles," The Sandbox, November 22, 2007, https://gocomics.typepad.com/the_sandbox/2007/11/thanksgiving-in.html.
78. Lair, 27.
79. Parnell, 218.
80. Christ, 74.
81. Kindsvatter, 252.
82. Anders, 292.
83. Parnell, 294.
84. Parnell, 219; Christ, 116.
85. Parnell, 220.
86. Christ, 105.
87. Lair, 27.
88. Parnell, 372.
89. Thorpe, Soldier Girls, 170.
90. Parnell, 372.
91. Darling, 162.
92. Reid Geary in "As Withdrawal Date Approaches, UNLC Veterans Recount a Day in Afghanistan," The Rebel Yell: University of Nevada- Las Vegas, February 25, 2013.
93. John Alderton in Young, 141.
94. Chase Salmela, in Spiller, 64.
95. Aaron Ruona quoted in Walling, 210–211.
96. Quoted in Junger, 81.
97. Downtime activities are the same for U.S. troops deployed in Iraq. See Mundey, in Bailey and Immerman, 188. Lair describes similar behaviors in Vietnam, Lair, 31.
98. Jacob Barnes (pseudonym), Interview by Lisa M. Mundey, May 22, 2020, personal transcript; Romesha, 91. Several memoirs and interviews mention binge-watching entire seasons of television shows; Arietta interview.
99. Jenkins in Skovlund, 145.
100. McGarry, 201, 233; Romesha, 83, Jenkins, in Skovlund, 140; Darling, 5; Parnell, 221.
101. McGarry, 227.

102. Jenkins, in Skovlund, 145.
103. Rico, xiii–xiv.
104. Quoted in Junger, 54.
105. Junger, 151.
106. Erwin interview. It was similar in Vietnam, see Lair, 30.
107. Scott Cunningham, Interview by Lisa Beckenbaugh, Operational Leadership Experiences Project, Combat Studies Institute, Ft. Leavenworth, Kansas, August 15, 2013, http://cgsc.contentdm.oclc.org/cdm/singleitem/collection/p4013coll13/id/3095/rec/5.
108. Jenkins, Lest We Forget, 69.
109. Romesha, 97.
110. Junger, 222.
111. Smith, 230.
112. Mark Feller quoted in Spiller, 101.
113. Kindsvatter, 91.
114. Lair, 158; Anders, 420.
115. Tupper, 140.
116. Nok-Noi Hauger, "Email Connects Soldiers to Home," Bangor Daily News, March 18, 2004.
117. Anders, 420.
118. Meyer, 11.
119. Wallace interview.
120. Walck interview.
121. Janke interview; Anderson interview.
122. Mundey, in Bailey and Immerman, 188.
123. Forsyth, 99.
124. Darling, 165.
125. Romesha, 90.
126. Forsyth, 121, 313; Skovlund, 32.
127. Tupper, 94.
128. Darling, 165.
129. Parnell, 223.
130. Anders, 203.
131. Meredith Fischer, "Soldiers Add Their Stamps to Requests/They're Hungry for Tastes of Home," Richmond Times Dispatch, July 24, 2004.
132. Fischer, "Soldiers Add Their Stamps to Requests"; Schellhaas, 256; Wallace inteview.
133. Wallace interview.
134. Anders, 269, 287.
135. Mary Beth Sheridan, "In Afghanistan, Troops Pause for a Special Memorial Day," Washington Post, May 28, 2002.
136. Rickard, 174.
137. Regan Morris, "Games, Tight Security Mark Holiday for Homesick U.S. Forces," Associated Press, July 4, 2002.
138. Smith, 211.
139. Herd, 175.
140. Mike Eckel, "Thanksgiving at Bagram Is Another Day Closer to Going Home," Associated Press, November 27, 2002; Mike Eckel, " Thanksgiving in the Middle of War on Terror," Associated Press, November 28, 2002; Jim Teeple, "U.S. Troops in Afghanistan Celebrate Thanksgiving," Voice of America News, November 28, 2002.
141. Thorpe, Soldier Girls, 180.
142. "Soldiers Feast on Turkeys They Raised," Chicago Daily Herald, November 27, 2009.

143. Forsyth, 217.

144. "Group of American and British Soldiers Celebrate Christmas at Bagram Air Base," CBS News Transcripts, December 25, 2001.

145. Catherine Callaway, "U.S. Troops Celebrating Christmas in Afghanistan," *CNN*, December 24, 2002.

146. Michael Kitchen, "U.S. Troops in Afghanistan Enjoy Holiday Festivities," *Voice of America News*, December 25, 2003.

147. Rickard, 39.

148. Jim Maceda, "Troops Mark Holiday Far from Home," NBC News Transcripts, December 25, 2009.

149. Rickard, 39.

Chapter 3

1. Eide and Gibler, 61.

2. Bird and Marshall, 6.

3. Doherty interview.

4. Bird and Marshall, 6.

5. Anders, 196.

6. Parnell, 25.

7. Waltz, 64–66.

8. Slusher interview.

9. Erwin interview.

10. ODA 553 Area Assessment: The Hazara Area (Central Mountainous Region of Afghanistan) and Friendly and Enemy Forces within the Area, 126 OEF D 006 CD, Civil Affairs & Psychological Operations, Operation Enduring Freedom: Historical Collection, 126th Military History Detachment, 2003, United States Army Education and Heritage Center, Carlisle Barracks, PA.

11. ODA 553 Area Assessment.

12. Gall, *Wrong Enemy*, 56, 80; Anand Gopal, *No Good Men Among the Living: America, the Taliban, and the War Through Afghan Eyes* (Minneapolis: HighBridge, 2015), 38.

13. Anders, 15.

14. Darling, 155; Christ, 54; See also Rico, 97; Herd, 164.

15. Anders, 95–96; See also Rico, 86.

16. Forsyth, 88; See also Doug Traversa, in Stanford, 83.

17. Thorpe, *Soldier Girls*, 140; Meg Jones, "Police Find Few Laws and Much Disorder," *Associated Press*, July 11, 2006.

18. Creedon interview; Forsyth, 221; Anders, 329.

19. Forsyth, 148.

20. Brown interview.

21. Forsyth, 152–153, 161.

22. Metin Gurcan, *What Went Wrong in Afghanistan? Understanding Counter-Insurgency Efforts in Tribalized Rural and Muslim Environments* (Helion & Company Limited, 2016), 57.

23. Tupper, 127.

24. Walck interview.

25. Rico, 146; Schroeder interview.

26. Christ, 220–221.

27. Herd, 137.

28. Tupper, 128.

29. Tupper, 177.

30. McGuire in Koontz, 406; For a fuller explanation of the tenets of *Pashtunwali*, see Aaron O'Connell, "Moving Mountains: Cultural Friction in the Afghan War," in O'Connell, 30–33.

31. Hunter in Koontz, 503. See also Reed oral history interview.

32. Augustine in Koontz, 436.

33. Rico 145–146.

34. Cariello interview.

35. Kimberly Evans, interviewed by J. Patrick Hughes and Lisa Mundey, February 13, 2007, U.S. Army Center of Military History, Ft. McNair.

36. Hunter in Koontz, 503.

37. Anders, 408.

38. Anders, 410.

39. Gall, *Wrong Enemy*, 60.

40. Edward Croot, Interview by John Bauer, Part II, Operational Leadership Experiences Project, Combat Studies Institute, Ft. Leavenworth, Kansas, February 17, 2007, http://cgsc.contentdm.oclc.org/cdm/singleitem/collection/p4013coll13/id/816/rec/2.

41. Gall, *Wrong Enemy*, 59–60; Bird and Marshall, 164; See also Mann, 50.

42. Doherty interview.

43. Gopal, 75–76.

44. Herd, 139.

45. Forsyth, 309.

46. Anders, 119; See also Doherty interview; Parnell, 14.

47. Smith, 208.

48. Christ, 288–289. UNICEF does not list Afghanistan as one of the countries where female genital mutilation is prevalent. "Female Genital Mutilation," UNICEF, accessed June 3, 2020, https://data.unicef.org/topic/child-protection/female-genital-mutilation/.

49. Doherty interview.

50. Allison M. Roberts, "Danville Area Marine Helps Develop Female Engagement Team in Afghanistan," *Danville Register & Bee*, May 19, 2013; Raymond T. Kareko, "Female Engagement Teams," *NCO Journal* (October 2019), accessed June 3, 2020, https://www.armyupress.army.mil/Portals/7/nco-journal/images/2019/October/FET/FET.pdf; Walling, 85–86; Colby Brown, "FET: Female Marines Build Relationships in Helmand," Defense Department Documents, U.S. Marine Corps Release, May 3, 2011; Elisabeth Bumiller, "New War Goal: Let Women Reach Women; Marine 'Female Engagement Teams' to Patrol in Afghanistan," *Pittsburgh Post-Gazette*, March 7, 2010.

51. "'FET' to Fight: Female Engagement Team Makes History," Defense Department Documents, U.S. Army Releases, April 18, 2013.

52. Michael J. Doidge, "Combat Multipliers: Tactical Female Engagement Teams in Paktika Province," in *Vanguard of Valor II: Small Unit Actions in Afghanistan*, ed. by Donald P. Wright

(Fort Leavenworth, KS: Combat Studies Institute, 2012), 107.

53. Bumiller, "New War Goal: Let Women Reach Women."

54. Eileen Rivers, *Beyond the Call: Three Women on the Front Lines in Afghanistan* (New York: Da Capo, 2018), 47; Doidge, "Combat Multipliers," in Wright, *Vanguard of Valor II*, 108–109.

55. Doidge, "Combat Multipliers," in Wright, *Vanguard of Valor II*, 106.

56. Rivers, 33.

57. Dwight A. Henderson, "Female Engagement Team Helps Establish Connection Between Marines and Afghan Women," Defense Department Documents, U.S. Marine Corps Releases, December 28, 2009; Doidge, "Combat Multipliers," in Wright, *Vanguard of Valor II*, 109, 112.

58. Rivers, 5; Doidge, "Combat Multipliers," in Wright, *Vanguard of Valor II*, 111–112, 116–118.

59. "Female Engagement Team Finds Strength Behind Burkas," States News Service, November 8, 2010. See also "Female Engagement Team Brings Aid to School, Orphanage," States News Service, February 14, 2011; and "Female Combat Troops Will Link to Afghan Women for New York National Guard's 27th Brigade," U.S. Fed News, June 6, 2011.

60. Allison M. Roberts, "Danville Area Marine Helps Develop Female Engagement Team in Afghanistan," *Danville Register & Bee*, May 19, 2013.

61. "Through Airmen's Eyes: Medic, Female Engagement Team Airman Recalls Horrors, Triumphs in Afghanistan," U.S. Fed News, July 2, 2013.

62. Sonja Childers quoted in "We Were Right," *Washington Post*, December 17, 2019; Sippi Azarbaijani-Moghaddam argues that FETs were largely unsuccessful in Afghanistan. "The Failure of Female Engagement Teams in Afghanistan," School of Public Policy, Central European University, accessed June 3, 2020, https://spp.ceu. edu/article/2014–03–19/failure-female-engage ment-afghnistan. Eileen Rivers argues that FETs were successful in Afghanistan and could be successful elsewhere. See Rivers, 187–200.

63. Medina interview.

64. Faris interview, Part I.

65. Eric Lanham, Interview by Laurence Lessard, Operational Leadership Experiences Project, Combat Studies Institute, Ft. Leavenworth, Kansas, February 22, 2007, http://cgsc.contentdm. oclc.org/cdm/singleitem/collection/p4013coll13/ id/1003/rec/1.

66. Thompson interview.

67. Farris interview, Part II.

68. Tabb interview, Part II.

69. Anders, 491.

70. Boesen interview; Christopher Plummer, Interview by James Evenson, Operational Leadership Experiences Project, Combat Studies Institute, Ft. Leavenworth, Kansas, June 6, 2006, http://cgsc.contentdm.oclc.org/cdm/singleitem/ collection/p4013coll13/id/206/rec/1.

71. Plummer interview; See also Berendsen interview.

72. Woodring interview.

73. Rickard, 194.

74. Davila interview.

75. Reed interview.

76. Darling, 20.

77. Anders, 477.

78. Anders, 486.

79. Anders, 258. Service members in Iraq had similar experiences. See Mundey, in Bailey and Immerman, 181–182.

80. Darling, 14.

81. Jenkins, in Skovlund, 142.

82. Parnell, 276.

83. Meredith Fischer, "Meeting Children of War," *Richmond Times Dispatch*, July 26, 2004.

84. Evan Wright in Willis, 133.

85. Michael Mormino in Spiller, 75–76.

86. Anderson interview.

87. Sellers in Koontz, 376–377; See also Rickard, 127.

88. Reed interview.

89. Rod Nordland, "Afghans Plan to Stop Recruiting Children as Police," *New York Times*, January 29, 2011, https://www.nytimes. com/2011/01/30/world/asia/30afghan.html; Rickard, 126.

90. Rod Norland, "Afghan Pedophiles Get Free Pass from U.S. Military, Report Says," *New York Times*, January 23, 2018, https:// www.nytimes.com/2018/01/23/world/asia/ afghanistan-military-abuse.html.

91. Rickard, 126.

92. Parnell, 29–33.

93. Christ, 51.

94. Toomer, in Stanford, 275.

95. Arrieta interview.

96. Boissonneau interview.

97. Anders, 247–248.

98. Woodring interview.

99. Doherty interview.

100. Augustine, in Koontz, 448.

101. Williams, 184; See also Parnell, 44–45.

102. Thorpe, *Soldier Girls*, 208.

103. Augustine, in Koontz, 448.

104. Clint Douglass, in Carroll, 80.

105. Reed interview; See also Cariello interview.

106. Will Mangham, in Stanford, 48.

107. Wallace interview.

108. Reed interview.

109. Anders, 40–43.

110. Anders, 258.

111. Parnell, 44–45.

112. Herd 140; See also Stanton, 212.

113. Dave Tukdarian, in Stanford, 23.

114. Herd, 138–139.

115. Mangham, in Stanford, 48.

116. Gregory Strong quoted in Spiller, 56.

117. Tilley interview.
118. Hendren and Cooper, in Willis, 66.
119. Anders, 396.
120. Augustine, in Koontz, 448.
121. Cariello interview.
122. Tilley interview; See also Medina interview.
123. Reed interview.
124. Farris interview, Part I.
125. Plummer interview.
126. Waltz, 114.
127. Plummer interview.
128. Parnell, 40.
129. Doherty interview.
130. Arrieta interview.
131. Cariello interview.
132. Medina interview.
133. Erwin interview.
134. Herd, 80; repeated in Meyer, 46; and Jacob Barnes, Interview by Lisa M. Mundey, May 20, 2020, personal transcript.
135. Mormino, in Spiller, 75–76.
136. Walck interview.
137. Christ, 201.
138. Golembesky, 153.
139. Hunter in Koontz, 502–503; See also Creedon interview.
140. Arrieta interview.
141. West, 244.
142. Deitra Korando, Interview by John McCool, Operational Leadership Experiences Project, Combat Studies Institute, Ft. Leavenworth, Kansas, October 5, 2005, http://cgsc.cdmhost.com/cdm/ref/collection/p4013coll13/id/39.
143. Erwin interview.
144. Tilley interview.
145. Ahmed Khan quoted in "Actions of U.S. Soldiers Hunting for Al-Qaeda and Taliban Fighters in Rural Afghanistan Cause Resentment Among Local Populace," *NPR All Things Considered*, September 13, 2002.
146. Quoted in "Culture Gap Cools U.S. Welcome," *St. Louis Post-Dispatch*, September 18, 2002.
147. Anders, 256; Edward Harris, "Foreign Presence Fuels Afghan Unrest," *St. Louis Post-Dispatch*, May 31, 2006.
148. Harris, "Foreign Presence Fuels Afghan Unrest."
149. Jason Straziuso, "Shots Further Shatter NATO Image," Associated Press reprinted in *Inland Valley Daily Bulletin* (Ontario, CA), June 16, 2007.
150. Lee-Anne Goodman, "Rogue U.S. Soldier's Massacre of Afghan Villagers Fuels Tensions for Obama," *Canadian Press*, March 11, 2012; Heidi Vogt, "Killing Villagers Imperils Mission," *St. Louis Post-Dispatch*, March 12, 2012.
151. Kindsvatter, 144.
152. Caputo, 133; Kindsvatter, 144–145.
153. Lair, 205.

Chapter 4

1. Historical trends for this combat to non-combat, or "tooth-to-tail" ratio can be found in John J. McGrath, "The Other End of the Spear: The Tooth-to-Tail Ratio (T3R) in Modern Military Operations," The Long War Series Occasional Paper 23 (Ft. Leavenworth, KS: Combat Studies Institute, 2007).
2. Rickard, 68.
3. Kindsvatter asserts, "memoirs reinforce this perception [of continuous action] by dwelling on the interesting, unusual, or dramatic events of combat while passing quickly over less memorable periods of boredom or relative quiet." Kindsvatter, 93–94.
4. Rickard, 4.
5. Anders, 468–469.
6. Dan Kearney quoted in Junger, 19.
7. Connors, Interview by Douglas Cubbison, 10th Mountain Division, January 2007, Operational Leadership Experiences Project, Combat Studies Institute, Ft. Leavenworth, KS, http://cgsc.contentdm.oclc.org/cdm/singleitem/collection/p4013coll13/id/1027/rec/22. The transcript does not provide a first name for this soldier.
8. Ripley, 14; Donatella Lorch, "The Green Berets Up Close," in Willis, 25–31; John Hendren and Richard T. Cooper, "Fragile Alliances in a Hostile Land," in Willis, 65–79; See also Stanton, *12 Strong*; Stewart, *Operation Enduring Freedom*.
9. ODA 553 Area Assessment: The Hazara Area (Central Mountainous Region of Afghanistan) and Friendly and Enemy Forces within the Area, 126 OEF D 006, Civil Affairs & Psychological Operations, Operation Enduring Freedom: Historical Collection, 126th Military History Detachment, 2003, U.S. Army Heritage and Education Center, Carlisle Barracks, PA.
10. Naylor, *Not a Good Day to Die*, 285.
11. Jason Purcell quoted in "Profile: Troops Pulled Back from the Battle Zone in Afghanistan Talk About Their Experiences and Feelings," NPR Morning Edition, March 11, 2002.
12. Jonathan Ewing, "Mud, Cold and Shells: A Trench-Level View of the War in Afghanistan," *Associated Press*, March 7, 2002. For an overview of the operation, see Stewart, *Operation Enduring Freedom*, 30–44; Naylor, *Not a Good Day to Die*; and Grau and Billingsley, *Operation Anaconda*.
13. Barry Bearak, "A National Challenged: The Battle," *New York Times*, March 12, 2002.
14. Nayor, *Not a Good Day to Die*, 294–296.
15. Naylor, *Not a Good Day to Die*, 311–377; Walling, 63–64; Call, 84. See also Malcolm MacPherson, *Robert's Ridge: A Story of Courage and Sacrifice on Takur Ghar Mountain, Afghanistan* (New York: Delacorte, 2005).
16. Walling, 84.
17. Herd, 96.
18. Romesha, 7.
19. Romesha, 110.
20. Herd, 97–98.

21. Rickard, 52.

22. Jimmy Settle and Don Reardon, *Never Quit* (New York: St. Martin's, 2017), 286.

23. Darling, 6.

24. Anders, 201.

25. Christ, 152.

26. Waltz, 241, 250. Waltz counted required approvals by the Special Forces company commander, Special Operations Task Force commander, Special Forces Group commander, Special Forces general in Kabul; local battle space battalion commander, his brigade commander, commander for Regional Command East; aviation battalion commander, aviation brigade commander; if the mission targeted Taliban leadership, approval from the ISAF commander or deputy commander; Afghan National Army battalion commander and Afghan National Army brigade commander.

27. Darling, 35.

28. Wallace interview.

29. Pamela Constable, "New Strategy Call for Wooding Some in Taliban; U.S. Forces in Afghanistan to Vary Tactics by Region," *Washington Post*, December 21, 2003.

30. Farris interview, Part I. The terms for enemy combatants changed over time. They were later known as "Anti-Afghan Forces" or AAF. For simplicity, I refer to them as insurgents or enemy forces.

31. Malcolm Garcia, "U.S. Forces Still Searching for Taliban, Al-Qaida in Afghanistan," *Knight Ridder Washington Bureau*, February 22, 2003.

32. Afghanistan Fatalities, *iCasualties. org*, accessed August 27, 2020, http://icasualties.org/App/AfghanFatalities?d-date-equals=2003&rows=0.

33. "Coalition in Afghanistan Wraps Up Mountain Blizzard," *American Forces Press Service*, March 13, 2004; Drew Brown, "4 Army Explosives Experts Killed While Destroying Afghan Arms," *San Jose Mercury News*, April 16, 2002.

34. Associated Press, "U.S. Soldiers Have a Blast Destroying Ammunition," *St. Louis Post-Dispatch*, November 3, 2002.

35. William Kennedy quoted in Walling, 247. *The Hurt Locker*, directed by Kathyrn Bigelow (Summit Entertainment, 2009). The film is about an EOD team in Iraq. Unrealistic scenes include the main character going out on his own and a single vehicle going out on an operation.

36. Marc Jones quoted in John Valceanu, "Military Police Soldiers Maintain Presence in Afghan Community," U.S. Department of Defense Information, February 21, 2005.

37. Wallace interview.

38. Farris interview, Part II.

39. Doherty interview.

40. Parnell, 152, 155.

41. Chandrasekaran, 140.

42. Anders, 14–15, 108, 386.

43. John Valceanu, "Military Police Soldiers Maintain Presence in Afghan Community," U.S. Department of Defense Information, February 21, 2005.

44. Quotes in Meredith Fischer, "On Patrol for Hearts and Minds," *Richmond Times Dispatch*, July 23, 2004.

45. Matthew Rosenberg, "U.S. Soldiers Refine Searches of Afghan Civilians for Weapons," *Associated Press*, October 19, 2002; Walling, 73.

46. Jenkins in Skovlund, 141.

47. Anders, 12, 197.

48. Waltz, 71.

49. Christ, 3, 13–14. See Headquarters, Department of the Army, *Soldier's Manual of Common Tasks: Warrior Skills Level 1*, 3–81.

50. Justin Sax, Interview by Douglas Cubbison, Operational Leadership Experiences Project, Combat Studies Institute, Ft. Leavenworth, Kansas, January 8, 2007, http://cgsc.contentdm.oclc.org/cdm/singleitem/collection/p4013coll13/id/1004/rec/1.

51. Connors interview.

52. Fontes, in Koontz, 479.

53. Greg Zoroya, "How the IED Changed the U.S. Military," *USA Today*, December 19, 2013, https://www.usatoday.com/story/news/nation/2013/12/18/ied-10-years-blast-wounds-amputations/3803017/; For the experience of service members with IEDs in Iraq, see Mundey, in Bailey and Immerman, 182–183.

54. Waltz, 93.

55. Parnell, 76.

56. Christ, 7.

57. Bradley, *Lions of Kandahar*, 75.

58. Daniel E. Baker, in Spiller 41.

59. Schellhaas, 243, 257.

60. Christ, 11.

61. Waltz, 94, 282.

62. Mark Melson, Interview by Angie Slattery, Operational Leadership Experiences Project, Combat Studies Institute, Ft. Leavenworth, Kansas, January 11, 2011, http://cgsc.contentdm.oclc.org/cdm/singleitem/collection/p4013coll13/id/2182/rec/1.

63. Waltz, 234.

64. Waltz, 261.

65. Schellhaas, 242–243.

66. Schellhaas, 243–244.

67. Linderman, 19; Kindsvatter, 82–83.

68. Christopher Hall, "Afghanistan: Georgia Army Guard Member Presented Award by Chairman of the Joint Chiefs," National Guard, February 23, 2012, accessed July 5, 2020, https://www.nationalguard.mil/News/Article/576152/afghanistan-georgia-army-guard-member-presented-award-by-chairman-of-the-joint/.

69. Beau Yarbrough, "Father of Five Earns Purple Heart," *Daily Press* (Victorville, CA), March 27, 2011.

70. Rickard, 108.

71. Tupper, 170.

72. Mullaney, 299. Emphasis in the original.

73. Quoted in Vishal Chandra, *The Unfinished War in Afghanistan, 2001–2014* (New Delhi:

Pentagon, 2015), 113; See also Jones, *Graveyard*, 230.

74. Brandon Griffin, Interview by Angie Slattery, Operational Leadership Experiences Project, Combat Studies Institute, Ft. Leavenworth, Kansas, February 2, 2012, http://cgsc.cdmhost.com/cdm/singleitem/collection/p4013coll13/id/2578/rec/3.

75. Walling, 129.

76. Barfield, 319; Neumann and Williams, 37.

77. Waltz, 140.

78. Parnell, 135, 148–150, 160.

79. Herd 111; Golembesky, 174.

80. Golembesky, 174.

81. Giustozzi, 153.

82. Romesha, 225.

83. Meyer, 155.

84. Mundey, in Bailey and Immerman, 181.

85. Sean D. Naylor, "Endless Pursuit? Taliban Fighters Blend In, Refuse to Play by the Rules," *Army Times*, October 24, 2005.

86. Parnell, 134.

87. Associated Press, "11,000-Plus Troops to Attack Taliban," *St. Louis Post-Dispatch*, June 14, 2006.

88. Quotes in Jason Straziuso, "Troops in Afghanistan: Mortars by Night, Water Shortages by Day," *Associated Press*, June 22, 2006. U.S. troops in Vietnam also complained that the war did not look like the World War II films they had grown up watching. See Lisa M. Mundey, *American Militarism and Anti-Militarism in Popular Media, 1945–1970* (Jefferson, NC: McFarland, 2012), 44–45.

89. Schellhaas, 245, 258.

90. "Paratroopers Deal Blow to Taliban in Remote Valley," U.S. Department of Defense Information, May 9, 2005.

91. R.J.S., "Skittles: A Sniper's Perspective," in Skovlund, 227.

92. Romesha, 199–200.

93. Romesha, 120–121.

94. Romesha, 122. Pro net, short for "Force Protection" for base defense.

95. Bradley, *Lions of Kandahar*, 255.

96. Charlie Faint, "The Swan Song," in Skovlund, 296.

97. Charlie Sherpa, "Quiet as TOC-Rats," Doonsbury's *The Sandbox*, accessed July 29, 2020, https://gocomics.typepad.com/the_sandbox/.

98. Laurence Critchell quoted in Linderman, 16.

99. McGarry, vi.

100. Mullaney, 295.

101. Doherty interview.

102. Meyer 92; Golembesky, 202; Doherty interview.

103. Rico 9, 11, 209; Junger also describes muzzle flashes as Christmas lights. Junger, 7; Kingsley, "Lost in the Sauce," in Skovlund, 373; Logan A. Lewis, "The Cave," in Skovlund, 384; Fick, 124; Stock in Leche, 117; Parnell, 288.

104. McGarry, 210; Anders, 198; Quoted in Christ, 246.

105. Anders 199, 208; Christ, 46, 169.

106. Linderman, 55–57; McGarry, 215; Waltz, 129; Rico, 201, 208, 210; Bradley, *Lions of Kandahar*, 3; Parnell, 84, 171; The first of the Indiana Jones film series, *Indiana Jones and the Raiders of the Lost Ark*, appeared in 1981; Quoted in Sean D. Naylor, "Not So Bulletproof: Troops on the Front Lines Lack Vital Piece of Body Armor," *Army Times*, March 4, 2002; Christ, 254–255, 259.

107. Mullaney, 290. Americans found machinery familiar in the Vietnam War as well. See Caputo, 83; Kingsley, "Lost in the Sauce," in Skovlund, 370; Romesha, 74, 109–110, 242; Golembesky, 50.

108. Beau Cleland, "Getting Shot At," in Stanford, 211; Meyer, 129, 132.

109. Parnell, 77.

110. Borge, "A Fight in the Mountains," in Skovlund, 306.

111. Bradley, *Lions of Kandahar*, 3; Cleland, in Stanford, 212; Golembesky, 55, 206; Mullaney, 283; Eide and Gibler, 87; Anders, 185; Romesha, 234.

112. Romesha, 109, 123.

113. Parnell, 192.

114. Kingsley, in Skovlund, 376–377.

115. Rico, 212.

116. Smenos, in Stanford, 217.

117. Anders, 195.

118. Bradley, *Lions of Kandahar*, 114.

119. Cleland, in Stanford, 213; Christ, 47; Settle and Reardon, 280–281, 287; Mullaney, 287, 315; Rico, 210; Golembesky, 257–258.

120. Parnell, 90; McGarry 284; Meyer 134; Rickard, 52; Romesha, 170; Bradley, *Lions of Kandahar*, 211.

121. Parnell, 112, 244, 320; McGarry, 276.

122. Romesha, 288–289; Golembesky, 219; McGarry, 278; Parnell, 179, 186; Lewis, in Skovlund, 386; Kevin Wallace in Walling, 227–228.

123. Romesha, 251–252; Kingsley, in Skovlund, 371; Rickard, 54; Corbin Chesley, "'Why Are You Leaving Now?'—A Rookie Afghan Policeman, a Combat Veteran, and a Share Loss of Naivety, *Task and Purpose*, April 18, 2021, https://taskandpurpose.com/news/afghanistan-war-veterans-pain-withdrawal/; Settle and Reardon, 291, 301.

124. Linderman, 346; Rico, 210. See Also Christ, 140; Troy Steward, in Stanford, 138; Cleland, in Stanford, 213; Parnell, 86; Antonio Delvecchio in Walling, 248–249; Settle and Reardon, 300.

125. Mark O'Neill, Interview by Jenn Vedder, Operational Leadership Experiences Project, Combat Studies Institute, Ft. Leavenworth, Kansas, February 15, 2011, http://cgsc.contentdm.oclc.org/cdm/singleitem/collection/p4013coll13/id/2214/rec/2.

126. Kingsley, in Skovlund, 378.

127. Bradley, *Lions of Kandahar*, 175.

128. Misha Pemble-Belkin Quoted in Junger, 105.

129. Junger, 109.

130. Caputo, 163.

131. Mullaney, 292, 294, 297.

132. Robert (Brian) Alexander, Interview by Leo Hirrel, Quartermaster School, October 25, 2011.

133. Meyer, 160.

134. Alexander Interview.

135. Smith, 237- 238; See Also Colby Bradley, in Skovlund, 343; Alexander Interview.

136. Kindsvatter, 247, 251–252; Combat Infantry Badge (CIB). Accessed February 3, 2020, https://www.hrc.army.mil/content/Combat%20 Infantry%20Badge%20CIB; Anders, 217; Kevin Lilley, "CAB for Past Conflicts? *Army Times*, April 4, 2015, https://www.armytimes.com/news/your-army/2015/04/04/cab-for-past-conflicts-5-things-you-should-know/; Arrieta Interview; the Number Comes from the Congressional Research Service. Cited in Richard Sisk, "Women in Combat: Silver Stars, Combat Action Badges, and Casualties," *Military.com*, August 31, 2015, https://www.military.com/daily-news/2015/08/31/women-in-combat-silver-stars-combat-action-badges-casualties.html; Taylor, 180. The Department of Defense opened all combat roles to women at the end of 2015. Matthew Rosenberg and Dave Philipps, "All Combat Roles Now Open to Women, Defense Secretary Says," *New York Times*, December 3, 2015, https://www.nytimes.com/2015/12/04/us/politics/combat-military-women-ash-carter.html; Revised Eligibility Criteria for Award of the Combat Action Ribbon (CAR), MARADMINS Number: 038/13, January 17, 2013, https://www.marines.mil/News/Messages/Messages-Display/Article/895299/revised-eligibility-criteria-for-award-of-the-combat-action-ribbon-car-and-upda/; Air Force Combat Action Medal, Air Force Personnel Center, accessed August 31, 2020, https://www.afpc.af.mil/About/Fact-Sheets/Display/Article/421918/air-force-combat-action-medal/; Combat Medical Badge, Code of Federal Regulations, Title 32, Chapter V, Subchapter F, Part 578.70, https://www.govinfo.gov/content/pkg/CFR-2008-title32-vol3/xml/CFR-2008-title32-vol3-sec578–70.xml; Rickard, 44.

Chapter 5

1. George Bochain quoted in Call, 37.

2. Ripley, 119.

3. Ripley, 120, 205, 126–127.

4. Quoted in Walling, 34–35.

5. Quoted in Ripley, 25.

6. Michael Zendejas, Interview with Jenna Fike, Operational Leadership Experiences Project, Combat Studies Institute, Ft. Leavenworth, Kansas, February 14, 2012, http://cgsc.contentdm. oclc.org/cdm/singleitem/collection/p4013coll13/id/2576/rec/1.

7. Smith, 244.

8. Ripley, 205.

9. Romesha, 264.

10. Quoted in Naylor, *Not a Good Day to Die*, 218.

11. Naylor, *Not a Good Day to Die*, 257–258. See also Walling, 59–60.

12. Pamela Constable, "Night Under Fire: A Lot of People Got Hit," *Washington Post*, March 9, 2002.

13. Ripley, 222.

14. Quoted in Walling, 60.

15. Quoted in Lance M. Bacon, " 'Flying Artillery' and Anaconda's Angels; Air Support—and Airmen Who Call It In—Prevented Moe Casualties in Shah-e-Kot," *Army Times*, April 8, 2002. For overviews of Operation Anaconda see Stewart, *Operation Enduring Freedom*, 30–44; Naylor, *Not a Good Day to Die*; Grau and Billingsley, *Operation Anaconda*.

16. Stanton, 143. For a more critical assessment of problems with close air support see Naylor, *Not a Good Day to Die*, 270–272. For as assessment of the strategic success of air power, see Rebecca Grant, "The Airpower of Anaconda," *Air Force Magazine*, September 1, 2002, https://www.airforcemag.com/article/0902anaconda/.

17. Stanton, 144.

18. Ripley, 132; Call, 19; Stanton, 144.

19. Golembesky, 107.

20. Andrew Kozar, Interviewed by Leo Hirrel, January 25, 2012, Quartermaster School.

21. Timothy Wollmuth, "Reserve C-130 Crews Critical to Front-Line Fighters," States News Service, April 21, 2004; Meredith Fischer, " 'Welcome,' Company C/Virginia National Guard Troops Become Part of Task Force Thunder," *Richmond Times Dispatch*, July 15, 2004.

22. Thomas W. Young, *The Speed of Heat: An Airlift Wing at War in Iraq and Afghanistan* (Jefferson, NC: McFarland, 2008), 49.

23. Mike Foley quoted in Young, 48.

24. Wollmuth, "Reserve C-130 Crews."

25. Fischer, " 'Welcome,' Company C."

26. Walker quoted in Young, 47.

27. Carla Riner quoted in Young, 51.

28. Young, 60.

29. Thorpe, *Soldier Girls*, 135.

30. Young, 60.

31. Smith, 226.

32. Bradley, *Lions of Kandahar*, 212.

33. Golembesky, 93–94.

34. Michael Millen quoted in *A-10 Thunderbolt II Units of Operation Enduring Freedom, 2008–14* Kindle Edition, by Gary Wetzel (Osprey, 2015), loc. 743.

35. Wetzel, loc. 1341.

36. Ripley, 126–127.

37. Smith, 197–198.

38. Meyer, 111–112; See also Doidge, "Flipping the Switch," in Wright, *Vanguard of Valor I*,

63. Helicopters could not see visible weapons on retreating insurgent forces, so they held their fire.

39. Chris Palmer quoted in Wetzel, loc. 1608.

40. Ed Schulman quoted in Call, 36.

41. Bradley, *Lions of Kandahar*, 173.

42. Romesha, 265; Ripley, 136.

43. Herd, 107.

44. Waltz, 136.

45. Golembesky, 77.

46. Horner and Stock quoted in Jeff Szczechowski, "A-10 Pilot Takes Aim on Terrorism," States News Service, March 23, 2004.

47. Parnell, 127–128.

48. Rickard, 117.

49. Golembesky, 75–76.

50. Rickard, 27.

51. Golembesky, 77.

52. Golembesky, 76; See also Matt M. Matthews, "Disrupt and Destroy: Platoon Patrol in Zhari District, September 2010," in *Vanguard of Valor: Small Unit Actions in Afghanistan*, ed. by Donald P. Wright (Fort Leavenworth, KS: Combat Studies Institute, 2012), 149–150.

53. Morgan, 426–432.

54. Ripley, 163; Call, 71.

55. Chris Spann quoted in Call, 72.

56. Rickard, 57–58.

57. Parnell, 205.

58. Michael Lowe quoted in Wetzel, loc 369.

59. Anthony Roe quoted in Wetzel, loc. 1250.

60. Bradley, *Lions of Kandahar*, 75–76, 212, 215.

61. Christopher Cisneros quoted in Wetzel, loc. 1439.

62. Romesha, 204.

63. Romesha, 289.

64. Parnell, 130.

65. Bradley, *Lions of Kandahar*, 263.

66. Rickard, 61, 64–65.

67. Parnell, 346.

68. Kindsvatter, 62. See also Charles R. Shrader, *Amicide: The Problem of Friendly Fire in Modern War* (Ft. Leavenworth: Combat Studies Institute, 1982).

69. Neumann and Williams, 40; "The Afghan War's Deadliest Friendly Fire Incident for U.S. Soldiers," *60 Minutes*, November 9, 2017, https://www.cbsnews.com/news/the-afghan-wars-deadliest-friendly-fire-incident-involving-u-s-soldiers/.

70. Walling, 72.

71. Carlotta Gall and David E. Sanger, "Civilian Deaths Sour Afghans' Mood," *New York Times* reprinted in *Pittsburgh Post-Gazette*, May 13, 2007.

72. Chandrasekaran, 338.

73. Millen quoted in Wetzel, loc. 1668.

74. Arrieta interview.

75. Zendejas interview. Class II supplies include clothing and equipment. Class IX includes parts for repair.

76. Zendejas interview.

77. Tapper, 329.

78. Matt Kelley, "Afghanistan's Mountains Push U.S. Helicopters to Their Limits," *Associated Press*, March 4, 2002.

79. Albano interview.

80. Ripley, 97–98.

81. Connie Lane, Interview by Jenna Fike, Operational Leadership Experiences Project, Combat Studies Institute, Ft. Leavenworth, Kansas, March 6, 2012, http://cgsc.contentdm.oclc.org/cdm/singleitem/collection/p4013coll13/id/2611/rec/20.

82. Zendejas interview.

83. McGrath, *Wanat*, 164.

84. Lane interview.

85. Smith, 227.

86. Dijon Rolle, "Air Assets Keep Troops in Afghanistan Moving, Supplied," U.S. Department of Defense Information, December 3, 2004.

87. Bradley, *Lions of Kandahar*, 176.

88. Rolle, "Air Assets."

89. Colby Bradley, in Skovlund, 336.

90. McGarry, 205–207; Kingsley, in Skovlund, 372.

91. Golembesky, 85, 118.

92. Kingsley, in Skovlund, 372.

93. Larry [last name withheld] quoted in Call, 77.

94. Jorgensen interview; See also Tapper, 81–83.

95. Jorgensen interview.

96. Jorgensen interview.

97. Anthony Nilon, Interviewed by Douglas Cubbinson, 10th Mountain Division, Fort Drum, New York, Combat Studies Institute, Ft. Leavenworth, KS, January 22, 2007, http://cgsc.contentdm.oclc.org/cdm/singleitem/collection/p4013coll13/id/1031/rec/1.

98. Zendejas interview.

99. Darling, 60–64.

100. Romesha, 221.

101. Smith, 203.

102. Smith, 190–191, 197.

103. Casey Blasingame quoted in West, 96.

104. Giustozzi, 155.

105. Golembesky, 162, 217, 219.

106. Darling, 138.

107. Darling, 127–132. According to FM 4–02.2: Army Medical Evacuation (Washington, DC, Army Publishing Directorate, 2007) these are the medevac categories: Category A (Urgent): Patient needs urgent medical attention within two hours for the preservation of life, limb, or eyesight. Category B (Urgent Surgical): Patient needs urgent surgical attention within two hours for the preservation of life, limb, or eyesight. Category C (Priority): Patient needs medical or surgical intervention within four hours for the preservation of life, limb, or eyesight. Category D (Routine): Patient needs medical attention within 24 hours. Category E (Convenience): Patient needs medical attention at the earliest possible convenience.

108. Darling, 137.

109. Romesha, 88.

110. Anders 373–375; See also Brian Delaplane in Matthew Currier Burden, *Blog of War: Front-Line Dispatches from Soldiers in Iraq and Afghanistan* (New York: Simon & Schuster, 2006), 55–59.

111. McGrath, *Wanat*, 175–176.

112. Antonio Delvecchio quoted in Walling, 248–249.

Chapter 6

1. For top-level criticism of the efforts to train Afghan security forces, see Craig Whitlock, "Unguarded Nation," *Washington Post*, December 9, 2019. See also Martin Loicano and Craig C. Felker, "In Our Own Image: Training the Afghan National Security Forces," in O'Connell, 112.

2. SIGAR, "Reconstructing the Afghan National Defense and Security Forces: Lessons from the U.S. Experience in Afghanistan," (Arlington, VA: SIGAR, September 2017), 15, 17; Obaid Younossi, Peter Dahl Thurelsen, Jonathan Vaccaro, Jerry M. Solinger, and Brian Grady, *The Long March: Building an Afghan National Army* (Santa Monica, CA: RAND, 2009), 14, 29.

3. SIGAR, "Reconstructing the Afghan National Defense and Security Forces," 22; See also Younossi, *et Al.*, 33; Medina interview.

4. Busy interview; Darling, 116.

5. Younossi, *et Al.*, 30; SIGAR, "Reconstructing the Afghan National Defense and Security Forces," 21.

6. David Rhode, "Training an Afghan Army That Can Shoot Straight," *New York Times*, June 6, 2002.

7. "Efforts in Afghanistan to Train National Army," *NPR Morning Edition*, July 23, 2002.

8. Schmidt quoted in Young, 151.

9. Rhode, "Training an Afghan Army."

10. Younossi, *et Al.*, 18.

11. Carlotta Gall, "Threats and Responses: Rebuilding Afghanistan," *New York Times*, January 25, 2003; Neumann and Williams, 22; See also Younossi, *et Al.*, 15.

12. SIGAR, "Reconstructing the Afghan National Defense and Security Forces," 19–20, 46, 49; Younossi, *et. Al.*, 15, 30, 58; "Troops on Leave Before Afghanistan Deployment," *Associated Press*, June 25, 2005.

13. SIGAR, "Reconstructing the Afghan National Defense and Security Forces," 45; Christopher Miller, Interview by Angie Slattery, Operational Leadership Experiences Project, Combat Studies Institute, Ft. Leavenworth, Kansas, April 11, 2012, http://cgsc.cdmhost.com/cdm/singleitem/collection/p4013coll13/id/2653/rec/1.

14. Medina interview.

15. Quotes in Frank Magni, "Training Afghan National Army Enhances Mission for ETT," U.S. Federal News, August 13, 2004. For the Military Decision-Making Process, see Center of Army Lessons Learned, *MDMP Handbook: Lessons and Best Practices*, No 15–06 (March 2015), https://usacac.army.mil/sites/default/files/publications/15–06_0.pdf.

16. Don Bishop, Interview by Lawrence Lessard, Operational Leadership Experiences Project, Combat Studies Institute, Ft. Leavenworth, Kansas, May 11, 2009, http://cgsc.contentdm.oclc.org/cdm/singleitem/collection/p4013coll13/id/2187/rec/1.

17. Tabb interview, Part II.

18. SIGAR, "Reconstructing the Afghan National Defense and Security Forces," 17.

19. Medina interview.

20. Johnson interview; See also Bates interview.

21. Doug Ross, Interview with Brad Helton, Operational Leadership Experiences Project, Combat Studies Institute, Ft. Leavenworth, Kansas, June 23, 2008, http://cgsc.contentdm.oclc.org/cdm/singleitem/collection/p4013coll13/id/1069/rec/1.

22. Bishop interview.

23. Michael Threatt, Interview by Doug Davids, Part II, Operational Leadership Experiences Project, Combat Studies Institute, Ft. Leavenworth, Kansas, December 17, 2007, http://cgsc.contentdm.oclc.org/cdm/singleitem/collection/p4013coll13/id/963/rec/2.

24. Woodring interview.

25. Meyer, 45.

26. Threatt interview.

27. Medina interview.

28. Threatt interview.

29. Tabb interview, Part II.

30. Threatt interview.

31. Threatt interview.

32. Ron Welsh quoted in Eric Schmitt, "Where Armies Must Be Built, It's Slow (Iraq) and Even Slower (Afghanistan), *New York Times*, September 25, 2005.

33. Medina Interview.

34. Miller Interview.

35. Lencz Interview.

36. Jeremy Galvez, "As Withdrawal Date Approaches, UNLV Veterans Recount a Day in Afghanistan," *Rebel Yell: University of Nevada-Las Vegas*, February 25, 2013.

37. Reed interview.

38. Christ, 39–42.

39. McGrath, *Wanat*, 151.

40. Plummer interview.

41. Gregory Strong, in Spiller, 58.

42. Creedon interview.

43. Medina interview.

44. John Bates, Interview by Brad Helton, Part II, Operational Leadership Experiences Project, Combat Studies Institute, Ft. Leavenworth, Kansas, June 24, 2008, http://cgsc.cdmhost.com/cdm/singleitem/collection/p4013coll13/id/1095/rec/2.

45. Christ, 219.

46. Medina interview.

47. Christ, 221–222.

48. Bates interview.

49. Special Inspector General of Afghanistan Reconstruction, "Corruption in Conflict: Lessons from the U.S. Experience in Afghanistan," (Arlington, VA: SIGAR, September 2016), https://www.sigar.mil/pdf/LessonsLearned/SIGAR-16–58-LL.pdf; See also Craig Whitlock, "Consumed by Corruption," *Washington Post,* December 9, 2019, https://www.washingtonpost.com/graphics/2019/investigations/afghanistan-papers/afghanistan-war-corruption-government/.

50. Medina interview.

51. Bishop interview; Tabb interview, Part II; Medina interview.

52. Marc Fleurant, Interview by Angie Slattery Hundley, Operational Leadership Experiences Project, Combat Studies Institute, Ft. Leavenworth, Kansas, February 6, 2013, http://cgsc.contentdm.oclc.org/cdm/singleitem/collection/p4013coll13/id/2988/rec/1.

53. Fleurant interview; See also Craig Whitlock, "Unguarded Nation," *Washington Post,* December 9, 2019.

54. Rickard, 18, 215.

55. Meyer, 56; See also Whitlock, "Unguarded Nation."

56. Woodring interview.

57. Lencz interview.

58. Tabb interview, Part II.

59. Walck interview.

60. Galvez, "As Withdrawal Date Approaches."

61. Kyle Gunn, "As Withdrawal Date Approaches, UNLV Veterans Recount a Day in Afghanistan," *Rebel Yell: University of Nevada-Las Vegas,* February 25, 2013.

62. Plummer interview.

63. Meyer, 45.

64. Mark O'Neill, Interview by Jenn Vedder, Operational Leadership Experiences Project, Combat Studies Institute, Ft. Leavenworth, Kansas, February 15, 2011, http://cgsc.contentdm.oclc.org/cdm/singleitem/collection/p4013coll13/id/2214/rec/2.

65. Lencz interview.

66. O'Neill interview.

67. O'Neill interview.

68. Boesen interview.

69. Eric Schmitt, "Where Armies Must Be Built, It's Slow (Iraq) and Even Slower (Afghanistan), *New York Times,* September 25, 2005.

70. Scott Edwards, in Spiller, 72.

71. Matt Lillibridge, Interview by Angie Slattery Hundley, Operational Leadership Experiences Project, Combat Studies Institute, Ft. Leavenworth, Kansas, October 5, 2012, http://cgsc.contentdm.oclc.org/cdm/singleitem/collection/p4013coll13/id/2779/rec/1.

72. Meyers, 41.

73. Edwards, in Spiller, 73.

74. Kindsvatter, 145, 153.

75. See Loicano and Felker in O'Connell, 117–122.

76. SIGAR, "Reconstructing the Afghan National Defense and Security Forces," 31; Giustozzi, 174; Jones, *Graveyard,* 165; Neumann and Williams, 24; Schmitt, "Where Armies Must Be Built."

77. Tabb interview, Part I.

78. SIGAR, "Reconstructing the Afghan National Defense and Security Forces," 37, 56; Pashtoon Atif, "The Impact of Culture on Policing in Afghanistan," in O'Connell, 145–146.

79. SIGAR, "Reconstructing the Afghan National Defense and Security Forces," 93.

80. Jason Thompson, in Spiller, 96.

81. Darling, 23, 26.

82. Davis interview.

83. Schellhaas, 219.

84. Daniel Baker, in Spiller, 38.

85. Heath Clark, in Spiller, 90.

86. Thompson, in Spiller, 95–97.

87. Crawley in Walling, 175–176.

88. Scott Cunningham, Interview by Lisa Beckenbaugh, Operational Leadership Experiences Project, Combat Studies Institute, Ft. Leavenworth, Kansas, August 15, 2013, http://cgsc.contentdm.oclc.org/cdm/singleitem/collection/p4013coll13/id/3095/rec/5; See also Whitlock, "Unguarded Nation."

89. Ross interview.

90. Schroeder interview.

91. Tabb interview, Part II.

92. Boesen interview.

93. Carlotta Gall, "A Slice of Afghanistan Secured Well by Afghans," *New York Times,* May 24, 2011.

94. Chandra, 172.

95. Mann, 33; Chandra, 173; Graham Bowley and Richard A. Oppel, Jr., "Afghan Police Recruit Turns His Weapon on His American Trainers, Killing 2," *New York Times,* August 18, 2012.

96. Golembesky, 250–251, 268.

97. Reed interview.

98. J.D. Browning quoted in West, 65.

99. Busy interview.

100. Graham Bowley and Rubin, "Americans Slain; Advisors to Exit Kabul Ministries," *New York Times,* February 26, 2012.

101. Bowley and Rubin, "Americans Slain."

102. Matthew Rosenberg, "As Trained Afghans Turn Enemy, a U.S.-Led Imperative Is in Peril," *New York Times,* May 16, 2012; Arrieta interview.

103. Quoted in "We Were Right," *Washington Post,* December 17, 2019.

104. Chandra, 173; SIGAR, "Report to the United States Congress," April 30, 2018, 93, accessed March 30, 2020, https://www.sigar.mil/pdf/quarterlyreports/2018–04–30qr-section3-security.pdf.

105. Rickard, 134.

Chapter 7

1. For a critique of U.S. reconstruction efforts in Afghanistan, see Jamie Lynn De Coster,

"Building and Undermining Legitimacy: Reconstruction and Development in Afghanistan," in O'Connell, 157–188.

2. Ripley, 204.

3. Jeff Coggin, "CHLC Operational Brief, CHLC 13/Gardeyz," October 30, 2002, 126 OEF D 084, Civil Affairs & Psychological Operations, Operation Enduring Freedom: Historical Collection, 126th Military History Detachment, 2003, Army Heritage and Education Center, Carlisle Barracks, PA. Coggin was later promoted to brigadier general and became the commanding general for the U.S. Army Civil Affairs and Psychological Operations Command (Airborne).

4. Olga Oliker, Richard Kauzlarich, James Dobbins, Kurt W. Basseuner, Donald L. Sampler, John G. McGinn, Michael J. Dziedzic, Adam R. Grisson, Bruce R. Pirnie, Nora Bensahel, A. Istar Guven, *Aid During Conflict: Interaction Between Military and Civilian Assistance Providers in Afghanistan, September 2001-June 2002* (RAND: Santa Monica, CA, 2004), 43; Center for Army Lessons Learned, *Afghanistan Provincial Reconstruction Handbook*, February 2011, Accessed April 2, 2020, https://usacac.army.mil/sites/default/files/publications/11–16.pdf; Walling, 74–76.

5. "A Day in the Life of a CJCMOTF Soldier," PowerPoint slides, OEF D-152 CD, Civil Affairs & Psychological Operations, Operation Enduring Freedom: Historical Collection, 126th Military History Detachment, 2003, U.S. Army Heritage and Education Center, Carlisle Barracks, PA.

6. "A Day in the Life."

7. "A Day in the Life."

8. "A Day in the Life."

9. "A Day in the Life."

10. "A Day in the Life."

11. "A Day in the Life."

12. "A Day in the Life."

13. "A Day in the Life."

14. "A Day in the Life."

15. "Narrative Justification for the Meritorious Unit Citation," Narrative for MUC-C 96 CA final (file name), "Narrative for Unit Citation" (folder name), 126-OEF-D-151 CD, Civil Affairs & Psychological Operations, Operation Enduring Freedom: Historical Collection, 126th Military History Detachment, 2003, U.S. Army Heritage and Education Center, Carlisle Barracks, PA.

16. James Dao, "GI's Fight Afghan Devastation with Plaster and Nails," *New York Times*, June 24, 2002.

17. "Deh Rawood," Multimedia Historical Monograph CD, Civil Affairs & Psychological Operations, Operation Enduring Freedom: Historical Collection, 126th Military History Detachment, 2003, U.S. Army Heritage and Education Center, Carlisle Barracks, PA; "Helmand River Valley," Multimedia Historical Monograph CD, Civil Affairs & Psychological Operations, Operation Enduring Freedom: Historical Collection, 126th Military History Detachment, 2003, U.S.

Army Heritage and Education Center, Carlisle Barracks, PA.

18. "Herat," Multimedia Historical Monograph CD, Civil Affairs & Psychological Operations, Operation Enduring Freedom: Historical Collection, 126th Military History Detachment, 2003, U.S. Army Heritage and Education Center, Carlisle Barracks, PA.

19. "Jalalabad," Multimedia Historical Monograph CD, Civil Affairs & Psychological Operations, Operation Enduring Freedom: Historical Collection, 126th Military History Detachment, 2003, U.S. Army Heritage and Education Center, Carlisle Barracks, PA.

20. Oliker, *et Al., Aid During Conflict*, 75–76.

21. James Dao, "GI's Fight Afghan Devastation with Plaster and Nails," *New York Times*, June 24, 2002.

22. Plummer interview.

23. Patrick Quinn, "Changes Dateline from Bagram; U.S. Army Hands Out Pencils, Toys and Other Supplies in Southern Afghanistan," *Associated Press*, May 22, 2002.

24. Sarah Daniel, "Reaching Out," *Sedalia Democrat*, April 10, 2006.

25. Katie Morris, Interview by Lisa Beckenbaugh, Operational Leadership Experiences Project, Combat Studies Institute, Ft. Leavenworth, Kansas, February 7, 2013, http://cgsc.contentdm.oclc.org/cdm/singleitem/collection/p4013coll13/id/3001/rec/9.

26. Quotes in "Logistics Soldiers Improve Afghan School," FDCH Federal Department and Agency Documents," July 29, 2004.

27. Craig Whitlock, "Built to Fail," *Washington Post*, December 9, 2019.

28. Arrieta interview.

29. Claudia Bullard, "Civil-Military Missions Helping Win War on Terrorism," U.S. Department of Defense Information, September 10, 2004.

30. Jenkins, in Skovlund, 156.

31. Quotes in Jennifer S. Emmons, "Medical-Assistance Visit Helps Give Afghan Children Bright Future," U.S. Department of Defense Information, November 4, 2004.

32. Herd, 167.

33. Center for Army Lessons Learned, *Afghanistan Provincial Reconstruction Handbook*, 3.

34. "Gardiz," Multimedia Historical Monograph CD, Civil Affairs & Psychological Operations, Operation Enduring Freedom: Historical Collection, 126th Military History Detachment, 2003, U.S. Army Heritage and Education Center, Carlisle Barracks, PA;

35. John Wade, Interview by Christopher K. Ives, Operational Leadership Experiences Project, Combat Studies Institute, Ft. Leavenworth, Kansas, February 14, 2008, http://cgsc.contentdm.oclc.org/cdm/singleitem/collection/p4013coll13/id/915/rec/1.

36. Center for Army Lessons Learned, *Afghanistan Provincial Reconstruction Handbook*, 1.

37. Russel L. Honoré and David V. Boslego,

"Forging Provincial Reconstruction Teams," *Joint Force Quarterly*, 44. No. 1 (2007), 86.

38. Quotes in Pamela Constable, "Courting Afghanistan Brick by Brick; Expanded Civil-Military Program Aims to Win Hearts and Minds," *Washington Post*, December 8, 2002.

39. Honoré and Boslego, 85–89; "Experts: Afghanistan Reconstruction Teams Succeed, Need More Work," *Inside the Army*, October 24, 2005; Government Accountability Office, "Provincial Reconstruction Teams in Afghanistan and Iraq," GAO-08–905RSU (Washington, D.C.: Sept. 26, 2008), 3, accessed April 2, 2020, https://www.gao.gov/new.items/d0986r.pdf.

40. Waltz, 99; Wade interview.

41. Morris interview.

42. Augustine interview, in Koontz, 429–430; Fontes interview, in Koontz, 459; Hunter interview, in Koontz, 484; Kimberly Evans, Interview by J. Patrick Hughes and Lisa Mundey, February 13, 2007, U.S. Army Center of Military History, Ft. McNair, Washington, DC., Unpublished transcript.

43. Wade interview.

44. Mike Varney, Interview by Christopher K. Ives, Operational Leadership Experiences Project, Combat Studies Institute, Ft. Leavenworth, Kansas, February 4, 2008, http://cgsc.contentdm.oclc.org/cdm/singleitem/collection/p4013coll13/id/906/rec/1.

45. Morris interview.

46. Walck interview.

47. Wade interview. Varney recounts the same story in his interview.

48. Varney interview.

49. Unnamed SIGAR Lessons Learned Interview, January 27, 2016, "The Afghanistan Papers Digital Document Archive," *Washington Post,* https://www.washingtonpost.com/graphics/2019/investigations/afghanistan-papers/documents-database/.

50. Wade interview.

51. Parnell, 40.

52. Forsyth, 156.

53. Fontes, in Koontz, 460–462.

54. Morris interview.

55. Evans interview.

56. Morris interview.

57. Fontes, in Koontz, 468.

58. Evans interview.

59. Fontes, in Koontz, 465.

60. "Remote Bases in Afghanistan Draw Minnesota Soldiers," *Associated Press*, November 29, 2004; See also Morris interview.

61. Jeremy A. Clawson, "Soccer Gives Afghans Positive Outlet with Soldiers' Help," U.S. Department of Defense Information, December 23, 2004.

62. Nicholas Dickson, Interview by Jenna Fike, Part II, Operational Leadership Experiences Project, Combat Studies Institute, Ft. Leavenworth, Kansas, October 1, 2009, http://cgsc.contentdm.oclc.org/cdm/singleitem/collection/p4013coll13/id/1628/rec/2.

63. Hunter, in Koontz, 495.

64. Waltz, 104.

65. Waltz, 104.

66. Anthony E. Carlson, "Forging Alliances at Yargul Village: A Lieutenant's Struggle to Improve Security," in *Vanguard of Valor: Small Unit Actions in Afghanistan*, ed. by Donald P. Wright (Fort Leavenworth, KS: Combat Studies Institute, 2012), 73–87.

67. Brian Elliot quoted in Carlson, "Forging Alliances," in Wright, *Vanguard of Valor I*, 87.

68. Evans interview.

69. Wade interview.

70. Varney interview.

71. Hunter, in Koontz, 509. Kimberly Evans used the exact same words, saying "I'd go back in a heartbeat." Evans interview.

72. Dickson interview.

73. Christoff Luehrs, "Provincial Reconstruction Teams: A Literature Review." *Prism*. Vol. 1, No. 1 (December 2009), 95, JSTOR. https://www.jstor.org/stable/10.2307/26469032; See also Robert E. Kemp, "Provincial Reconstruction Teams in Eastern Afghanistan: Utility as a Strategic Counterinsurgency Tool," *Military Review* (September-October 2011): 28- 36; Conor Keane, *U.S. Nation Building in Afghanistan* (NY: Routledge, 2016).

74. NATO, International Security Assistance Force History, accessed May 24, 2019, https://www.nato.int/cps/en/natohq/topics_69366.htm.

75. Arrieta interview; Creedon interview. For a case-study of the use of CERP funds in Afghanistan, see Anthony E. Carlson, "Gaining the Initiative in Musahi: Using CERP to Disrupt the Taliban in Kabul Province," in *Vanguard of Valor II: Small Unit Actions in Afghanistan,* ed. by Donald P. Wright (Fort Leavenworth, KS: Combat Studies Institute, 2012), 29–54.

76. For analyses of the CERP program and its effectiveness, see Gregory Johnson, Vijaya Ramachandran, and Julie Walz, "CERP in Afghanistan: Refining Military Capabilities in Development Activities," *PRISM* 3, no. 2 (2012): 81–98, accessed June 3, 2020, www.jstor.org/stable/26469731; SIGAR, "Commander's Emergency Response Program: DOD Has Not Determined the Full Extent to Which Its Program and Projects, Totaling $1.5 Billion in Obligations, Achieved Their Objectives and Goals in Afghanistan from Fiscal Years 2009 Through 2013," (Arlington, VA: SIGAR, April 2018), https://www.sigar.mil/pdf/audits/SIGAR-18–45-AR.pdf; Renard Sexton, "Did U.S. Aid Win Hearts and Minds in Afghanistan? Yes and No," *Washington Post*, January 6, 2017, https://www.washingtonpost.com/news/monkey-cage/wp/2017/01/06/did-u-s-nonmilitary-aid-win-hearts-and-minds-in-afghanistan-yes-and-no/.

77. SIGAR, "Counternarcotics: Lessons Learned from the U.S. Experience in Afghanistan," (Arlington, VA: SIGAR, June 2018), https://www.sigar.mil/interactive-reports/counternarcotics/index.html.

78. SIGAR, "Counternarcotics"; See also Craig Whitlock, "Overwhelmed by Opium," *Washington Post*, December 9, 2019.

79. Whitlock, "Overwhelmed by Opium."

80. Matthew Brown, Interview by Jenna Fike, Operational Leadership Experiences Project, Combat Studies Institute, Ft. Leavenworth, Kansas, July 30, 2012, http://cgsc.cdmhost.com/cdm/singleitem/collection/p4013coll13/id/2742/rec/1.

81. Bates interview.

82. Ross interview.

83. Gregory Strong, in Spiller, 57.

84. Government Accountability Office, "Afghanistan Governance: Performance-Data Gaps Hinder Overall Assessment of U.S. Efforts to Build Financial Management Capability," GAO-11–907 (September 2011), accessed April 10, 2020, https://www.gao.gov/assets/330/323502.html; Giustozzi, 203; For a critique of these efforts, see Abigail T. Linnington and Rebecca D. Patterson, "Rule of Law and Governance in Afghanistan, 2001–2014," in O'Connell, 189–212.

85. Forsyth, 76, 93.

86. Arrieta interview.

Chapter 8

1. Robert E. Kemp, "Provincial Reconstruction Teams in Eastern Afghanistan: Utility as a Strategic Counterinsurgency Tool," *Military Review* (September-October 2011), 33.

2. Waltz, 230.

3. Heath Clark, in Spiller, 85.

4. For the Stryker deployment, see Kevin M. Hymel, *Strykers in Afghanistan: Battalion, 17th Infantry Regiment in Kandahar Province, 2009, Vanguard of Valor IV* (Ft. Leavenworth, KS: Combat Studies Institute, 2014). For problems with the deployment, see "Report Blames Lapses on Stryker Commander," *Military Times*, March 27, 2013, https://www.militarytimes.com/2013/03/27/report-blames-lapses-on-stryker-commander-532-page-report-finds-colonel-ignored-doctrine-proper-procedure-in-leading-undisciplined-bct/; Fairweather, 317; Waltz, 235, 248.

5. Chandrasekaran, 167.

6. Greg Jaffe, "The Battle for Highway 1: U.S. Troops and Taliban Insurgents Are in the Last Throes of a Fight for One of Afghanistan's Vital Arteries, *Pittsburgh Post-Gazette*, April 16, 2012.

7. Colby Bradley in Skovlund, 323.

8. Karin Brulliard, "From Kandahar, a Different View of War," *Pittsburgh Post-Gazette*, October 10, 2010.

9. Chandrasekaran, 288.

10. Kingsley in Skovlund, 373.

11. Brenden McEvoy, Interview by Joey Strudnicka, Operational Leadership Experiences Project, Combat Studies Institute, Ft. Leavenworth, Kansas, November 13, 2013, http://cgsc.

contentdm.oclc.org/cdm/singleitem/collection/p4013coll13/id/3124/rec/7.

12. D. Scott Mann, *Game Changers: Going Local to Defeat Violent Extremists Special Forces & Law Enforcement Edition* (Leesburg, VA: Tribal Analysis Center, 2015), 64, 66; Maurer, "Witness to a War"; Daniel R. Green, "Organizing Like the Enemy: Special Operations Forces, Afghan Culture, and Village Stability Operations," in O'Connell, 246.

13. Mann, *Game Changers*, 66.

14. Quoted in Maurer, "Witness to a War."

15. Edward Woodall, Interview with Joey Strudnicka, Operational Leadership Experiences Project, Combat Studies Institute, Ft. Leavenworth, Kansas, December 3, 2013, http://cgsc.contentdm.oclc.org/cdm/singleitem/collection/p4013coll13/id/3159/rec/2.

16. Waltz, 343. He cites several examples of successful VSOs and claims the Taliban and Haqqani leadership viewed them as a strategic threat to their insurgencies. Waltz, 344–345.

17. Mann, *Game Changers*, 74; See also Green, in O'Connell, 260–269; Scott J. Gaitley, "Securing Dan Patan: A U.S. Infantry Squad's Counterinsurgency Program in an Afghan Village," in *Vanguard of Valor II: Small Unit Actions in Afghanistan*, ed. by Donald P. Wright (Fort Leavenworth, KS: Combat Studies Institute, 2012), 127, 136–137; Waltz, 346.

18. Mann, *Game Changers*, 75.

19. Mann, *Game Changers*, 75–76: See also Bradley Moses, SIGAR Lessons Learned Interview, "The Afghanistan Papers Digital Document Archive," *Washington Post*, https://www.washingtonpost.com/graphics/2019/investigations/afghanistan-papers/documents-database/.

20. Maurer, "Witness to a War."

21. Scott Mann, SIGAR Lessons Learned Interview, "The Afghanistan Papers Digital Document Archive," *Washington Post*, https://www.washingtonpost.com/graphics/2019/investigations/afghanistan-papers/documents-database/.

22. Unnamed SIGAR Lessons Learned Interview, September 7, 2016, "The Afghanistan Papers Digital Document Archive," *Washington Post*, https://www.washingtonpost.com/graphics/2019/investigations/afghanistan-papers/documents-database/. Gaitley focuses on positive outcomes, Gaitley, "Securing Dan Patan," in Wright, *Vanguard of Valor II*, 141–142.

23. Amin Saikal, *Modern Afghanistan: A History of Struggle and Survival* (New York: L.B. Tauris, 2012), 260; Chandrasekaran, 145, 342; Walling, 179; Heath Druzin, "A Look at How the U.S.-Led Coalition Lost Afghanistan's Marjah District to the Taliban," *Stars and Stripes*, January 16, 2016; "Report Blames Lapses on Stryker Commander," *Military Times*.

24. John Motter, quoted in "We Were Right," *Washington Post*, December 17, 2019.

25. Druzin, "A Look at How"; Steele, 34; Chandrasekaran, 70.

26. James Clark, "For Those Who Fought in Marjah, It Was More Than Just a Battle," *Task & Purpose*, February 13, 2015, accessed June 14, 2020, https://taskandpurpose.com/leadership/fought-marjah-just-battle.

27. Clark, "For Those Who Fought in Marjah."

28. Chandrasekaran, 139–140.

29. Clark, "For Those Who Fought in Marjah."

30. E3D blog post, November 4, 2014, accessed April 14, 2020, http://battlerattle.marinecorpstimes.com/2012/02/13/remembering-the-battle-of-marjah-two-years-later/. Misspellings in the original. Some of the Marines nicknamed it "Operation Bloody Valentine." See Vincent Liberatore, blog post, February 14, 2012, accessed April 14, 2020, http://battlerattle.marinecorpstimes.com/2012/02/13/remembering-the-battle-of-marjah-two-years-later/.

31. Chandrasekaran, 144, 151; Clark, "For Those Who Fought in Marjah"; Druzin, "A Look at How"; Steele, 34.

32. Clark, "For Those Who Fought in Marjah."

33. Druzin, "A Look at How."

34. Fairweather, 317; Steele, 33; See also Neumann and Williams, 62–63.

35. Clint Thoman quoted in West, 35.

36. Linderman, 13; See also Kindsvatter, 78–92.

37. J.D. Browning, quoted in West, 142.

38. Chandrasekaran, 287.

39. Lewis, in Skovlund, 382.

40. Dominic Esquibel quoted in West, 49.

41. Walling, 215–216; Steele, 25.

42. Colby Bradley, in Skovlund, 323.

43. Colby Bradley, in Skovlund, 348–352.

44. Colby Bradley, in Skovlund, 327.

45. Golembesky, 25; Waltz, 310.

46. Waltz, 269; Colby Bradley, in Skovlund, 335.

47. Michael Hastings, "Runaway General: The Profile That Brought Down McChrystal," *Rolling Stones*, June 22, 2010, accessed April 15, 2020, https://www.rollingstone.com/politics/politics-news/the-runaway-general-the-profile-that-brought-down-mcchrystal-192609/. See also Tom Bowman and Renee Montagne, "Rules of Engagement Are a Dilemma for U.S. Troops," *NPR Morning Edition*, December 11, 2009, accessed April 15, 2020, https://www.npr.org/templates/story/story.php?storyId=121330893.

48. Meyer, 103.

49. Waltz, 10.

50. Quoted in Waltz, 313.

51. Michael Hastings, "Runaway General: The Profile That Brought Down McChrystal," *Rolling Stones*, June 22, 2010, accessed April 15, 2020, https://www.rollingstone.com/politics/politics-news/the-runaway-general-the-profile-that-brought-down-mcchrystal-192609/; Chandrasekaran, 290; Barnes interview, May 20, 2020; Fairweather, 318.

52. Alvin Tilley, Interview by Angie Slattery, Operational Leadership Experiences Project, Combat Studies Institute, Ft. Leavenworth, Kansas, June 29, 2011, http://cgsc.contentdm.oclc.org/cdm/singleitem/collection/p4013coll13/id/2373/rec/1.

53. Marvin Linson, Interview by Angie Slattery, Operational Leadership Experiences Project, Combat Studies Institute, Ft. Leavenworth, Kansas, April 20, 2011, http://cgsc.contentdm.oclc.org/cdm/singleitem/collection/p4013coll13/id/2319/rec/1.

54. Chandrasekaran, 286.

55. Chandrasekaran, 167. For some of the small unit offensive operations, see Matthews, "Disrupt and Destroy," in Wright, *Vanguard of Valor I*, 131–156 and Kevin M. Hymel, "Trapping the Taliban at OP Dusty: A Scout Platoon in the Zhari District," in *Vanguard of Valor: Small Unit Actions in Afghanistan* (Fort Leavenworth, KS: Combat Studies Institute, 2012), 157–178.

56. Darling, 163.

57. Chandrasekaran, 297.

58. Benjamin F. Jones, "Leaving Afghanistan," in O'Connell, 286; Heidi Vogt, "The Less-Highlighted Part of the U.S. Drawdown in Afghanistan: Fewer Advisers and Trainers," *Canadian Press*, July 2, 2012; "Defense Secretary Panetta Announces Completion of Afghanistan Surge Drawdown," U.S. Fed News, September 21, 2012; Saikal 261; See Craig Whitlock, "Stranded Without a Strategy, *Washington Post*, December 9, 2019.

59. Rod Nordland, "Troop 'Surge' in Afghanistan Ends with Mixed Results," *New York Times*, September 22, 2012.

60. Miles Lagoze, quoted in Camille Baker, "A Veteran's War Movie Sheds Damning Light on How the Marines Fight in Afghanistan," *Intercept*, April 7, 2019, accessed May 11, 2020, https://theintercept.com/2019/04/07/combat-obscura-afghanistan-war-documentary/.

61. Victoria Areerob, "As Withdrawal Date Approaches, UNLC Veterans Recount a Day in Afghanistan," *Rebel Yell: University of Nevada-Las Vegas*, February 25, 2013.

62. Matthew Jarzin, "As Withdrawal Date Approaches, UNLC Veterans Recount a Day in Afghanistan," *Rebel Yell: University of Nevada-Las Vegas*, February 25, 2013.

63. C. Todd Lopez, "'Team of Teams' Draws Down Afghan Bases, Equipment," U.S. Army Releases, April 8, 2015.

64. "For U.S.-Led Force in Afghanistan, Time to Pack Up," *Agence France Presse*, June 18, 2014.

65. Arrieta interview.

66. Barnes interview, May 20, 2020.

67. Christine Hannigan quoted in "We Were Right," *Washington Post*, December 17, 2019.

68. "American Units Adapting to New Missions in Afghanistan," *State News Service*, May 2, 2014.

69. Ahmed Azam, "2 Coalition Soldiers Killed

by Attackers in Afghan Uniforms," *New York Times*, February 13, 2014; Jones, "Leaving Afghanistan," 288.

70. Azam Ahmed, "Apathy and Fear of Taliban Combine to Keep Rural Voters Away from the Polls," *New York Times*, April 6, 2014.

71. Alissa J. Rubin, "Taliban Wage Deadly Attacks in 3 Afghan Provinces," *New York Times*, May 13, 2014.

72. Azam Ahmed, "Taliban Making Military Gains in Afghanistan," *New York Times*, July 27, 2014.

73. Declan Walsh and Azam Ahmed, "Mending Alliance, U.S. and Afghanistan Sign Lon-Term Security Agreement," *New York Times*, October 1, 2014; Missy Ryan, "Afghan Training Mission Means a Sprint for U.S. Troops," *Washington Post*, December 8, 2014.

74. "U.S. Still Losing Soldiers as It Prepares to Exit," *Leader-Post* (Regina, Saskatchewan), October 14, 2014.

75. "3ID HQ to Deploy to Afghanistan as Drawdown, Retrograde Continues," *Army News Service*, October 29, 2014.

76. Drew Brooks, "Army Leaders Say There's No Drawdown in Costs as U.S. Troops Leave Afghanistan," *Fayetteville Observer*, December 17, 2014.

77. Rod Nordland, "Taliban Push Into Afghan Districts That U.S. Forces Secured," *New York Times*, December 23, 2014; Ahmed Azam, "Hour's Drive Outside Kabul, Taliban Reign," *New York Times*, November 23, 2014; Rod Norland, "For Afghans, the Fighting Now Knows No Season," *New York Times*, November 29, 2014; Mark Mazzetti and Eric Schmitt, "In a Shift, Obama Extends U.S. Role in Afghan Combat," *New York Times*, November 22, 2014; Malkasian, *The American War*, 385.

78. Lynne O'Donnell, "Afghanistan Mire in War and U.S. Combat Command Ends," *St. Louis Post-Dispatch*, December 9, 2014; Williams, 251.

79. NATO, Resolute Support Mission in Afghanistan, accessed May 24, 2019, https://www.nato.int/cps/en/natohq/topics_113694/htm; NATO, Resolute Support Mission in Afghanistan," accessed May 7, 2020, https://rs.nato.int/about-us/mission.aspx.

80. Pamela Constable, "A Formal End to NATO's Combat Role in Afghanistan," *Washington Post*, December 29, 2014.

81. Williams, 252; Jessica Donati, *Eagle Down: The Last Special Forces Fighting in the Forever War* (New York: Public Affairs, 2021), 1, 6; Morgan, 415, 420, 469.

82. Doherty interview.

83. Maurer, "Witness to a War"; Donati, 48; Morgan, 479; Malkasian, *The American War*, 416–417.

84. Donati, 115–117, 195–196; Morgan 470, 483; Malkasian, *The American War*, 384–385.

85. Donati, 236–237, 266–267; Morgan 490; Malkasian, *The American War*, 404–411; 423–447.

Chapter 9

1. Susannah George, "What You Need to Know About the U.S.-Taliban Peace Deal," *Washington Post*, February 29, 2020, accessed March 2, 2020, https://www.washingtonpost.com/world/asia_pacific/what-you-need-to-know-about-the-us-taliban-peace-deal/2020/02/29/e63e062c-5a67-11ea-8efd-0f904bdd8057_story.html; Donati, 266–267; Malkasian, *The American War*, 445.

2. Missy Ryan, Susannah George, and Haq Nawaz Khan, "Violence in Afghanistan Will Probably Continue Despite Deal, U.S. Military Leaders Say," *Washington Post*, March 2, 2020, accessed May 8, 2020, https://www.washingtonpost.com/world/violence-in-afghanistan-will-probably-continue-despite-deal-us-military-leaders-say/2020/03/02/6f82577c-5c97-11ea-ac50-18701e14e06d_story.html.

3. Sharif Hassan and Susannah George, "Taliban Attacks in Afghanistan Surge After U.S. Peace Deal, Inflicting Heavy Casualties," *Washington Post*, April 30, 2020, accessed May 7, 2020, https://www.washingtonpost.com/world/asia_pacific/taliban-attacks-in-afghanistan-surge-after-us-peace-deal-inflicting-heavy-casualties/2020/04/30/1362fb40-88c0-11ea-80df-d24b35a568ae_story.html.

4. Greg Jaffe, "Following Withdrawal Announcement, Battle to Determine Afghanistan War's Legacy Begins," *Washington Post*, April 13, 2021, https://www.washingtonpost.com/national-security/afghanistan-war-legacy-us-military/2021/04/13/a2f4bf70-9c7c-11eb-8005-bffc3a39f6d3_story.html; Wooston, Lamothe, and Wagner, "Biden Forcefully Defends Afghan Pullout."

5. Gordon Lubold and Yaroslav Trofimov, "Afghan Government Could Collapse Six Months After U.S. Withdrawal, New Intelligence Assessment Says," *Wall Street Journal*, June 23, 2021, https://www.wsj.com/articles/afghan-government-could-collapse-six-months-after-u-s-withdrawal-new-intelligence-assessment-says-11624466743; Lara Seligman, "Sources: U.S. Troop Withdrawal from Afghanistan Complete 'For All Intents and Purposes,'" *Politico*, July 7, 2021, https://www.politico.com/news/2021/07/07/us-troop-withdrawal-afghanistan-498671.

6. Cameron Sellers, "Goodbye, Afghanistan," in *Operation Homecoming*, ed. Carroll, 317.

7. Jenkins, iii. Other veterans have invoked the same sentiment for their war. Philip Caputo quotes the same passage in his memoir. Caputo, 66.

8. Linderman, 263.

9. Fick, 369.

10. Parnell, ix, 370.

11. Romesha, 14.

12. Anders, vii, 497–498.

13. Cariello interview.

14. Janke interview.

15. Rico, 306.

16. Tupper, 253.

17. Bradley, xi, 279–280.

18. Marine Chad Mauger, blog post, February 14, 2012, accessed April 14, 2020, http://battlerattle.marinecorpstimes.com/2012/02/13/remembering-the-battle-of-marjah-two-years-later/.

19. Kindsvatter, 184–185.

20. Creedon interview.

21. McGarry, 4.

22. Meyer, 188.

23. Jeff Sibley quoted in West, 200.

24. Waltz, xvi.

25. Golembesky, xiv–xv, 281.

26. West, 244.

27. Arietta interview.

28. Jay O'Brian quoted in quoted in "We Were Right," *Washington Post*, December 17, 2019.

29. David Bently quoted in "We Were Right," *Washington Post*, December 17, 2019.

30. Paul Szoldra, "There's a New 'Father and Son Served in Afghanistan' Puff Piece, and Boy Is It Depressing," *Task and Purpose*, July 17, 2018, accessed May 11, 2020, https://taskandpurpose.com/code-red-news/theres-a-new-father-and-son-served-in-afghanistan-puff-piece-and-boy-is-it-depressing. Army Staff Sgt. Will Blackburn served in Afghanistan in 2004, and his son served there in 2020. See Russ Bynum, "'Let's Go Home': Afghan War Vets Torn on U.S.-Taliban Deal," *Military Times*, March 1, 2020, accessed May 11, 2020, https://www.militarytimes.com/news/your-military/2020/03/01/lets-go-home-afghan-war-vets-torn-on-us-taliban-deal/.

31. Miles Lagoze quoted in Camille Baker, "A Veteran's War Movie Sheds Damning Light on How the Marines Fight in Afghanistan," *Intercept*, April 7, 2019, accessed May 11, 2020, https://theintercept.com/2019/04/07/combat-obscura-afghanistan-war-documentary/.

32. Thomas Gibbons-Neff, "At War," *New York Times*, October 2, 2020.

33. Carter Malkasian observes these mixed feelings from the troops from his deployments in Afghanistan, too. See, Malkasian, *The American War*, 453.

34. Michael Flynn quoted in Craig Whitlock, "At War with the Truth," *Washington Post*, December 9, 2017.

35. Meyer, 177.

36. Jeff Schogol, "'It Bothers Me a Little Bit That It's Just Going to End Like This'—The Pain Felt by Afghanistan War Veterans," *Task and Purpose*, April 24, 2021, https://taskandpurpose.com/news/afghanistan-war-veterans-pain-withdrawal/.

37. Tony Villa quoted in Schogol, "It Bothers Me."

38. William Monahan quoted in Schogol, "It Bothers Me."

39. Peter Lucier quoted in Dan Lamothe and Alex Horton, "For Afghanistan Veterans, Old Feelings of Frustration and Loss Surface as the U.S. Prepares to End Its Longest War," *Washington Post*, April 14, 2021, https://www.washingtonpost.com/national-security/afghanistan-withdrawal-veterans-biden/2021/04/14/92ce7798–9c96–11eb-8a83–3bc1fa69c2e8_story.html.

40. Amber Chase quoted in Lamothe and Horton, "For Afghanistan Veterans."

41. Tyler Burdick quoted in Lamothe and Horton, "For Afghanistan Veterans."

42. RJ Reinhart, "U.S. Views Mixon on War in Afghanistan," *Gallup*, September 11, 2019, accessed May 11, 2020, https://news.gallup.com/poll/266546/views-mixed-war-afghanistan.aspx.

43. Shibley Telhami and Connor Kopchick, "This Recent Poll Shows How Americans Think About the War in Afghanistan," *Washington Post*, January 5, 2020, accessed May 11, 2020, https://www.washingtonpost.com/politics/2020/01/05/this-recent-poll-shows-how-americans-think-about-war-afghanistan/.

44. Ruth Igielnik and Kim Parker, "Majorities of U.S. Veterans, Public Say the Wars in Iraq and Afghanistan Were Not Worth Fighting," Pew Research Center, July 10, 2019, accessed May 11, 2020, https://www.pewresearch.org/fact-tank/2019/07/10/majorities-of-u-s-veterans-public-say-the-wars-in-iraq-and-afghanistan-were-not-worth-fighting/.

45. "Do Voters Know We're Still at War in Afghanistan?" Rasmussen Reports, July 30, 2018, accessed May 11, 2020, https://www.rasmussenreports.com/public_content/politics/current_events/afghanistan/do_voters_know_we_re_still_at_war_with_afghanistan.

46. Jaffe, "Following Withdrawal Announcement."

47. Max Boot, "Opinion: Biden's Afghanistan Withdrawal Could Be the First Step to a Taliban Takeover," *Washington Post*, April 13, 2021, https://www.washingtonpost.com/opinions/2021/04/13/bidens-afghanistan-withdrawal-could-be-first-step-taliban-takeover/

48. Pamela Constable, "If the Taliban Take Power Again, Will Afghans Have Died in Vain?" *Washington Post*, April 16, 2021, https://www.washingtonpost.com/outlook/if-the-taliban-take-power-again-will-afghans-have-died-in-vain/2021/04/16/b30f60ae-9e5c-11eb-8005-bffc3a39f6d3_story.html.

49. Susannah George and Aziz Tassal, "The Taliban Is Targeting Areas Around Key Provincial Capitals, Looking for Weak Spots as Foreign Troops Withdraw," *Washington Post*, May 8, 2021, https://www.washingtonpost.com/world/2021/05/08/afghanistan-taliban-attacks/

50. Fazelminallah Qazizai, "The Taliban Are Getting Stronger in Afghanistan as U.S. and NATO Forces Exit," *NPR Morning Edition*, June 8, 2021.

51. Joseph Choi, "Partisan Splits Seen in New Poll on Withdrawal from Afghanistan," *Hill*, July

14, 2021, https://thehill.com/homenews/562897-partisan-split-seen-in-new-poll-on-withdrawal-from-afghanistan.

52. Karlyn Bowman, "The War in Afghanistan: A Polling Post-Mortem," *Forbes,* July 8, 2021, https://www.forbes.com/sites/bowmanmarsico/2021/07/08/the-war-in-afghanistan-a-polling-post-mortem/?sh=d4834136214b.

53. Kathy Frankovic, "Americans Support Decision to Withdrawal U.S. Forces from Afghanistan," YouGovAmerica, April 23, 2021, https://today.yougov.com/topics/politics/articles-reports/2021/04/23/americans-support-withdraw-afghanistan; See also Jim Golby and Peter Feaver, "It Matters If Americans Call Afghanistan a Defeat," *Atlantic,* August 17, 2019, accessed May 11, 2020, https://www.theatlantic.com/ideas/archive/2019/08/will-americans-call-afghanistan-victory/596188/.

54. Jeffrey P. Kimball, "The Stab-in-the-Back Legend and the Vietnam War," *Armed Forces & Society,* vol. 14 no. 3 (1988), 433–458. https://doi.org/10.1177/0095327X8801400306.

55. Schogol, "It Bothers Me."

56. Craig Whitlock, "The War in Afghanistan: Promises to Win, but No Vision for Victory," *Washington Post,* April 14, 2021, https://www.washingtonpost.com/investigations/the-war-in-afghanistan-promises-to-win-but-no-vision-for-victory/2021/04/14/89acb8d6–9c6f-11eb-b7a8–014b14aeb9e4_story.html.

57. Whitlock, "The War in Afghanistan"; Jaffe, "Following Withdrawal Announcement"; Qazizai, "The Taliban Are Getting Stronger"; Boot, "Biden's Afghanistan Withdrawal."

58. Andrew Bacevich, *The New American Militarism: How Americans Are Seduced by War,* Updated Ed. (New York: Oxford University Press, 2013), 108–117. Caleb S. Cage argues that "heroes and Victims" is a narrative of the Iraq and Afghan wars, though I believe Bacevich establishes the heroism component pre-dates either war. See Caleb S. Cage, *War Narratives: Shaping Beliefs, Blurring Truths in the Middle East* (College Station: Texas A&M University Press, 2019), 79–90.

59. *Zero Dark Thirty,* directed by Kathryn Bigelow (Columbia Pictures, 2012).

60. Manohla Dargis, "By Any Means Necessary," *New York Times,* December 17, 2012, https://www.nytimes.com/2012/12/18/movies/jessica-chastain-in-zero-dark-thirty.html; Although these are imperfect measures of public opinion, Rotten Tomatoes and the Internet Movie Database are convenient for tracking their users' preferences in a general sense. I use these as proxies, as imprecise as they are, for general public sentiment. The film has a 91% positive critic score and 80% positive audience score on Rotten Tomatoes. "Zero Dark Thirty," *Rotten Tomatoes,* accessed June 22, 2020, https://www.rottentomatoes.com/m/zero_dark_thirty; It has a 7.4.10 stars and 95 metacritic score on IMDb. "Zero Dark Thirty," *IMDb.com,* accessed June 22, 2020, app.

61. *Lone Survivor,* directed by Peter Berg (Universal, 2013); Marcus Luttrell with Patrick Robinson, *Lone Survivor: The Eyewitness Account of Operation Redwing and the Lost Heroes of SEAL Team 10* (New York: Back Bay, 2008).

62. Junger, 51.

63. Morris Kessler, "Lone Survivor: What Really Happened During Operation Redwings," *Esquire,* April 2, 2014, https://www.esquire.com/uk/culture/news/a5665/lone-survivor/.

64. It has a 75% positive critic rating and 87% positive audience rating. "Lone Survivor," *Rotten Tomatoes,* accessed June 26, 2020, https://www.rottentomatoes.com/m/lone_survivor; It has a 7.5/10 audience rating and 60 metacritic rating. "Lone Suvivor," *Imdb.com,* accessed June 26, 2020, app.

65. *12 Strong,* directed by Nicolai Fuglsig (Warner Brothers Pictures, 2018).

66. Gary Thompson, "What Does '12 Strong' Actor Rob Riggle Know About the War in Afghanistan? A Lot. He Was One of the First Guys There," *Philadelphia Inquirer,* January 12, 2018, https://www.inquirer.com/philly/columnists/gary_thompson/12-strong-rob-riggle-christmas-hemsworth-horse-soldiers-20180112.html.

67. For the elements of the combat war genre, see Jeanine Basinger, *The World War II Combat Film: Anatomy of a Genre* updated ed. (Middletown, CT: Wesleyan University Press, 2003).

68. It garners 50% positive critic reviews and 62% positive audience reviews. "12 Strong," *Rotten Tomatoes,* accessed June 25, 2020, https://www.rottentomatoes.com/m/12_strong; It has 6.6/10 stars for audiences and 54 metacritic score. "12 Strong," *IMDb.com,* accessed June 25, 2020, app.

69. *War Machine* film poster, Imdb.com, accessed May 11, 2020, https://www.imdb.com/title/tt4758646/?ref_=fn_al_tt_1; Michod, David. *War Machine,* directed by David Michod (Netflix, 2017).

70. Michael Hastings, "Runaway General: The Profile That Brought Down McChrystal," *Rolling Stones,* June 22, 2010, accessed April 15, 2020, https://www.rollingstone.com/politics/politics-news/the-runaway-general-the-profile-that-brought-down-mcchrystal-192609/.

71. It garnered a 48% critic rating and a 34% audience rating. "War Machine," *Rotten Tomatoes,* accessed June 24, 2020, https://www.rottentomatoes.com/m/war_machine_2016#audience_reviews; It rated 6.0/10 stars for audiences and 56 metacritic score. "War Machine," *IMDB.com,* accessed June 24, 2020, app.

72. *The Kill Team,* directed by Dan Krauss (Nostromo Pictures, 2019).

73. Critics preferred Krauss's documentary on the incident, but still gave a 70% positive rating. Audiences only gave it 40%. "The Kill Team," *Rotten Tomatoes,* accessed June 24, 2020,

https://www.rottentomatoes.com/m/the_kill_team_2019; It has a 5.9/10 audience ranking and 60 metacritic score on IMDb. "The Kill Team," *IMDb.com,* accessed June 24, 2020, app.

74. Mark Schone and Matthew Cole, "Calvin Gibbs, Leader of 'Thrill Kill' Soldiers, Guilty of Murder," *ABC News,* November 10, 2011, https://abcnews.go.com/Blotter/leader-thrill-kill-soldiers-found-guilty/story?id=14924863; Simon Thompson, "Fact, Fiction and the Importance of Seeking the Truth with 'The Kill Team,'" *Forbes,* October 24, 2019, https://www.forbes.com/sites/simonthompson/2019/10/24/fact-fiction-and-the-importance-of-seeking-the-truth-with-the-kill-team/#71f1fcb14cbb. Cage would argue the narrative of this film fits with the "victims" narrative prevalent in the Iraq and Afghan Wars. See Cage, 79–90.

75. Stoney Portis, "At War," *New York Times,* July 3, 2020, email distribution; "The Outpost," *IMDb.com,* accessed July 7, 2020, app.

76. Rod Lurie, " 'The Outpost' Director Rod Lurie on Looking Beyond Box Office Numbers to Find Validation in Films Released During Pandemic—Guest Column," *Deadline,* July 6, 2020, https://deadline.com/2020/07/the-outpost-movie-military-families-reaction-rod-lurie-guest-column-1202978655/.

77. Ann Hornaday, "'The Outpost' Is Both a Riveting War Movie and a Cautionary Tale," *Washington Post,* July 1, 2020, https://www.washingtonpost.com/goingoutguide/movies/the-outpost-movie-review/2020/07/01/c53a969e-b713–11ea-aca5-ebb63d27e1ff_story.html?arc404=true. It has a 90% positive critic rating on Rotten Tomatoes. Very few audience members have rated it thus far—only 85—but they have liked it with 85% positive reviews. "The Outpost," *Rotten Tomatoes,* accessed July 7, 2020, https://www.rottentomatoes.com/m/the_outpost_2019. On IMDB, the film has a Metacritic rating of 71. Once again, very few audience members have rated it. It stands at present at 6.6/10. From the user reviews, it appears that many audience members expect Hollywood storytelling with character arcs and plot development. "The Outpost" User Reviews *IMDB.com,* app.

78. *Restrepo,* directed by Tim Heatherington and Sebastian Junger (National Geographic Entertainment, 2010).

79. It has 97% positive critic reviews and 88% positive audience reviews on Rotten Tomatoes. "Restrepo," *Rotten Tomatoes,* accessed June 22, 2020, https://www.rottentomatoes.com/m/restrepo; It has a 7.5/10 stars on IMDb and a critic metascore of 85. "Restrepo," *IMDb.com,* accessed June 22, 2020, IMDb app.

80. *Legion of Brothers,* directed by Greg Barker (CNN Films, 2017).

81. Only seven critics reviewed the documentary as reported by Rotten Tomatoes at the time of this research. All gave it a positive review. Audience ratings were 66% with only 300 reporting.

In comparison, 13,496 people rated *Restrepo.* "Legion of Brothers," *Rotten Tomatoes,* accessed June 30, 2020, https://www.rottentomatoes.com/m/legion_of_brothers; "Restrepo," *Rotten Tomatoes.* Similarly, only 286 audience members rated *Legion of Brothers* on IMDb, and gave it a mere 5.7/10 rating. In comparison, 21,646 rated *Restrepo.* "Legion of Brothers," *IMDb.com,* accessed June 30, 2020, app; "Restrepo," *IMDB.com.*

82. Lagoze quoted in Baker, "A Veteran's War Movie Sheds Damning Light on How the Marines Fight in Afghanistan."

83. Critics have 100% positive reviews. Only 22 audience members rated it. They give it 77% positive rating, though it is not terribly representative. "Combat Obscura," *Rotten Tomatoes,* accessed July 1, 2020, https://www.rottentomatoes.com/m/combat_obscura. Only five critics are included on IMDb. They gave it a 56 metascore. Another 233 audience members gave it 6.8/10 stars. "Combat Obscura," *IMDb,* accessed July 1, 2020, app.

84. *Taking Fire* (Discovery Channel, 2016). "Taking Fire," *IMDB.com,* accessed June 30, 2020, app. 252 people gave ratings as of this date, giving it 8.1/10 stars.

85. Kindsvatter, 287; 286–293.

Conclusion

1. Dan Lamothe, "Top U.S. Commander in Afghanistan Steps Down, Marking a Symbolic End to 20 Years of War," *Washington Post,* July 12, 2021, https://www.washingtonpost.com/national-security/2021/07/12/last-us-general-afghanistan/.

2. Barnes interview, May 20, 2020.

3. "Summary of War Spending," Watson Institute, Brown University, accessed July 29, 2020, https://watson.brown.edu/costsofwar/figures/2019/budgetary-costs-post-911-wars-through-fy2020–64-trillion. This figure includes expected spending on veterans' medical and disability through FY2059. Direct spending reaches $5.4 trillion.

4. "Afghan Fatalities by Country," iCasualties, accessed July 19, 2021, http://icasualties.org/chart/Chart.

5. Davidson, "The Costs of War," 3.

6. Neta C. Crawford and Catherin Lutz, "Human and Budgetary Costs to Date of the U.S. War in Afghanistan," Costs of War, Watson Institute, Brown University, April 15, 2021, https://watson.brown.edu/costsofwar/files/cow/imce/figures/2021/Human%20and%20Budgetary%20Costs%20of%20Afghan%20War%2C%202001–2021.pdf.

7. Colby Bradley, quoted in *75th Ranger Regiment,* 348.

8. Parnell, 372.

9. Isabel Debre, "Counting the Costs of

America's 20-Year War in Afghanistan," *Associated Press*, April 20, 2021, https://apnews.com/article/asia-pacific-afghanistan-middle-east-business-5e850e5149ea0a3907cac2f282878dd5.

10. "Afghanistan: Women's Empowerment and Gender," USAID, updated July 9, 2021, accessed July 18, 2021, https://www.usaid.gov/afghanistan/gender-participant-training.

11. Major Dan, "CODA," Doonsbury's The Sandbox, accessed July 29, 2020, https://gocomics.typepad.com/the_sandbox/. Emphasis in the original.

Bibliography

Archival Materials

"The Afghanistan Papers Digital Document Archive." *The Washington Post*. https://www.washingtonpost.com/graphics/2019/investigations/afghanistan-papers/documents-database/.

Civil Affairs & Psychological Operations, "Operation Enduring Freedom: Historical Collection," 126th Military History Detachment, 2003. United States Army Education and Heritage Center. Carlisle Barracks, PA.

Films

Barker, Greg, dir. *Legion of Brothers*. CNN Films. 2017. Amazon Prime.

Berg, Peter, dir. *Lone Survivor*. Universal Pictures. 2013. Amazon Prime.

Bigelow, Kathryn, dir. *Zero Dark Thirty*. Columbia Pictures. 2012. Amazon Prime.

Fuglsig, Nicolai, dir. *12 Strong*. Warner Brothers Pictures. 2018. Amazon Prime.

Hetherington, Tim, and Sebastian Junger, dirs. *Restrepo*. National Geographic Entertainment. 2010. Amazon Prime.

Junger, Sebastian, dir. *Korengal*. Gold Crest Films. 2014. Amazon Prime.

Krauss, Dan, dir. *The Kill Team*. Nostromo Pictures. 2019. Amazon Prime.

Lagoze, Miles, dir. *Combat Obscura*. Oscilloscope Laboratories. 2019. Amazon Prime.

Lurie, Rod, dir. *The Outpost*. Screen Media Films. 2020. Amazon Prime.

Mactavish, Scott, dir. *Murph: The Protector*. Starz. 2013. Amazon Prime.

Michod, David, dir. *War Machine*. Netflix. 2017. Netflix.

Television Series

Battleground Afghanistan. National Geographic Channel. 2013.

Taking Fire. Discovery Channel. 2016.

Newspapers

Army Times, 2002–2021.
Military Times, 2002–2021.
New York Times, 2001–2021.
Washington Post, 2001–2021.

Oral History Interviews

Albano, Lou. Interview by Laurence Lessard. Operational Leadership Experiences Project. Combat Studies Institute. Ft. Leavenworth, Kansas. January 29, 2009. http://cgsc.contentdm.oclc.org/cdm/singleitem/collection/p4013coll13/id/1726/rec/6.

Alexander, Robert (Brian). Interview by Leo Hirrel. Quartermaster School. October 25, 2011.

Anderson, Christian. Interview by Angie Slattery. Operational Leadership Experiences Project. Combat Studies Institute. Ft. Leavenworth, Kansas. November 10, 2010. http://cgsc.cdmhost.com/cdm/singleitem/collection/p4013coll13/id/2125/rec/1.

Arietta, Neil. Interview by Lisa M. Mundey. August 18, 2019. Personal transcript.

Barnes, Jacob (Pseudonym). Interview by Lisa M. Mundey. May 20, 2020. Personal transcript.

_____. Interview by Lisa M. Mundey. May 22, 2020. Personal transcript.

Bates, John. Interview by Brad Helton. Part II. Operational Leadership Experiences Project. Combat Studies Institute. Ft. Leavenworth, Kansas. June 24, 2008. http://cgsc.cdmhost.com/cdm/singleitem/collection/p4013coll13/id/1095/rec/2.

Berendsen, Anton. Interview by Michael Anderson. Operational Leadership Experiences Project. Combat Studies Institute. Ft. Leavenworth, Kansas. February 8, 2015. http://cgsc.contentdm.oclc.org/cdm/singleitem/collection/p4013coll13/id/3263/rec/1.

Bishop, Don. Interview by Lawrence Lessard. Operational Leadership Experiences Project. Combat Studies Institute. Ft. Leavenworth,

Kansas. May 11, 2009. http://cgsc.contentdm. oclc.org/cdm/singleitem/collection/ p4013coll13/id/2187/rec/1.

Boesen, Stephen. Interview by Shawn O'Brien. Operational Leadership Experiences Project. Combat Studies Institute. Ft. Leavenworth, Kansas. July 7, 2008. http://cgsc.contentdm.oclc. org/cdm/singleitem/collection/p4013coll13/ id/1360/rec/1.

Boissonneau, Andrew. Interview by Joey Strudnicka. Operational Leadership Experiences Project. Combat Studies Institute. Ft. Leavenworth, Kansas. September 17, 2014. http:// cgsc.cdmhost.com/cdm/singleitem/collection/ p4013coll13/id/3242/rec/1.

Brown, Matthew. Interview by Jenna Fike. Operational Leadership Experiences Project. Combat Studies Institute. Ft. Leavenworth, Kansas. July 30, 2012. http://cgsc.cdmhost.com/cdm/ singleitem/collection/p4013coll13/id/2742/ rec/1.

Buckingham, William. Interview by Angie Slattery. Operational Leadership Experiences Project. Combat Studies Institute. Ft. Leavenworth, Kansas. February 2, 2010. http://cgsc. contentdm.oclc.org/cdm/singleitem/collection/ p4013coll13/id/1794/rec/4.

Busy, Kevin. Interview by Allen Skinner. Operational Leadership Experiences Project. Combat Studies Institute. Ft. Leavenworth, Kansas. May 18, 2012. http://cgsc.cdmhost.com/cdm/ singleitem/collection/p4013coll13/id/2683/ rec/1.

Cariello, Dominic. Interview by John McCool. Operational Leadership Experiences Project. Combat Studies Institute. Ft. Leavenworth, Kansas. February 16, 2007. http://cgsc. contentdm.oclc.org/cdm/singleitem/collection/ p4013coll13/id/720/rec/1.

Connors. Interview by Douglas Cubbison. 10th Mountain Division. January 2007. Operational Leadership Experiences Project. Combat Studies Institute. Ft. Leavenworth, KS. http:// cgsc.contentdm.oclc.org/cdm/singleitem/ collection/p4013coll13/id/1027/rec/22.

Creedon, Michael. Interview by Lisa M. Mundey. June 3, 2020. Personal Transcript.

Croot, Edward. Interview by John Bauer, Part II. Operational Leadership Experiences Project. Combat Studies Institute. Ft. Leavenworth, Kansas. February 17, 2007. http:// cgsc.contentdm.oclc.org/cdm/singleitem/ collection/p4013coll13/id/816/rec/2.

Davila, Diego. Interview by Shawn O'Brien. Operational Leadership Experiences Project. Combat Studies Institute. Ft. Leavenworth, Kansas. June 10, 2008. http://cgsc.cdmhost.com/cdm/ singleitem/collection/p4013coll13/id/1484/ rec/1.

Davis, Ross. Interview by William Adler. Operational Leadership Experiences Project. Combat Studies Institute. Ft. Leavenworth, Kansas. December 19, 2007. http://cgsc.contentdm.

oclc.org/cdm/singleitem/collection/ p4013coll13/id/900/rec/1.

Diana, Gabriel. Interview by Lisa Beckenbaugh. Operational Leadership Experiences Project. Combat Studies Institute. Ft. Leavenworth, Kansas. May 14, 2013. http://cgsc.contentdm. oclc.org/cdm/singleitem/collection/ p4013coll13/id/3072/rec/1.

Dickson, Nicholas. Interview by Jenna Fike. Part II. Operational Leadership Experiences Project. Combat Studies Institute. Ft. Leavenworth, Kansas. October 1, 2009. http:// cgsc.contentdm.oclc.org/cdm/singleitem/ collection/p4013coll13/id/1628/rec/2.

DiGuadio, Adam. Interview by Angie Slattery. Operational Leadership Experiences Project. Combat Studies Institute. Ft. Leavenworth, Kansas. December 1, 2011. http://cgsc.cdmhost. com/cdm/singleitem/collection/p4013coll13/ id/2526/rec/1.

Doherty, Thomas. Interview by Lisa M. Mundey. December 28, 2018. Personal transcript.

Erwin, Christy. Interview by Lisa Beckenbaugh. Operational Leadership Experiences Project. Combat Studies Institute. Ft. Leavenworth, Kansas. October 21, 2013. http:// cgsc.contentdm.oclc.org/cdm/singleitem/ collection/p4013coll13/id/3126/rec/1.

Evans, Kimberly. Interview by J. Patrick Hughes and Lisa Mundey. February 13, 2007. U.S. Army Center of Military History. Ft. McNair, Washington, D.C. Unpublished transcript.

Fanning, Bryan. Interview by Joey Strudnicka. Operational Leadership Experiences Project. Combat Studies Institute. Ft. Leavenworth, Kansas. October 10, 2013. http:// cgsc.contentdm.oclc.org/cdm/singleitem/ collection/p4013coll13/id/3111/rec/6.

Farris, Stuart. Interview by Laurence Lessard. Part I. Operational Leadership Experiences Project. Combat Studies Institute. Ft. Leavenworth, Kansas. December 6, 2007. http:// cgsc.contentdm.oclc.org/cdm/ref/collection/ p4013coll13/id/1019.

Farris, Stuart. Interview by Laurence Lessard. Part II. Operational Leadership Experiences Project. Combat Studies Institute. Ft. Leavenworth, Kansas. December 6, 2007. http:// cgsc.contentdm.oclc.org/cdm/singleitem/ collection/p4013coll13/id/1020/rec/2.

Fleurant, Marc. Interview by Angie Slattery Hundley. Operational Leadership Experiences Project. Combat Studies Institute. Ft. Leavenworth, Kansas. February 6, 2013. http:// cgsc.contentdm.oclc.org/cdm/singleitem/ collection/p4013coll13/id/2988/rec/1.

Gray, Michael. Interview by Joey Strudnicka. Part II. Operational Leadership Experiences Project. Combat Studies Institute. Ft. Leavenworth, October 15, 2014. http://cgsc.contentdm.oclc. org/cdm/singleitem/collection/p4013coll13/ id/3247/rec/4.

Griffin, Brandon. Interview by Pete Boisson. Part

II. Operational Leadership Experiences Project. Combat Studies Institute. Ft. Leavenworth, Kansas. July 25, 2006. http://cgsc.contentdm.oclc.org/cdm/singleitem/collection/p4013coll13/id/484/rec/4.

_____. Interview by Angie Slattery. Operational Leadership Experiences Project. Combat Studies Institute. Ft. Leavenworth, Kansas. February 2, 2012. http://cgsc.cdmhost.com/cdm/singleitem/collection/p4013coll13/id/2578/rec/3.

Hollar, John. Interview by Angie Slattery. Operational Leadership Experiences Project. Combat Studies Institute. Ft. Leavenworth, Kansas. May 25, 2011. http://cgsc.contentdm.oclc.org/cdm/singleitem/collection/p4013coll13/id/2359/rec/1.

Janke, Jeff. Interview by Laurence Lessard. Operational Leadership Experiences Project. Combat Studies Institute. Ft. Leavenworth, Kansas. February 16, 2007. http://cgsc.cdmhost.com/cdm/singleitem/collection/p4013coll13/id/734/rec/1.

Johnson, Hurel. Interview by Laurence Lessard. Operational Leadership Experiences Project. Combat Studies Institute. Ft. Leavenworth, Kansas. September 17, 2007. http://cgsc.contentdm.oclc.org/cdm/singleitem/collection/p4013coll13/id/777/rec/1.

Jorgensen, Erik. Interview by Douglas Cubbison, 10th Mountain Division, Fort Drum, New York. January 22, 2007. http://cgsc.contentdm.oclc.org/cdm/singleitem/collection/p4013coll13/id/1005/rec/1.

Kivioja, Kyle. Interview by Sean Kaubisch. Operational Leadership Experiences Project. Combat Studies Institute. Ft. Leavenworth, Kansas. April 10, 2015. http://cgsc.contentdm.oclc.org/cdm/singleitem/collection/p4013coll13/id/3269/rec/1.

Korando, Deitra. Interview by John McCool. Operational Leadership Experiences Project. Combat Studies Institute. Ft. Leavenworth, Kansas. October 5, 2005. http://cgsc.cdmhost.com/cdm/ref/collection/p4013coll13/id/39.

Kozar, Andrew. Interviewed by Leo Hirrel. January 25, 2012. Quartermaster School.

Lachicotte, George. Interview by Jenna Fike. Operational Leadership Experiences Project. Combat Studies Institute. Ft. Leavenworth, Kansas. November 1, 2011. http://cgsc.contentdm.oclc.org/cdm/singleitem/collection/p4013coll13/id/2467/rec/1.

Lane, Connie. Interview by Jenna Fike. Operational Leadership Experiences Project. Combat Studies Institute. Ft. Leavenworth, Kansas. March 6, 2012. http://cgsc.contentdm.oclc.org/cdm/singleitem/collection/p4013coll13/id/2611/rec/20.

Lanham, Eric. Interview by Laurence Lessard. Operational Leadership Experiences Project. Combat Studies Institute. Ft. Leavenworth, Kansas. February 22, 2007. http://cgsc.contentdm.oclc.org/cdm/singleitem/collection/p4013coll13/id/1003/rec/1.

Lee, Robert. Interview by Jenna Fike. Operational Leadership Experiences Project. Combat Studies Institute. Ft. Leavenworth, Kansas. March 21, 2011. http://cgsc.contentdm.oclc.org/cdm/singleitem/collection/p4013coll13/id/2271/rec/5.

Lencz, Rich. Interview by Brad Helton. Operational Leadership Experiences Project. Combat Studies Institute. Ft. Leavenworth, Kansas. September 5, 2008. http://cgsc.contentdm.oclc.org/cdm/singleitem/collection/p4013coll13/id/1240/rec/1.

Lillibridge, Matt. Interview by Angie Slattery Hundley. Operational Leadership Experiences Project. Combat Studies Institute. Ft. Leavenworth, Kansas. October 5, 2012. http://cgsc.contentdm.oclc.org/cdm/singleitem/collection/p4013coll13/id/2779/rec/1.

Linson, Marvin. Interview by Angie Slattery. Operational Leadership Experiences Project. Combat Studies Institute. Ft. Leavenworth, Kansas. April 20, 2011. http://cgsc.contentdm.oclc.org/cdm/singleitem/collection/p4013coll13/id/2319/rec/1.

Long, Eric. Interview by Leo Hirrel. January 24, 2012. Quartermaster School.

Lovett, Daniel. Interview by Jenn Vedder. Operational Leadership Experiences Project. Combat Studies Institute. Ft. Leavenworth, Kansas. March 19, 2010. http://cgsc.cdmhost.com/cdm/singleitem/collection/p4013coll13/id/1853/rec/1.

McEvoy, Brendan. Interview by Joey Strudnicka. Operational Leadership Experiences Project. Combat Studies Institute. Ft. Leavenworth, Kansas. November 13, 2013. http://cgsc.contentdm.oclc.org/cdm/singleitem/collection/p4013coll13/id/3124/rec/7.

Medina, José. Interviewed by Leo Hirrel. Quartermaster School. December 12, 2011.

Melson, Mark. Interview by Angie Slattery. Operational Leadership Experiences Project. Combat Studies Institute. Ft. Leavenworth, Kansas. January 11, 2011. http://cgsc.contentdm.oclc.org/cdm/singleitem/collection/p4013coll13/id/2182/rec/1.

Miller, Christopher. Interview by Angie Slattery. Operational Leadership Experiences Project. Combat Studies Institute. Ft. Leavenworth, Kansas. April 11, 2012. http://cgsc.cdmhost.com/cdm/singleitem/collection/p4013coll13/id/2653/rec/1.

Morris, Katie. Interview by Lisa Beckenbaugh. Operational Leadership Experiences Project. Combat Studies Institute. Ft. Leavenworth, Kansas. February 7, 2013. http://cgsc.contentdm.oclc.org/cdm/singleitem/collection/p4013coll13/id/3001/rec/9.

Nilon, Anthony. Interview by Douglas Cubbinson. 10th Mountain Division. Fort Drum, New York. January 22, 2007. http://cgsc.contentdm.oclc.

org/cdm/singleitem/collection/p4013coll13/
id/1031/rec/1.

O'Neill, Mark. Interview by Jenn Vedder. Operational Leadership Experiences Project. Combat Studies Institute. Ft. Leavenworth, Kansas. February 15, 2011. http://cgsc.contentdm.oclc.org/cdm/singleitem/collection/p4013coll13/id/2214/rec/2.

Plummer, Christopher. Interview by James Evenson. Operational Leadership Experiences Project. Combat Studies Institute. Ft. Leavenworth, Kansas. June 6, 2006. http://cgsc.contentdm.oclc.org/cdm/singleitem/collection/p4013coll13/id/206/rec/1.

Reed, Robert. Interview by Angie Slattery. Operational Leadership Experiences Project. Combat Studies Institute. Ft. Leavenworth, Kansas. May 18, 2011. http://cgsc.contentdm.oclc.org/cdm/singleitem/collection/p4013coll13/id/2341/rec/1.

Reynolds, Jennifer. Interview by Angie Slattery. Operational Leadership Experiences Project. Combat Studies Institute. Ft. Leavenworth, Kansas. April 13, 2011. http://cgsc.contentdm.oclc.org/cdm/singleitem/collection/p4013coll13/id/2306/rec/3.

Ross, Doug. Interview with Brad Helton. Operational Leadership Experiences Project. Combat Studies Institute. Ft. Leavenworth, Kansas. June 23, 2008. http://cgsc.contentdm.oclc.org/cdm/singleitem/collection/p4013coll13/id/1069/rec/1.

Sax, Justin. Interview by Douglas Cubbison. Operational Leadership Experiences Project. Combat Studies Institute. Ft. Leavenworth, Kansas. January 8, 2007. http://cgsc.contentdm.oclc.org/cdm/singleitem/collection/p4013coll13/id/1004/rec/1.

Schroeder, John. Interview by John McCool. Operational Leadership Experiences Project. Combat Studies Institute. Ft. Leavenworth, Kansas. February 16, 2007. http://cgsc.cdmhost.com/cdm/singleitem/collection/p4013coll13/id/733/rec/1.

Slusher, Michael. Interview by Laurence Lessard. Operational Leadership Experiences Project. Combat Studies Institute. Ft. Leavenworth, Kansas. February 16, 2007. http://cgsc.cdmhost.com/cdm/singleitem/collection/p4013coll13/id/504/rec/1.

Tabb, John. Interview by Marty Deckard. Part I. Operational Leadership Experiences Project. Combat Studies Institute. Ft. Leavenworth, Kansas. May 27, 2008. http://cgsc.contentdm.oclc.org/cdm/singleitem/collection/p4013coll13/id/1108/rec/1.

———. Interview by Marty Deckard. Part II. Operational Leadership Experiences Project. Combat Studies Institute. Ft. Leavenworth, Kansas. May 27, 2008. http://cgsc.contentdm.oclc.org/cdm/singleitem/collection/p4013coll13/id/1109/rec/2.

Thompson, David. Interview by Laurence Lessard.

Operational Leadership Experiences Project. Combat Studies Institute. Ft. Leavenworth, Kansas. June 16, 2009. http://cgsc.cdmhost.com/cdm/singleitem/collection/p4013coll13/id/1949/rec/1.

Threatt, Michael. Interview by Doug Davids. Part II. Operational Leadership Experiences Project. Combat Studies Institute. Ft. Leavenworth, Kansas. December 17, 2007. http://cgsc.contentdm.oclc.org/cdm/singleitem/collection/p4013coll13/id/963/rec/2.

Tilley, Alvin. Interview by Angie Slattery. Operational Leadership Experiences Project. Combat Studies Institute. Ft. Leavenworth, Kansas. June 29, 2011. http://cgsc.contentdm.oclc.org/cdm/singleitem/collection/p4013coll13/id/2373/rec/1.

Toolan, Paul. Interview by Pete Boisson. Operational Leadership Experiences Project. Combat Studies Institute. Ft. Leavenworth, Kansas. July 24, 2006. http://cgsc.contentdm.oclc.org/cdm/singleitem/collection/p4013coll13/id/362/rec/1.

Varney, Mike. Interview by Christopher K. Ives. Operational Leadership Experiences Project. Combat Studies Institute. Ft. Leavenworth, Kansas. February 4, 2008. http://cgsc.contentdm.oclc.org/cdm/singleitem/collection/p4013coll13/id/906/rec/1.

Wade, John. Interview by Christopher K. Ives. Operational Leadership Experiences Project. Combat Studies Institute. Ft. Leavenworth, Kansas. February 14, 2008. http://cgsc.contentdm.oclc.org/cdm/singleitem/collection/p4013coll13/id/915/rec/1.

Walck, Ronald. Interview by Shawn O'Brien. Operational Leadership Experiences Project. Combat Studies Institute. Ft. Leavenworth, Kansas. May 21, 2008. http://cgsc.contentdm.oclc.org/cdm/singleitem/collection/p4013coll13/id/1270/rec/1.

Wallace, Steven. Interview by Jenna Fike. Operational Leadership Experiences Project. Combat Studies Institute. Ft. Leavenworth, Kansas. October 6, 2010. http://cgsc.cdmhost.com/cdm/singleitem/collection/p4013coll13/id/2055/rec/1.

Wells, Chris. Interview by Pete Boisson. Operational Leadership Experiences Project. Combat Studies Institute. Ft. Leavenworth, Kansas. July 25, 2005. http://cgsc.contentdm.oclc.org/cdm/singleitem/collection/p4013coll13/id/317/rec/1.

Woodall, Edward. Interview with Joey Strudnicka. Operational Leadership Experiences Project. Combat Studies Institute. Ft. Leavenworth, Kansas. December 3, 2013. http://cgsc.contentdm.oclc.org/cdm/singleitem/collection/p4013coll13/id/3159/rec/2.

Woodring, William. Interview by Laurence Lessard. Operational Leadership Experiences Project. Combat Studies Institute. Ft. Leavenworth, Kansas. December 12, 2006. http://

cgsc.contentdm.oclc.org/cdm/singleitem/
collection/p4013coll13/id/648/rec/1.

Young, Judd. Interview with Angie Slattery. Operational Leadership Experiences Project. Combat Studies Institute. Ft. Leavenworth, Kansas. January 6, 2011. http://cgsc.contentdm.oclc.org/cdm/singleitem/collection/p4013coll13/id/2176/rec/1.

Zendejas, Michael. Interview with Jenna Fike. Operational Leadership Experiences Project. Combat Studies Institute. Ft. Leavenworth, Kansas. February 14, 2012. http://cgsc.contentdm.oclc.org/cdm/singleitem/collection/p4013coll13/id/2576/rec/1.

Published Primary Sources

Anders, Robert S. *Winning Paktika: Counterinsurgency in Afghanistan*. Bloomington, IN: AuthorHouse, 2013.

Bradley, Rusty, and Kevin Maurer. *Lions of Kandahar: The Story of a Fight Against All Odds*. New York: Bantam, 2015.

Browder, Laura, and Sascha Pflaeging. *When Janes Comes Marching Home: Portraits of Women Combat Veterans*. Chapel Hill: University of North Carolina Press, 2010.

Burden, Matthew Currier. *The Blog of War: Front-Line Dispatches from Soldiers in Iraq and Afghanistan*. New York: Simon & Schuster, 2006.

Carroll, Andrew, ed. *Operation Homecoming: Iraq, Afghanistan, and the Home Front, in the Words of U.S. Troops and Their Families*. New York: Random House, 2006.

Christ, James F. *ETT... Embrace the Suck! Embedded Tactical Trainers with the Afghan National Army*. Independently Published, 2017.

Darling, Paul. *Taliban Safari: One Day in the Surkhagan Valley*. Lawrence: University Press of Kansas, 2019.

Eide, Marian, and Michael Gibler. *After Combat: True War Stories from Iraq and Afghanistan*. Lincoln: University of Nebraska Press, 2018.

Fick, Nathaniel. *One Bullet Away: The Making of a Marine Officer*. Boston: Houghton Mifflin, 2005.

Forsyth, Michael J. *A Year in Command in Afghanistan: Journal of a United States Army Battalion Commander, 2009–2010*. Jefferson, NC: McFarland, 2017.

Golembesky, Michael, and John R. Bruning. *Level Zero Heroes: The Story of U.S. Marine Special Operations in Bala Murghab, Afghanistan*. New York: St. Martin's, 2014.

Herd, Walter Morris. *Unconventional Warrior: Memoir of a Special Operations Commander in Afghanistan*. Jefferson, NC: McFarland, 2013.

Jenkins, Leo. *Lest We Forget: A Ranger Medic's Story*. 2nd ed. Self-published, 2017.

Jones, William Gardner. *My Year of Living Dangerously: An American Soldier in Afghanistan*. Charleston, SC: William Jones, 2009.

Koontz, Christopher, ed. *Enduring Voices: Oral Histories of the U.S. Army Experience in Afghanistan, 2003–2005*. Washington, D.C.: Center of Military History, United States Army, 2008.

Leche, Christine Dumaine, ed. *Outside the Wire: American Soldiers' Voices from Afghanistan*. Charlottesville: University Press of Virginia, 2013.

Luttrell, Marcus with Patrick Robinson. *Lone Survivor: The Eyewitness Account of Operation Redwing and the Lost Heroes of SEAL Team 10*. New York: Back Bay, 2008.

McGarry, Grant. *A Night in the Pech Valley: A Memoir of a Member of the 75th Ranger Regiment in the Global War on Terrorism*. LTRC Publishing, 2016.

Meyer, Dakota, and Bing West. *Into the Fire: A Firsthand Account of the Most Extraordinary Battle in the Afghan War*. New York: Random House, 2012.

Mullaney, Craig. *The Unforgiving Minute: A Soldier's Education*. New York: Penguin, 2009.

Parnell, Sean, and John R. Bruning. *Outlaw Platoon: Heroes, Renegades, Infidels, and the Brotherhood of War in Afghanistan*. New York: William Morrow, 2013.

Rickard, Chad. *Mayhem 337: Memoir of a Combat Advisor in Afghanistan*. BookBaby, 2019.

Rico, Johnny. *Blood Makes the Grass Grow Green: A Year in the Desert with Team America*. New York: Presidio, 2007.

Romesha, Clinton. *Red Platoon: A True Story of American Valor*. New York: Dutton, 2016.

Schellhaas, Kristine. *15 Years of War: How the Longest War in U.S. History Affected a Military Family in Love, Loss, and the Cost of Service*. Life Publishing, 2016.

Settle, Jimmy, and Don Rearden. *Never Quit: From Alaskan Wilderness Rescues to Afghanistan Firefights as an Elite Special Ops PJ*. New York. St. Martin's, 2017.

Skovlund, Marty, Jr. *Violence of Action: The Untold Stories of the 75th Ranger Regiment in the War on Terror*. Colorado Springs: Blackside Concepts, 2014.

Smith, Amber. *Danger Close: My Epic Journey as a Combat Helicopter Pilot in Iraq and Afghanistan*. New York: Atria, 2016.

Spiller, Harry. *Veterans of Iraq and Afghanistan: Personal Accounts of 22 Americans Who Served*. Jefferson, NC: McFarland, 2014.

Stanford, David, ed. *Doonesbury.com's the Sandbox: Dispatches from Troops in Iraq and Afghanistan*. Kansas City: Andrews McMeel, 2007.

Tupper, Benjamin. *Greetings from Afghanistan, Send More Ammo: Dispatches from Taliban Country*. New York: Neil Caliber, 2011.

Waltz, Michael G. *Warrior Diplomat: A Green Beret's Battles from Washington to Afghanistan*. Lincoln, NE: Potomac Books, 2014.

Young, Thomas W. *The Speed of Heat: An Airlift*

Wing at War in Iraq and Afghanistan. Jefferson, NC: McFarland, 2008.

Articles, Reports, and Online Sources

Center for Army Lessons Learned. *Afghanistan Provincial Reconstruction Handbook.* February 2011. https://usacac.army.mil/sites/default/files/publications/11–16.pdf. Accessed April 2, 2020.

Clark, James. "For Those Who Fought in Marjah, It Was More Than Just a Battle." *Task & Purpose.* February 13, 2015. https://taskandpurpose.com/leadership/fought-marjah-just-battle. Accessed June 14, 2020.

Davidson, Jason W. "The Costs of War to United States Allies Since 9/11." Watson Institute. Brown University. May 12, 2021. https://watson.brown.edu/costsofwar/files/cow/imce/papers/2021/Davidson_AlliesCostsofWar_Final.pdf. Accessed May 13, 2021.

Department of Defense. "Selected Manpower Statistics FY 2001." Selected Manpower Statistics. Historical Reports FY 1994–2009. https://www.dmdc.osd.mil/appj/dwp/dwp_reports.jsp. Accessed September 20, 2019.

_____. "Selective Reserve by Rank/Grade." September 30, 2001. https://www.dmdc.osd.mil/appj/dwp/dwp_reports.jsp. Accessed February 24, 2020.

Government Accountability Office. "Actions Needed to Further Improve the Consistency of Combat Skills Training Provided to Army and Marine Corps Support Forces." GAO-10–465. Government Accountability Office. April 2010. https://www.gao.gov/assets/310/303355.html. Accessed August 26, 2020.

_____. "Afghanistan Governance: Performance-Data Gaps Hinder Overall Assessment of U.S. Efforts to Build Financial Management Capability." GAO-11–907. September 2011. https://www.gao.gov/assets/330/323502.html. Accessed April 10, 2020.

_____. "Provincial Reconstruction Teams in Afghanistan and Iraq." GAO-08–905RSU. Washington, D.C.: Sept. 26, 2008. https://www.gao.gov/new.items/d0986r.pdf. Accessed April 2, 2020.

Holder, Kelly Ann. "They Are Half the Size of the Living Vietnam Veteran Population," Census Bureau. April 11, 2018. Census.gov/programs-surveys/acs/. Accessed June 18, 2019.

Hsia, Timothy. "A Quick Review of Combat Outposts." *Small Wars Journal,* November 27, 2008. https://smallwarsjournal.com/blog/journal/docs-temp/138-hsia.pdf.

Johnson, Gregory, Vijaya Ramachandran, and Julie Walz. "CERP in Afghanistan: Refining Military Capabilities in Development Activities." *PRISM* 3, no. 2 (2012): 81–98. www.jstor.org/stable/26469731. Accessed June 3, 2020.

Kemp, Robert E. "Provincial Reconstruction Teams in Eastern Afghanistan: Utility as a Strategic Counterinsurgency Tool." *Military Review* (September-October 2011): 28- 36.

Kirell, Jay. "Here's What Happens When Your Local Porta Potty Cleaner Just Up and Leaves." *Task and Purpose.* September 18, 2018. https://taskandpurpose.com/afghanistan-porta-potty-truck/. Accessed March 13, 2019.

Lowe, Miranda Summers. "The Gradual Shift to an Operational Reserve: Reserve Component Mobilizations in the 1990s." *Military Review.* May-June 2019. https://www.armyupress.army.mil/Journals/Military-Review/English-Edition-Archives/May-June-2019/Summers-Lowe-Reserve-1990s/.

Luehrs, Christoff. "Provincial Reconstruction Teams: A Literature Review." *Prism.* Vol. 1, No. 1 (December 2009): 95–102. JSTOR. https://www.jstor.org/stable/10.2307/26469032.

Maurer, Kevin. "Witness to a War." *The Washington Post Magazine.* September 9, 2019. Accessed September 18, 2019. https://www.washingtonpost.com/news/magazine/wp/2019/09/09/feature/the-afghanistan-war-is-likely-ending-one-longtime-correspondent-asks-was-it-worth-it/.

McGrath, John J. "The Other End of the Spear: The Tooth-to-Tail Ratio (T3R) in Modern Military Operations." The Long War Series Occasional Paper 23. Ft. Leavenworth, KS: Combat Studies Institute Press, 2007.

North Atlantic Treaty Organization. International Security Assistance Force History. https://www.nato.int/cps/en/natohq/topics_69366.htm. Accessed May 24, 2019.

_____. Resolute Support Mission in Afghanistan. Accessed May 24, 2019. https://www.nato.int/cps/en/natohq/topics_113694/htm.

O'Brien, C.P., M. Oster, and E. Morden, editors. *Substance Use Disorders in the U.S. Armed Forces.* Washington, D.C.: National Academies Press, 2013. https://www.ncbi.nlm.nih.gov/books/NBK207276/. Accessed June 5, 2020.

Oliker, Olga, Richard Kauzlarich, James Dobbins, Kurt W. Basseuner, Donald L. Sampler, John G. McGinn, Michael J. Dziedzic, Adam R. Grisson, Bruce R. Pirnie, Nora Bensahel, and A. Istar Guven. *Aid During Conflict: Interaction Between Military and Civilian Assistance Providers in Afghanistan, September 2001-June 2002.* RAND: Santa Monica, CA, 2004.

Reynolds, George M., and Amanda Shendruk. "Demographics of the U.S. Military." Council on Foreign Relations. https://www.cfr.org/article/demographics-us-military. Accessed October 15, 2019.

Special Inspector General for Afghanistan Reconstruction. "Commander's Emergency Response Program: DOD Has Not Determined the Full Extent to Which Its Program and Projects, Totaling $1.5 Billion in Obligations, Achieved Their Objectives and Goals in Afghanistan from Fiscal Years 2009 Through 2013." https://www.sigar.mil/pdf/audits/SIGAR-18–45-AR.pdf. Arlington, VA: SIGAR, April 2018.

_____. "Corruption in Conflict: Lessons from the US Experience in Afghanistan." Arlington, VA: SIGAR, September 2016.

_____. "Counternarcotics: Lessons Learned from the U.S. Experience in Afghanistan." Arlington, VA: SIGAR, June 2018.

_____. "Reconstructing the Afghan National Defense and Security Forces: Lessons from the U.S. Experience in Afghanistan." Arlington, VA: SIGAR, September 2017.

_____. "Report to the United States Congress." April 30, 2018. https://www.sigar.mil/pdf/quarterlyreports/2018–04–30qr-section3-security.pdf. Accessed March 30, 2020.

"Taliban Admit Covering Up Death of Mullah Omar." *BBC.* August 31, 2015. https://www.bbc.com/news/world-asia-34105565. Accessed March 13, 2019.

Vongkiatkajorn, Kanyakrit, Alex Horton, Meryl Kornfield, Jenn Abelson, and Ted Muldoon. "We Were Right." *The Washington Post.* December 17, 2019. https://www.washingtonpost.com/graphics/2019/investigations/afghanistan-papers/veterans-reaction/. Accessed April 22, 2020.

Wenger, Jennie W., Caolionn O'Connell, and Linda Cottrell. "Examination of Recent Deployment Experience Across the Services and Components." RAND. https://www.rand.org/pubs/research_reports/RR1928.html?adbsc=social_20180320_2212921&adbid=97592816763333 4272&adbpl=tw&adbpr=22545453. Accessed February 24, 2020.

Whitlock, Craig. "The Afghanistan Papers: A Secret History of the War." *The Washington Post.* December 2019. https://www.washingtonpost.com/graphics/2019/investigations/afghanistan-papers/afghanistan-war-confidential-documents/. Accessed April 22, 2020.

Younossi, Obaid, Peter Dahl Thurelsen, Jonathan Vaccaro, Jerry M. Solinger, and Brian Grady. *The Long March: Building an Afghan National Army.* Santa Monica, CA: RAND, 2009.

Books

Bacevich, Andrew J. *The New American Militarism: How Americans Are Seduced by War.* Updated ed. New York: Oxford University Press, 2013.

Bailey, Beth. *America's Army: Making the All-Volunteer Force.* Cambridge, MA: Belknap, 2009.

Bailey, Beth, and Richard H. Immerman, eds. *Understanding the U.S. Wars in Iraq and Afghanistan.* New York: New York University Press, 2015.

Barfield, Thomas. *Afghanistan: A Cultural and Political History.* Princeton: Princeton University Press, 2010.

Basinger, Jeanine. *The World War II Combat Film: Anatomy of a Genre.* Updated ed. Middletown, CT: Wesleyan University Press, 2003.

Bellesiles, Michael A. *A People's History of the U.S. Military: Ordinary Soldiers Reflect on Their Experience of War, from the American Revolution to Afghanistan.* New York: New, 2012.

Bird, Tim, and Alex Marshall. *Afghanistan: How the West Lost Its Way.* New Haven: Yale University Press, 2011.

Blehm, Eric. *The Only Thing Worth Dying For: How Eleven Green Berets Fought for a New Afghanistan.* New York: Harper Perennial, 2010.

Cage, Caleb S. *War Narratives: Shaping Beliefs, Blurring Truths in the Middle East.* College Station: Texas A&M University Press, 2019.

Call, Steve. *Danger Close: Tactical Air Controllers in Afghanistan and Iraq.* College Station: Texas A&M University Press, 2007.

Caputo, Philip. *A Rumor of War.* 40th anniversary ed. New York: Picador, 1996.

Cavanna, Thomas P. *Hubris, Self-Interest, and America's Failed War in Afghanistan: The Self-Sustaining Overreach.* Lanham, MD: Lexington, 2015.

Chandra, Vishal. *The Unfinished War in Afghanistan, 2001–2014.* New Delhi: Pentagon, 2015.

Chandrasekaran, Rajiv. *Little America: The War Within the War for Afghanistan.* New York: Alfred A. Knopf, 2012.

Chivers, C.J. *The Fighters: Americans in Combat in Afghanistan and Iraq.* New York: Simon & Schuster, 2018.

Department of the Army. Headquarters. *Warrior Skills Level 1: Soldier's Manual of Common Tasks.* Soldier Training Publication No. 21–1-SMCT. Washington, D.C.: Department of the Army, May 2011.

Donati, Jessica. *Eagle Down: The Last Special Forces Fighting in the Forever War.* New York: Public Affairs, 2021.

Eichstaedt, Peter H. *Above the Din of War: Afghans Speak About Their Lives, Their Country, and Their Future—And Why America Should Listen.* Boston: Houghton Mifflin Harcourt, 2014.

Fairweather, Jack. *The Good War: Why We Couldn't Win the War or the Peace in Afghanistan.* New York: Basic, 2014.

Fergusen, James. *Taliban: The Unknown Enemy.* Cambridge, MA: Da Capo, 2011.

Filkins, Dexter. *The Forever War.* New York: Alfred A. Knopf, 2008.

Gall, Carlotta. *The Wrong Enemy: America in Afghanistan, 2001–2014.* New York: Houghton Mifflin Harcourt, 2014.

Gezari, Vanessa M. *The Tender Soldier: A True Story of War and Sacrifice.* New York: Simon & Schuster, 2013.

Giustozzi, Antonio. *Koran, Kalashnikov, and Laptop: The Neo-Taliban Insurgency in Afghanistan.* New York: Columbia University Press, 2008.

Gopal, Anand. *No Good Men Among the Living: America, the Taliban, and the War Through Afghan Eyes.* Minneapolis: HighBridge, 2015.

Grau, Lester W., and Dodge Billingsley. *Operation Anaconda: America's First Battle in Afghanistan.* Lawrence: University Press of Kansas, 2011.

Grey, Stephen. *Into the Viper's Nest: The First Pivotal Battle of the Afghan War.* Minneapolis: Zenith Press, 2010.

Gurcan, Metin. *What Went Wrong in Afghanistan? Understanding Counter-Insurgency Efforts in Tribalized Rural and Muslim Environments.* Helion, 2016.

Hymel, Kevin M. *Strykers in Afghanistan: Battalion, 17th Infantry Regiment in Kandahar Province, 2009. Vanguard of Valor IV.* Ft. Leavenworth, KS: Combat Studies Institute Press, 2014.

Jalali, Ali Ahmad. *A Military History of Afghanistan: From the Great Game to the Global War on Terror.* Lawrence: University Press of Kansas, 2017.

Jones, Seth G. *Counterinsurgency in Afghanistan.* Santa Monica, CA: RAND, 2008.

_____. *In the Graveyard of Empires: America's War in Afghanistan.* New York: W.W. Norton, 2009.

Junger, Sebastian. *War.* New York: Twelve, 2010.

Kaplan, Fred M. *The Insurgents: David Petraeus and the Plot to Change the American Way of War.* New York: Simon & Schuster, 2013.

Keane, Conor. *US Nation Building in Afghanistan.* NY: Routledge, 2016.

Kindsvatter, Peter S. *American Soldiers: Ground Combat in the World Wars, Korea, and Vietnam.* Lawrence: University Press of Kansas, 2003.

Lair, Meredith H. *Armed with Abundance: Consumerism & Soldiering in the Vietnam War.* Chapel Hill: University of North Carolina Press, 2018.

Linderman, Gerald. *The World Within War: America's Combat Experience in World War II.* New York: Free, 1997.

MacPherson, Malcolm. *Robert's Ridge: A Story of Courage and Sacrifice on Takur Ghar Mountain, Afghanistan.* New York: Delacorte, 2005.

Malkasian, Carter. *The American War in Afghanistan: A History.* New York: Oxford University Press, 2021.

_____. *War Comes to Garmser: Thirty Years of Conflict on the Afghan Frontier.* New York: Oxford University Press, 2013.

Mann, D. Scott. *Game Changers: Going Local to Defeat Violent Extremists Special Forces & Law Enforcement Edition.* Leesburg, VA: Tribal Analysis Center, 2015.

McGrath, John. *Wanat: Combat Action in Afghanistan, 2008.* Fort Leavenworth, KS: Combat Studies Institute, 2010.

Millett, Allan R., Peter Masklowski, and William B. Feis. *For the Common Defense: A Military History of the United States from 1607 to 2012.* 3rd ed. New York: Free, 2012.

Morgan, Wesley. *The Hardest Place: The American Military Adrift in Afghanistan's Pech Valley.* New York: Random House, 2021.

Mundey, Lisa M. *American Militarism and Anti-Militarism in Popular Media, 1945–1970.* Jefferson, NC: McFarland, 2012.

Naylor, Sean. *Not a Good Day to Die: The Untold Story of Operation Anaconda.* New York: Berkley Caliber, 2005.

Neumann, Brian F. and Colin J. Williams. *The U.S. Army in Afghanistan: Operation Enduring Freedom, May 2005-January 2009.* Washington, D.C.: U.S. Army Center of Military History, 2020.

Neumann, Brian F., Lisa Mundey, and Jon Mikolashek. *Operation Enduring Freedom, March 2002-April 2005.* Washington, D.C.: U.S. Army Center of Military History, 2013.

Neumann, Ronald E. *The Other War: Winning and Losing in Afghanistan.* Washington, D.C.: Potomac, 2009.

O'Connell, Aaron B., ed. *Our Latest Longest War: Losing Hearts and Minds in Afghanistan.* Reprint ed. Chicago: University of Chicago Press, 2018.

Pool, H.J. *Expeditionary Eagles: Outmaneuvering the Taliban.* Emerald Isle, NC: Posterity, 2010.

Ripley, Tim. *Operation Enduring Freedom: America's Afghan War 2001–2002.* Pen & Sword, 2011.

Rivers, Eileen. *Beyond the Call: Three Women on the Front Lines in Afghanistan.* New York: Da Capo, 2018.

Rubin, Barnett R. *Afghanistan from the Cold War Through the War on Terror.* New York: Oxford University Press, 2013.

Saikal, Amin. *Modern Afghanistan: A History of Struggle and Survival.* New York: L.B. Tauris, 2012.

Schilling, Dan, and Lori Longfritz. *Alone at Dawn.* Kindle Edition. New York: Grand Central Publishing, 2019.

Shrader, Charles R. *Amicide: The Problem of Friendly Fire in Modern War.* Ft. Leavenworth: Combat Studies Institute, 1982.

Stanton, Doug. *12 Strong: The Declassified True Story of the Horse Soldiers.* New York: Scribner's, 2017.

Steele, Jonathan. *Ghosts of Afghanistan: Hard Truths and Foreign Myths.* Berkeley, CA: Counterpoint, 2011.

Stewart, Richard W., ed. *American Military History Volume II: The United States Army in a Global Era, 1917–2003.* Washington, D.C.: United States Army Center of Military History, 2005.

_____. *Operation Enduring Freedom: The United States Army in Afghanistan, October 2001-March 2002.* Washington, D.C.: U.S. Army Center of Military History, 2004.

Tapper, Jake. *The Outpost: An Untold Story of American Valor.* New York: Little, Brown and Co., 2012.

Taylor, William A. *Military Service and American Democracy: From World War II to the Iraq and Afghanistan Wars.* Lawrence: University Press of Kansas, 2016.

Thorpe, Helen. *Soldier Girls: The Battles of Three Women at Home and at War.* New York: Scribner's, 2014.

Tucker-Jones, Anthony. *The Afghan War: Operation Enduring Freedom, 2001–2014.* Barnsley, South Yorkshire: Pen & Sword, 2014.

Wadle, Ryan. *Hammer Down: The Battle for the Watapur Valley, 2011.* Fort Leavenworth, KS: Combat Studies Institute Press, 2014.

Walling, Michael G. *Enduring Freedom, Enduring Voices: US Operations in Afghanistan.* New York: Osprey, 2015.

West, Bing. *One Million Steps: A Marine Platoon at War.* New York: Random House, 2015.

Wetzel, Gary. *A-10 Thunderbolt II Units of Operation Enduring Freedom, 2008–14.* Kindle Edition. Osprey, 2015.

Williams, Brian Glyn. *Afghanistan Declassified: A Guide to America's Longest War.* Philadelphia: University of Pennsylvania Press, 2012.

Willis, Clint, ed. *Boots on the Ground: Stories of American Soldiers from Iraq and Afghanistan.* New York: Thunder Mountain, 2004.

Wright, Donald P. *A Different Kind of War: The United States Army in Operation Enduring Freedom (OEF), October 2001-September 2005.* Fort Leavenworth, KS: Combat Studies Institute, 2010.

_____. *Vanguard of Valor II: Small Unit Actions in Afghanistan.* Fort Leavenworth, KS: Combat Studies Institute, 2012.

Wright, Donald P., ed. *Vanguard of Valor: Small Unit Actions in Afghanistan.* Fort Leavenworth, KS: Combat Studies Institute Press, 2012.

Index

Numbers in *bold italics* indicate pages with illustrations.